No More Rules

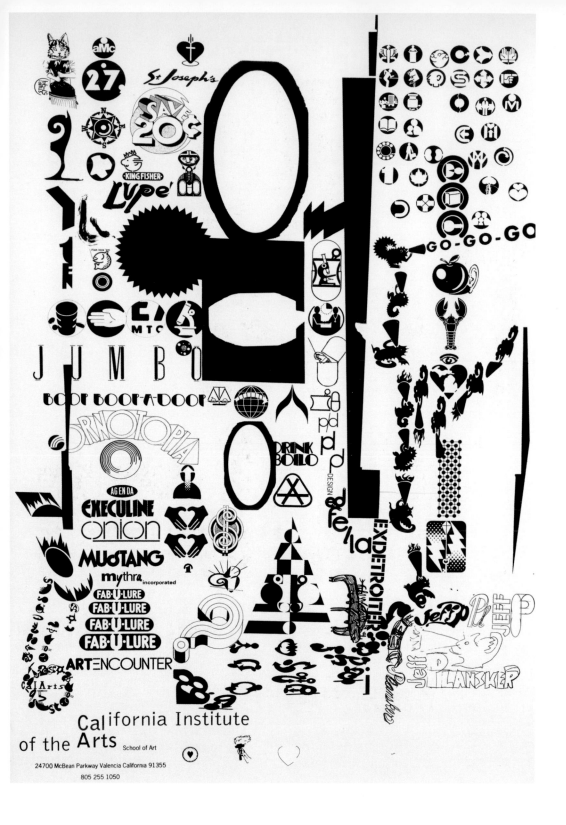

California Institute
of the Arts School of Art

24700 McBean Parkway Valencia California 91355

805 255 1050

No More Rules

Graphic Design and Postmodernism

Rick Poynor

Laurence King Publishing

LAURENCE KING

First published in 2003
This mini edition published in 2013 by
Laurence King Publishing Ltd
361-373 City Road
London ECIV ILR
United Kingdom
Tel: +44 20 7841 6900
Fax: +44 20 7841 6910
e-mail: enquiries@laurenceking.com
www.laurenceking.com

A catalogue record for this book is available
from the British Library

ISBN 978 1 78067 103 1

Jacket design by David Pearson
Book design by Kerr|Noble
Edited by Nell Webb
Picture research by Helen McFarland
Additional photography by Nigel Jackson
Printed in China

Text set in Eureka by Peter Bil'ak, Pop by Neville Brody
and Pop modified by Kerr|Noble

Frontispiece : Edward Fella. Poster for Jeffery Plansker lecture at California
Institute of the Arts, 1994

Contents

Preface   6

Introduction   8

1   Origins   18

2   Deconstruction   38

3   Appropriation   70

4   Techno   96

5   Authorship   118

6   Opposition   148

Notes   172

Selected Bibliography   180

Index   184

Picture Credits   192

Preface

No More Rules has its starting point in a close engagement with graphic design of the postmodern era that began, for me, in the early 1980s. It deals with recent events in design history, but it is not a history as such. It doesn't set out to argue that there shouldn't be any more rules in graphic design, only that during this period many designers, including some influential ones, have proceeded as though this were the case. Contemplating the mass of material and reviewing how it has been treated in other accounts, often by individual designer and by stylistic tendency, it seemed most useful to identify some key themes in design's rule-defying relationship with postmodernism – origins, deconstruction, appropriation, technology, authorship and opposition – and organize the book on this basis. Some of the examples shown and considered here, and some of the ideas and arguments discussed, were selected because they played a central role in design thinking during this period. Any critical survey that did not include them would be making a serious oversight. Others feature because they are representative of approaches that became typical.

What made these years so stimulating for someone observing and writing about graphic design was the high level of discussion that the work generated, particularly in the late 1980s and early 1990s when many of these ideas were novel and unfamiliar in design circles and the technology was changing rapidly. I am especially indebted to a number of designers and design writers who, in different ways, have played a significant role in the development of my own thinking about this material: Ellen Lupton, J. Abbott Miller, Robin Kinross, Neville Brody, Peter Saville, Rudy VanderLans, Michael Rock, Steven Heller,

Katherine McCoy, Edward Fella and Jeffery Keedy. It would
amaze me if I have said nothing in these pages with which they
want to disagree strenuously. My thanks to these colleagues
and my thanks also to all the individuals and organizations that
have shown their support for the fundamental principle of free
discussion by permitting their work to be reproduced in this book.

Warm thanks must also go to Laurence King and Jo
Lightfoot at Laurence King Publishing; to Nell Webb, the book's
tirelessly conscientious editor; and to Amelia Noble and Frith Kerr,
its designers, who kept faith with the project from the start.

Rick Poynor

Introduction

Twenty years after the term started to be used widely, postmodernism remains a difficult, slippery and, for some, infuriating topic. There is already a vast literature devoted to every aspect of postmodernism and new books arrive all the time. By the late 1980s, it was common to see the word used in newspapers and magazines and some publications ran whole series of articles attempting to explain what it meant. Sometimes they just ridiculed it. For a while it was voguish to drop this clever-sounding buzzword into cultural conversations and it even started to show up in television commercials. The widespread assumption now, outside the academy, is that postmodernism has gone the way of so many other intellectual fads. Many people never understood what it was supposed to mean and even the most knowledgeable observers are sometimes inclined to treat it with suspicion. For Judith Williamson, author of *Decoding Advertisements*, interviewed in a design journal, the term is too vague to be useful in anything other than a stylistic sense.[1] Richard Kostelanetz, author of *A Dictionary of the Avant-Gardes*, is even blunter: 'My personal opinion holds that anything characterized as postmodern, whether by its author or its advocates, is beneath critical consideration, no matter how immediately popular or acceptable it might be.'[2]

So why write a critical survey of postmodernism and graphic design at this point? First, because no matter how awkward, problematic and uncertain the concept of postmodernism might appear to be, it is now so well established as a way of thinking about our time and our 'condition' that it cannot be simply ignored. Second, because despite a certain amount of discussion in design magazines and chapters about postmodern graphic design in a few books, there has, surprisingly, never been a book devoted to the

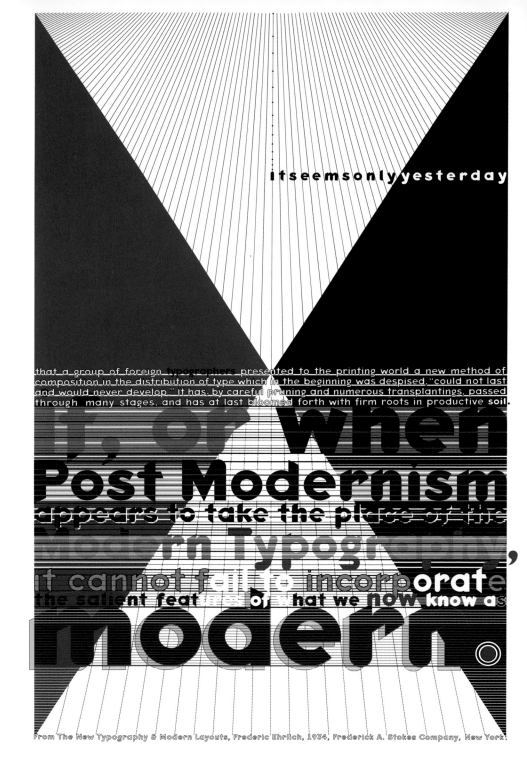

itseemsonlyyesterday that a group of foreign typographers presented to the printing world a new method of composition in the distribution of type which in the beginning was despised, "could not last and would never develop." It has, by careful pruning and numerous transplantings, passed through many stages, and has at last bloomed forth with firm roots in productive soil. If, or when Post Modernism appears to take the place of the Modern Typography, it cannot fail to incorporate the salient features of what we now know as modern.

From The New Typography & Modern Layouts, Frederic Ehrlich, 1934, Frederick A. Stokes Company, New York.

Jeffery Keedy. Emigre Type Specimen Series
Booklet No. 4: Keedy Sans, typographic
illustration, Emigre, USA, 2002

topic. I say surprisingly because it could be argued that graphic design, as currently practised, is a prime example of a popular, accessible medium exhibiting symptoms of postmodernism. In the last 15 years, graphic designers have created some of the most challenging examples of postmodernism in the visual arts. For the most part, though, despite their cheerful embrace of 'low' popular culture, cultural studies commentators have overlooked these communications and products. Critical introductions to postmodernism and the arts routinely deal with literature, architecture, fine art, photography, pop music, fashion, film and television, but they show little sign of even noticing, still less attempting to 'theorize', any form of design, despite its obviously central role as a shaper of contemporary life.[3]

For their part, few graphic designers have been eager to define their output as postmodern. Those who have laid most positive and even argumentative claim to the label have tended to be American. Many of the designers, American and non-American, who are identified in *No More Rules* as producing work which relates to postmodernism and its themes would reject the term vehemently. For many others, the word would be no more comprehensible as a description than it would be to ordinary members of the public. Graphic design as a profession has long had an aversion to theory and many of the key postmodernist texts are highly demanding even for those who possess a basic sympathy for their arguments and intentions. For other designers, postmodernism is too closely identified with a particular historicist style of architecture current in the 1980s and it is consequently rejected on grounds of æsthetic taste as much as anything. As chapter 1 argues, this essentially stylistic view of postmodernism by some design commentators has inhibited an understanding of the way in which postmodern tendencies continued to influence design throughout the 1990s.

It is not this book's purpose to provide an overview of postmodernism and all attempts at summary inevitably run up against the multitude of sometimes conflicting interpretations that postmodernism has generated. (Some suggestions for further reading are given in the bibliography.) A few key postmodernist ideas can, however, be sketched here and some of these will be developed in the book as they relate to graphic design. Postmodernism cannot be understood without reference to modernism. While the 'post' prefix might seem to suggest that postmodernism comes after modernism, or that it replaces or rejects it, many commentators point out that postmodernism is a kind of parasite, dependent on its modernist host and displaying many of the same features – except that the meaning has changed. Where postmodernism differs, above all, is in its loss of faith in the progressive ideals that sustained the modernists, who inherited the eighteenth-century Enlightenment's belief in the possibility of continuous human progress through reason and science. The Enlightenment project, writes David Harvey in *The Condition of Postmodernity*, 'took it as axiomatic that there was only one possible answer to any question. From this it followed that the world could be controlled and rationally ordered if we could only picture and represent it rightly. But this presumed a single mode of representation which, if we could uncover it ... would provide the means to Enlightenment ends.'[4] For postmodern thinkers, it is no longer possible to believe in absolutes, in 'totalizing' systems, in universally applicable values or solutions. They view with incredulity the claims of grand or metanarratives – as Jean-François Lyotard termed them in *The Postmodern Condition: A Report on Knowledge* – that seek to explain the world and control the individual through religion, science or politics.[5]

The products of postmodern culture may sometimes bear similarities to modernist works, but their inspiration and purpose is fundamentally different. If modernism sought to create a better world, postmodernism – to the horror of many observers – appears to accept the world as it is. Where modernism frequently attacked commercial mass culture, claiming from its superior perspective to know what was best for people, postmodernism enters into a complicitous relationship with the dominant culture. In postmodernism, modernism's hierarchical distinctions between worthwhile 'high' culture and trashy 'low' culture collapse and the two become equal possibilities on a level field. The erosion of the old boundaries allows new hybrid forms to blossom and many changes seen within design in recent years, as it took on some of art's self-expressive characteristics, only make sense in these terms.

The dissolution of authoritative standards creates fluid conditions in which all appeals to universality, expertise, set ways of doing things and unbreakable rules look increasingly dubious and untenable, at least in the cultural sphere. As many cultural critics have noted, the products of postmodern culture tend to be distinguished by such characteristics as fragmentation, impurity of form, depthlessness, indeterminacy, intertextuality, pluralism, eclecticism and a return to the vernacular. Originality, in the imperative modernist sense of 'making it new', ceases to be the goal; parody, pastiche and the ironic recycling of earlier forms proliferate. The postmodern object 'problematizes' meaning, offers multiple points of access and makes itself as open as possible to interpretation.

No More Rules' central argument is that one of the most significant developments in graphic design, during the last two decades, has been designers' overt challenges to the conventions or rules that were once widely regarded as constituting good practice. Towards the end of his life, the modernist poet T.S. Eliot observed that 'It's not wise to violate rules until you know how to observe them' and the commonly held view that one should master one's discipline before seeking to disrupt it also held true for design.[6] In *Typography: Basic Principles* (1963), John Lewis, a British designer and graphic design teacher, includes a chapter titled 'Rules are Made to be Broken'. 'Before you start breaking rules,' he writes, 'you should know what they are. Once one knows what are the correct procedures one can look at them critically and see whether by deliberately flouting them anything can be added to methods of communication.'[7] Lewis believed that there was even a place for illegibility, for mixing up fonts and mutilating letters, if it would serve the message by adding some excitement. However, when it came to book design, no interference between author and reader could ever be justified. 'The book page is not a medium for self expression,' he decrees.[8] For this generation of designers, the rules of page layout and typographic craft distilled from 500 years of printing history provided an essential framework, though knowing when and how to break them was acknowledged as vital to creative design. In 1981, the American designer Bob Gill summarized the thinking behind his 25 years as a designer with a two-sentence book title that was virtually a manifesto in itself: *Forget All the Rules about Graphic Design. Including the Ones in this Book.*[9] Graphic designers have continued to invoke the need first to absorb, but then to resist and transcend the rules of professional design. 'Rules are good. Break them,' Tibor Kalman urged colleagues, as recently as 1998.[10]

By this time, as Kalman well knew, the idea of rules had become highly contentious. The late 1980s and early 1990s had seen a huge body of work, much of it created by young designers, in which every principle and ordinance heeded by earlier generations had been subjected to continuous assault. As chapter 2 shows, this process began mainly at Cranbrook Academy of Art, under the influence of writing by postmodern theorists. Edward Fella, an American designer then in his late forties, has a pivotal place in these developments. Fella, like Kalman, was essentially self-taught, but his rule-breaking method was grounded, as T.S.Eliot had advised, in a thorough acquaintance with design's conventions. David Carson, probably the most widely adulated designer to emerge in the 1990s, took a different view, arguing without embarrassment that it was his ignorance of rules, with all their prescriptions and constraints, that allowed him to produce designs that seemed to many to resemble nothing ever encountered before in commercial print media. 'I never learned all the things you're not supposed to do, I just do what makes the most sense ...' Carson explained. 'There's no grid, no format. I think it ends up in a more interesting place than if I just applied formal design rules.'[11]

For many young designers, this was a hugely beguiling idea. In Carson's case, it produced extremely striking and visually exciting results, seeming to some, at least for a while, to confirm the total irrelevance of rules: the designer trusts to his intuitive sense of what will work, what feels right, and everything falls into place. 'By unmooring the page from the grid, each design element operates through an associative illogic, arresting the eye and pulling attention into an adventure of the senses across the open field of the page,' enthused one reviewer in a British style and fashion magazine.[12] Such an approach was enough to provoke several years of soul-searching in the design schools, since every foundational principle they taught now seemed open to question.

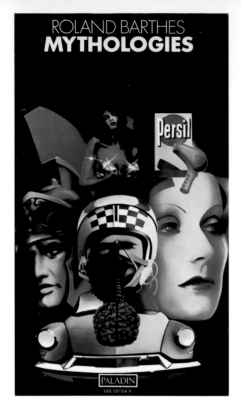

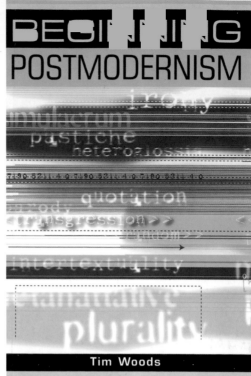

Phillip Castle. Mythologies by Roland Barthes, book cover, Granada Publishing, UK, 1976

[Right] **River Design Company. Beginning Postmodernism** by Tim Woods, book cover, Manchester University Press, UK, 1999

It soon became clear, looking at the work pouring from legions of imitators, that without a very particular kind of talent, 'associative illogic' was most likely to lead to work that was simply a mess. Intuition alone was not enough, but there was no doubt that appeals to this mysterious internal guidance system, which was the unique property of the individual designer or viewer, reflected a wider reluctance in society to submit to any form of imposed, external authority. Was this sufficient, though, to explain the widespread enthusiasm for signifiers that, in the new atomized digital typography, no longer signified in any established, collective sense? The literary critic Fredric Jameson notes how in schizophrenia – a term that he uses as description rather than as diagnosis – as temporal continuities and spoken language break down, 'the signifier in isolation becomes ever more material ... As meaning is lost, the materiality of words becomes obsessive, as is the case when children repeat a word over and over again until its sense is lost ... a signifier that has lost its signified has thereby been transformed into an image.'[13] Something similar seems to be at work in much of the rule-defying design produced during this period, as the materiality of typographic form takes precedence over linguistic sense.

One only has to look at cover designs of books about postmodernism to see how, from the mid-1990s, the unmoored

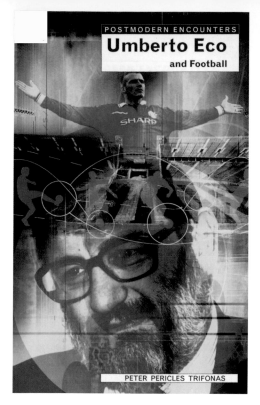

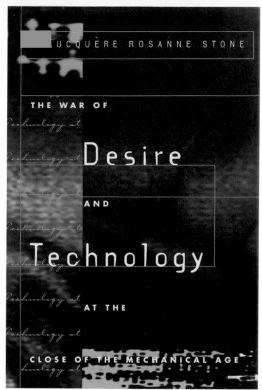

Steve Rawlings. Umberto Eco and Football by
Peter Pericles Trifonas, book cover, Icon Books,
UK, 2001

[Right] **Mimi Ahmed.** The War of Desire and
Technology at the Close of the Mechanical
Age by Allucquère Rosanne Stone, book cover,
MIT Press, USA, 1995

page and its nebulous, associative space became the defining trope
when representing this subject matter. In the 1970s, montage – a
modernist device – was still the most contemporary-looking way
of depicting the collisions and fusions of the postmodern cultural
landscape. In Phillip Castle's airbrush illustration for a paperback
edition of Roland Barthes' *Mythologies*, conventional reference points
are becoming unfixed and jostling each other in new configurations,
suggesting the possibility of new cultural relationships, but each
shiny element is distinct in itself, retaining its own clear boundaries.
In fully postmodern representational space, all that is solid often
melts into an intoxicating, semi-abstract blur. *Beginning Postmodernism*
(1999), an introductory text aimed at students, dissolves postmodern
keywords such as irony, pastiche and intertextuality into a
hyperactive field of shooting horizontal lines. On covers for the
'Postmodern Encounters' series of essays, dealing with topical
themes in the work of Foucault, Baudrillard, Eco, Derrida and others,
the thinkers' heads meld with a tempestuous electronic space, boiling
over with logos, images and word fragments, as though the Zeitgeist
itself is gushing from their brains. On the cover of Allucquère
Rosanne Stone's *The War of Desire and Technology at the Close of the
Mechanical Age* (1995), the title type, contained by a precise-seeming
but arbitrary framework of pink rules, hangs above foggy images
in which nothing definite can be perceived.

Since the mid-1990s, there has been a retreat from the total repudiation of rules, not that this ever held much appeal for most established practitioners. David Carson looks increasingly like a coruscating one-off, rather than the harbinger of a new school of untutored designing driven by raw talent and unfettered intuition. Graphic designers did not need to look far to see that, whatever its merits as a critique of design, the argument that no special know-how was needed to become a designer would encourage anyone who felt like it to buy a copy of QuarkXpress and a few fonts and set up as competition. Designers who have spent several years and run up large debts acquiring a college education have every reason to believe that there are many aspects of being a designer that can only be properly absorbed through study.

If there were sound commercial reasons to preserve the idea of design as a craft, the nature of craft was also undergoing intellectual reassessment. In a perceptive analysis of what it means to possess craft knowledge, published in 1994, the British critic Peter Dormer argues that the 'constitutive rules' that govern a particular kind of craft activity are not external to it. These rules are the activity: they give it its own internal logic, which the practitioner must follow, and, taken together, they add up to a body of knowledge. To divorce them from the activity would be to destroy it.[14] Graphic design without any rules would cease to be graphic design and this is even more the case with typography. As this introduction was written, signs of a growing backlash against rule-less design were starting to emerge from the typographic establishment. A book titled *About Face: Reviving the Rules of Typography*, published in 2002, contends that 'Rules can be broken but never ignored' and this phrase from its introduction is emblazoned in large letters across its title spread, as a guiding principle.[15] The text reiterates conventions of effective typographic practice with which every guide-writer from Jan Tschichold to John Lewis would concur. There is no discussion of postmodernism in the book (ours is a 'modernist society', claims the author) and the typographic experiments of the last 20 years go largely unmentioned.[16]

Yet this period has seen an explosion of creative activity in visual communication, as designers re-examined existing rules and forged new approaches. Graphic design is a much more open, diverse, inclusive and, perhaps too, inventive field as a result of these challenges. Inspired by a revised conception of authorship, which ran counter to postmodern assumptions, graphic work became more self-assertive, idiosyncratic and sometimes extreme, as many examples in this book clearly show. Design now embraces a broad range of stylistic possibilities, from informal approaches inspired by the vernacular – admired for its energy and anti-professionalism – to virtuoso forms of digital image-making that push graphic technology to the limit. The complexity of construction that has been a feature of postmodern design from the start, leading, at the high point of rule-breaking zeal, to the paradox of meaningless complexity finds expression today in spectacularly detailed designs that radiate a commanding sense of expertise.

As a professional activity, graphic design faces an uncertain future now that new technology has opened up graphic production and expression to many more people. Its role in postmodern society is, however, likely to remain central. Postmodern graphic designers are deeply implicated in a consumer culture that makes ever more ingenious use of design as a beacon of identity and a tool of seduction. At the same time, they are freer than ever to question, oppose and perhaps begin to reframe design's future role.

1 Origins

When postmodernism first began to be mentioned in connection with graphic design, the search, among commentators, was for a definable style that could be labelled 'postmodern graphic design'. To an extent these observers succeeded in their aim and by the end of the 1980s, when this 'style' had seemingly run its course, it was possible to believe that postmodern design was over and that other stylistic approaches had taken its place. Most surveys and histories of graphic design covering this period continue to take this view. While there was a kind of graphic design that bore some relation to trends in architecture also labelled 'postmodern', the use of postmodern graphic design as a contained stylistic category is misleading because it implies that the design that succeeded it in stylistic terms no longer has a relationship with postmodernism. Yet if there was, and is, a cultural condition that can be called postmodernism, there is no reason for believing that it came to a sudden halt around 1990 and proponents of postmodernism as a graphic style do not argue that it did. They don't have to, since their analysis confines itself mainly to questions of æsthetics; having defined the style, it is enough that it stops. The cultural factors that gave rise to postmodernism did not disappear in the 1990s and it could be argued that many of them have intensified.

One of the earliest uses of the term 'postmodern' in relation to design in a general sense appeared in 1968, in the British magazine *Design*. A year earlier, art historian and critic Nikolaus Pevsner had described certain tendencies in architecture as postmodern, and design critic Corin Hughes-Stanton proposed to apply the description to 'freewheeling' forms of design thinking previously labelled 'Pop'.[1] The tendency's later eclecticism was already apparent in its use of Art Nouveau, 1920s moderne and pseudo-space age imagery. Hughes-Stanton laments postmodern design's lack of originality and the fact that it has not produced its own contemporary style. He welcomes it, however, not as a rejection of modern design, but as a logical step in its development. 'As an attitude, it is closer to people and what they want: it is prepared to meet all their legitimate needs without moralising about what those needs should be. Its roots are thus deeper embedded in society than those of the Modern school.'[2] He predicts the continuing breakdown of modernist boundaries in design, suggests that design will become more æsthetically adventurous and sees a dawning integration of pleasure-giving and ergonomic factors.

In the 1970s, the term 'postmodern' continued to be applied to architecture by various critics and architects, but it was Charles Jencks who did most to establish the idea, with his book *The Language of Post-Modern Architecture* (1977). Postmodern architects, he argues, are still partly modern in terms of sensibility and use of technology. Consequently, the postmodern style is 'hybrid, double-coded, based on fundamental dualities'.[3] This could entail the juxtaposition of old and new, or the witty inversion of the old, and it nearly always meant the architecture had something strange and paradoxical about it. For Jencks, postmodernism represented the demise of modernism's avant-garde extremism and a partial return to tradition. It was an acknowledgement, too, that contemporary society is composed of different groups with different tastes. Postmodern architecture's hybrid, double-coded forms attempted to communicate both with the elite professional class, able to decipher the references, and the general public, which would enjoy the playful elements. If the dynamiting of the modernist Pruitt-Igoe housing scheme in St Louis, Missouri, on 15 July 1972 spelled the death of modern architecture, as Jencks liked to argue, then, in his view, Michael Graves' controversial, competition-winning Portland building (1982), with its giant, decorative keystone, was postmodern architecture's first major monument.[4]

In graphic design, Wolfgang Weingart was a seminal figure in the development of the 'new wave' that came, in time, to be called postmodernist. Weingart trained as a typesetter in Basle, Switzerland, and from 1968 he was a tutor at Basle's

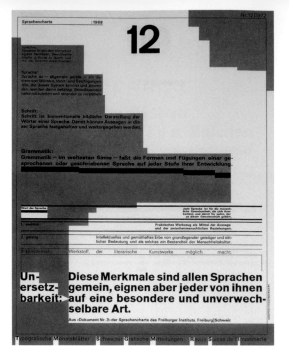

Wolfgang Weingart. *Typografische Monatsblätter*, no. 12, magazine cover, Switzerland, 1972

Kunstgewerbeschule. As a typesetting apprentice, he had been obliged to memorize and regurgitate dozens of 'correct' answers to design problems set out in teaching manuals for typography. 'It seemed as if everything that made me curious was forbidden: to question established typographic practice, change the rules, and to reevaluate its potential,' he writes. 'I was motivated to provoke this stodgy profession and to stretch the typeshop's capabilities to the breaking point, and finally, to prove once again that typography is an art.'[5] In 1964, in an article for the trade journal *Druckspiegel*, he wrote that 'Phototypesetting with its technical possibilities is leading today's typography into a game without game rules.'[6] The editors declined to publish his text in full, fearing they would lose their readers. Weingart was determined not to be constrained by the reductive conventions of Swiss modernist typography, which in his view had hardened into orthodoxy and formula. Using lead type and letterpress, he began to investigate basic typographic relationships, such as size, weight, slant, and the limits of readability. He was fascinated by the effects of letterspacing and he stretched words and lines until the text came close to being unintelligible. In 1972 and 1973, he designed a series of 14 related covers for *Typografische Monatsblätter* magazine, which introduced his challenging ideas to Swiss and international readers.

Weingart's work was spontaneous, intuitive, deeply infused with feeling and it had a significant influence on American design. In 1968, soon after Weingart started at the Kunstgewerbeschule, Dan Friedman began his studies at the school, and from 1970 to 1971,

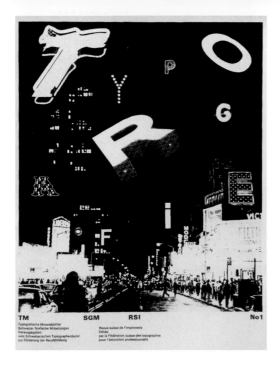

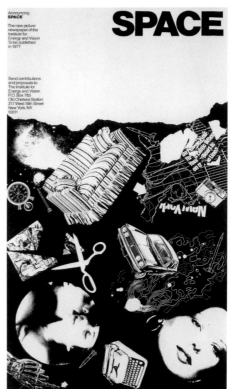

Dan Friedman. Typografische Monatsblätter,
no. 1, magazine cover, Switzerland, 1971

[Right] **Dan Friedman.** Space, promotional
poster for a picture newspaper, USA, 1976

April Greiman also undertook postgraduate work. In 1972, at
Friedman's instigation, Weingart toured the United States,
speaking about his work in Philadelphia, Columbus, Cincinnati,
Princeton, New Haven and Providence.[7] Two early pieces by
Friedman show how his own approach evolved during this period.
A minimalist poster based on the letter 'N', created in 1968 for
a film showing at the Hochschule für Gestaltung in Ulm (where
Friedman also studied), is, in his own words, 'simple, restrained,
orderly, static, exclusive, abstract, pure, reduced, harmonious,
systematic, and integrated'.[8] By contrast, a 1971 cover for *Typografische
Monatsblätter*, in which a series of letterforms found in Times Square,
Manhattan, float above the city, is 'complex, excessive, chaotic,
dynamic, inclusive, vernacular, contextual, expanded, dissonant,
random, and fractured' – qualities that would be seen, with growing
frequency, in the years ahead.[9] After they met in 1972, Friedman
and Greiman had a considerable impact on each other's approach
to design. In a 1976 poster by Friedman for a new picture newspaper,
Space, to be published by the Institute for Vision and Energy, found
images such as a sofa, a typewriter and a pair of lovers float and
revolve around each other like so much debris adrift in deep space.
It was a sign that design was beginning to break from its moorings,
question its commitment to rationalism and determinacy and take
on increasingly unfixed and open-ended new forms.

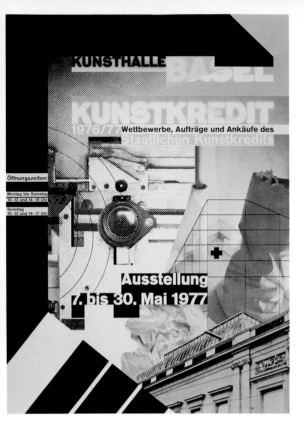

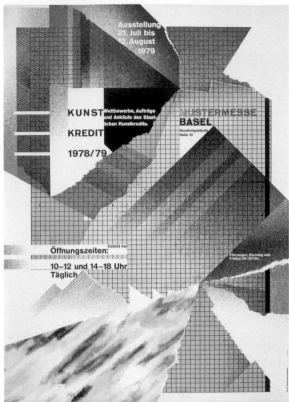

Wolfgang Weingart. Kunstkredit 1976|77, exhibition poster, Switzerland, 1977

[Right] **Wolfgang Weingart.** Kunstkredit 1978|79, exhibition poster, Switzerland, 1979

In the late 1970s, Weingart started to receive commissions to design posters for museums and other cultural organizations and his work changed direction. The collage-like 'Kunstkredit' exhibition poster (1977) was contructed from separate pieces of film layered together and fixed to a film base, then transferred directly to the offset litho printing plate. Weingart's complex pictorial spaces, unprecedented at the time, fused typography, graphic elements and fragments of photographs on equal terms. He exposed sections of the grid, violating its purity with jagged outlines, torn edges, random shapes and imploding sheets of texture, as in the second 'Kunstkredit' poster (1979). Weingart ruptured, twisted and layered his surfaces into multifaceted cubist geometries that embodied a new kind of self-referential graphic space. His photomechanical expressionism, discovered in the darkroom and at the lightbox in the process of working, acted on the viewer's senses and emotions to show that, in the right hands, graphic design could sometimes be a medium for autonomous artistic expression.

An early use of 'postmodernism' specifically in reference to graphic design occurred in 1977, when the American designer Wilburn Bonnell curated an exhibition titled 'Postmodern Typography: Recent American Developments' at the Ryder Gallery in Chicago.[10] Bonnell's decision to label the work 'postmodern' was

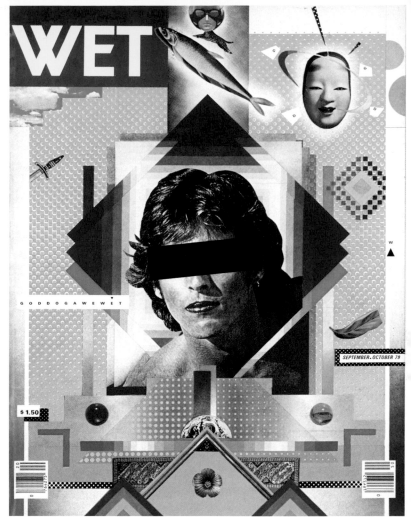

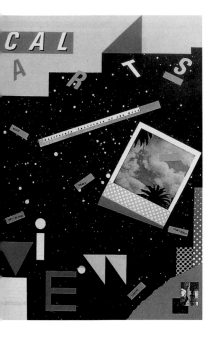

inspired by the term's use in architectural writing. The show featured work by Friedman, Greiman, Steff Geissbuhler, Willi Kunz, Bonnell himself, and others, although its participants did not necessarily regard themselves then (or later) as practitioners of postmodern design, tending to see the term as too limiting or too vague. As so often with design work of an experimental nature, their clients came mainly from the cultural and educational sectors and there seemed little chance at first that it would be taken up in the corporate sphere. Greiman's covers for the *CalArts Viewbook* and for an issue of the West Coast magazine *Wet* in 1979 exemplify many of the characteristics of the new work. Her eclectic visual language draws from Surrealism, Art Deco and ornamental pattern-making. For *Wet*, Greiman and Jayme Odgers, a regular collaborator at this time, collage the various elements together to form an angular, richly detailed graphic setting – a kind of shrine – for the picture of pop singer Ricky Nelson at its centre. In a poster|brochure for California Institute of the Arts, which has become emblematic of the period, Greiman and Odgers present a paradoxical interior space in which gravity is suspended, relationships of scale are overturned and the illusory nature of the panorama is underlined by the presence of a hand, holding up the scene for inspection. A woman's face, gazing out of this world at the viewer, suggests that this rule-free zone should be understood as a mental space with boundless possibilities. Greiman's reflections in interview highlight the subjective concerns of her early designs. 'I'm a feeling person. Obviously the optimum situation is to have a balance between mind and heart and between body and spirit. … I think culturally we're seeing that the forms being expressed in New Wave are very female.'[11] Greiman contrasts the mystery, irrationality and unexplainable aspect of her work with the masculine linearity of Swiss design; her aim, though, was to build additional layers on this sense of order and structure rather than to abandon it.

A poster by Willi Kunz, created in 1978 for an exhibition of photographs by Fredrich Cantor, was also hailed as a quintessential example of postmodern design. Kunz, too, had studied at the Kunstgewerbeschule in Basle before moving in 1970 to the United States. At first sight 'Strange Vicissitudes' is much closer to the linearity that Greiman resisted. It is certainly highly organized: the large type used for the photographer's name contrasts with the tiny type used for the picture's title, which hinges from the 'F' in a vertical white band. The main photograph of actor Marcello Mastroianni plays against the smaller image of an anonymous woman and the black bars at either side lock the two images in place. However, the red title, letterspaced across the main picture, introduces an element of subtle disturbance and the grid of dots (an allusion, Kunz notes, to the lights in the Mastroianni picture) also reads as somewhat arbitrary and strange.[12] The woman looks out from under her fringe with a single eye – a rogue dot that has escaped from the grid – while Mastroianni's eyes are shut tight. In Kunz's poster, the idea of the grid, which had been so central to Swiss design in the 1950s and 1960s, is simultaneously acknowledged and subverted. The vertical cut in the corner of the Mastroianni

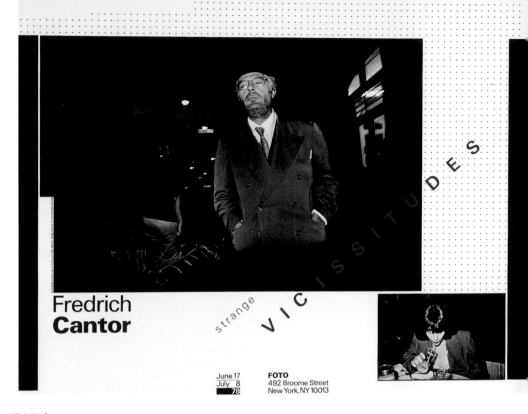

Fredrich
Cantor

strange *VICISSITUDES*

June 17
July 8
78

FOTO
492 Broome Street
New York, NY 10013

Willi Kunz. **Strange Vicissitudes,**
exhibition poster, USA, 1978.
Photographs by Fredrich Cantor

image gives the composition a destabilized 'stepping' movement
often seen in the work of Weingart and other exponents of
typography's new wave.

To appreciate the new wave's impact on design in the
United States, it is necessary to understand how constrained
prevailing conceptions of design had become. An issue of *Print*
magazine devoted to communication design in the 1970s is
titled 'The Triumph of the Corporate Style' and there is a striking
homogeneity in the examples of design and advertising it shows.
Company literature produced by corporations such as Mobil,
Exxon, North American Rockwell and Aristar was orderly, well
structured, undeniably clear, but totally predictable and lifeless
in its use of watered-down modernist forms. 'The 1970s was marked
by the rise of the Corporate Style in communications design and
the subsequent enfeeblement of imaginative activity,' concludes
the issue's introduction. 'It was a period in which security and
safety replaced risk as the dominant selling tool.'[13] The writer
wonders whether anything can be done to bring about a
transformation of attitudes in the 1980s, though, as we have
seen, such changes were already under way. However necessary
these changes might have been, early responses to the new wave
were often negative. Older designers, accustomed to rigorously

suppressing the personal, registered concern at the eruption of wayward subjectivity and resisted the idea, expressed by Weingart and Greiman, that design might be a form of art. These critics saw the new wave's stylistic elements and effects as obstacles to the lucid transmission of the client's message and they dismissed these experiments as a passing fad. An early article about the new wave, titled 'Play and Dismay in Post-Modern Graphics', quotes a senior New York designer: 'I don't consider graphic design to be an opportunity to advance art forms. It has to advance the client's interest.'[14] For the critic Marc Treib, postmodernism's assault on the eye with pages of blips, slits, dots and zits was initially enjoyable, an exhilarating relief from ordinary design, but rapidly became exhausting and tedious. 'It is like listening to six radios playing at once, each with a different station. This is not charged complexity; it is noise.'[15]

Yet the cultural ideas surfacing in the work of Friedman, Greiman and others had been around for some time, even if they were unfamiliar in graphic design. In his book *Complexity and Contradiction in Architecture*, first published in 1966, Robert Venturi presents a 'gentle manifesto' for an architecture that would reflect the richness and ambiguity of contemporary experience. Architects, he argues, can no longer allow themselves to be intimidated by orthodox modern architecture's puritanical injunctions and restrictions. Among other preferences, Venturi favours elements that are hybrid rather than pure, distorted rather than straightforward, ambiguous rather than articulated, accommodating rather than excluding, redundant rather than simple, and inconsistent and equivocal rather than direct and clear. Architecture, he declares, should evoke many levels of meaning; it should be possible to read it and use it in several ways at the same time. 'I am for messy vitality over obvious unity,' writes Venturi. 'I include the non sequitur and proclaim the duality.'[16] More, he concludes, inverting the well-worn modernist axiom, is not less. In their famous study *Learning from Las Vegas* (1972), Venturi, Denise Scott Brown and Steven Izenour applied some of these ideas to a detailed, illustrated analysis of the Las Vegas Strip, which they addressed non-judgementally purely as a phenomenon of architectural communication.[17] The attention they gave to brash roadside signs usually dismissed by the cultured as debased and ugly encouraged graphic designers to look more sympathetically at vernacular design as a way of breaking free from modernism, particularly at Cranbrook Academy of Art (see chapter 2).

When measured against the radical challenges directed at architectural practice in Venturi's manifesto, much of the graphic design first labelled 'postmodern' now looks far from shocking. In the late 1980s and early 1990s, designers would go much further in their attempts to create multilayered communications that captured the complexity and ambiguity of modern experience. Despite Weingart's experiments with text setting, most early postmodern designers accepted the established rules of intelligible typographic delivery and they concentrated their attention on what happened around the edges of the text rather than on new ways of handling text itself. This distinction can be seen in *Fetish*, a magazine started by Jane Kosstrin and David Sterling, former students of Cranbrook Academy of Art and founders of Doublespace, based in New York. The shortlived, large-format publication, aimed at metropolitan sophisticates with a fascination for material culture, was a postmodern proposition in its own right. A special issue on synthetics, published in 1980, features articles about plastics, pocket cameras, astro turf, Barbie dolls, and synthesizer music. Picture material, feature titles and pull-quotes underscored by heavy rules are set on the slant and irregular chunks of striped pattern punctuate the issue; one spread features swathes of zebra pattern. A feature titled 'Machine Music' employs some of the new wave's most familiar typographic gestures – letterspacing, mixed type weights – and an inventive repertoire of devices and symbols evokes the unfamiliar notation and sounds of contemporary electronic music. While the pages are busy with activity and 'noise', the main text is presented in five conventionally set, sanserif columns. In an interview with fashion designer Betsey Johnson, seven narrow text columns, treated as a graphic component of the spread alongside other elements, descend in a series of roughly equal steps, but the unconventional text block still retains a high degree of clarity.

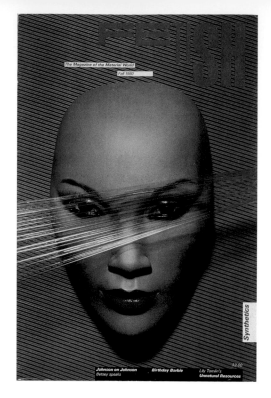

[Right & opposite] **Doublespace. Fetish**, no. 2, magazine cover and spreads, USA, 1980. Cover photograph by Jere Cockrell. Betsey Johnson photograph by Stephen Ruehr

[Top & bottom] **Christoph Radl.** Memphis logos, Italy, 1982 and 1983

[Middle] **Valentina Grego.** Memphis logo, Italy, 1983

In *Fetish*, graphic design is the medium of a new sensibility: informal, playful, ironic, synthetic, pluralist, referential, and confident in the intrinsic interest and value of everyday popular culture. In late 1980, this emerging global sensibility saw the birth of a three-dimensional design phenomenon that would have far-reaching international influence, even in the sphere of graphic design. The Memphis design group founded in Milan by Ettore Sottsass, Michele De Lucchi and others took its name – according to Memphis chronicler Barbara Radice – from the Bob Dylan song 'Stuck Inside of Mobile with the Memphis Blues Again'. Memphis objects were most striking for their use of plastic laminates printed with a wild variety of colourful patterns. Like roadside neon signs, laminates were identified with ordinary, 'undesigned' environments: coffee shops, ice cream parlours, milk bars, fast-food restaurants, and kitchens and bathrooms in the home. Memphis applied this cheap-looking material to luxurious pieces for the living room that were as wilful and bizarre as they were æsthetically compelling. Memphis designs, Radice observes, are 'assemblages, agglomerates ... deposits of decorations that overlap, intersect, add up and flow together ...'[18] She goes on to explain: 'The whole Memphis idea is oriented toward a sensory concentration based on instability, on provisional representation of provisional states and of events and signs that fade, blur, fog up and are consumed.... Communication – true communication – is not

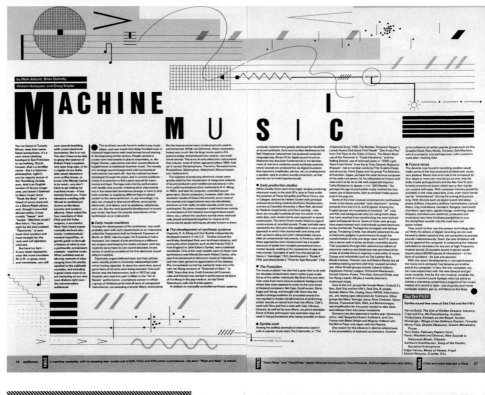

M A C H I N E M U S I C

by Mark Abbott, Brian Doherty, William Hohauser, and Doug Snyder

You've heard of Tuxedo Moon, seen that name listed somewhere, it's a new-wave clothing boutique in San Francisco or something; Stockhausen, that's a familiar name—(he's a German philosopher, right?)—and who's that guy in the Throbbing Gristle, sure, that's an English version of Scrape imaginin; you haven't listened to disco music since "Rock the Boat" and a friend of yours once put on a Steve Reich album and, though it sounded almost pretty, it was mostly "beeps" and "boops." Machine music? Not into it. You gaze right by the bins marked "Electronic" at your local vinyl vendors and head straight for the rock-and-roll alphabet-card area.

But here's a fact—if your taste represents even the most munchane M.O.R. or grass-roots anti-trendiness, you still own records building with covert electronic innovation, like it or not. You don't have to be able to grasp the essence of Robert Fripp's explanatory tape-loop raps, or be a regular at any SoHo side-street laboratory-cum-coffee house, or know who Wendy Carlos is (or was)—you don't have to go looking for machine music—it has already found you. From elevators creeping with Muzak to synthesized drums on the latest country and western albums. Fetish asked the four members of Slick Dick and the Volkswagens, a successful, New York-based experimentally-inclined electronic/mechanical/musical expedition, to gently guide us through a history of what is now a profoundly omnipresent creature—machine music. What unfolded was an alluring network of tales ranging from the starkly seminal to the sublimely complex, and including a great mass most of us are harboring on our very own shelves right now—the commonplace subliminal.

The synthetic sounds found in today's pop music (disco and new wave) have deep founded roots in classical experiments with mechanized sound starting in the beginning of this century. People wanted to create new instruments to play in ensembles, or, like Edgar Varese, used siren and other sound effects as supplements to traditional chamber music. The novelty of a strange sound incorporated with conventional instruments has worn off—but the method has been developed through the years, and in current academic music it is common to find a piece scored for transverse and tape. The tape runs into the performance with totally new sounds, imitating other instruments not in the ensemble (sometimes strange or hard-to-find instruments), or supplying different figures played earlier by the same performer. In pop recordings, it is also not unusual to find sound effects, some purely electronic, and others, such as airplanes, telephones, cars, etc. But the most powerful development in recent pop music has been the popular assimilation of the synthesizer as an instrument.

The logistics of producing electronic music were greatly aided by the introduction of integrated systems of sound producers and modifiers (modulators) in the form called synthesizers (first marketed by R. A. Moog in 1964), and later by computer-controlled sound generators. Some composers, however, didn't like the aesthetic results of these instruments, since most of the sounds and organizations were too identifiable, and since at first really complex sounds could not be synthesized. So some composers used machines mainly as extensions of the classical sound generators (oscillators, etc.), where the resultant sounds were meticulously pieced and layered together by means of the commercial studio techniques already known to them.

● Early music machines

Tracing the development of the synthesizer, one could probably start with early experiments on an instrument called the Trautonium built by Frederick Trautwein of Berlin in 1928. Like the organ, the Trautonium had a keyboard, but instead of just switching to a different set of pipes and keeping the scales constant, each key could be set to have its own sound and pitch. In one sense, it could be considered the first electronic sound effects machine.

Electronic organs followed soon, but their pitches were usually preset in chromatic relationships (with minor tuning capacity). At about the same time, sound generators of all sorts were being invented. One such device was the Instaurumon, built in 1913 by Luigi Russolo and used that year in Milan in the "Art of Noises" performance, a symphony concert in which a group of Dadaists performed all sorts of unexpected instruments, not excluding a bicycle. Many instruments like the Instaurumon were constructed and used in performances. While not electronic, these resonators looked very much like the large horns used in P.A. systems today, and produced very unique, non-traditional sounds. The array of early electronic instruments that ensued, most of which appeared before 1950, had sci-fi names: Dynamophone, Theremin, Rumanimaphonti, Russolofono, Sphyrophon, Melochord, Mixtur-teremum, Electronium.

● The development of synthesis systems

Originally, R. A. Moog and Don Buchla independently developed systems in the U.S. Studies around the world also developed their own synthesis systems, and eventually other systems, such as the Putney VCS-3 from England or John Eaton's Syn-tet, were marketed worldwide. One of the most notable users of these new synthesizers was Wendy (formerly Walter) Carlos, who was first introduced to electronic music at Columbia, and then later gained an appreciation of the classics. She immediately turned her particular taste into a hit with her Moog versions of "Switched-on Bach," in 1968. Since that time, Keith Emerson (of Emerson, Lake and Palmer) has worked in performance renditions of the Moog in the pop medium, as has David Rosenboom with the Buchla system.

In addition to manually controlled synthesis systems, computer systems have greatly advanced the flexibility of sound synthesis. Early work by Max Mathews at the Bell Telephone Laboratories has produced computer languages (eg. Music IV) for digital sound structure. Mathews has also been fundamental in the development of real-time computer sound synthesis systems, where sounds are produced live via digital (numbers that represent amplitudes, pitches, etc.) to analog (what a speaker uses to produce sound) conversion, so that sounds can be heard spontaneously.

● Early production studios

While usually there were three major studios producing electronic music in the early 90's, (one in Paris under the direction of Pierre Schaeffer and Pierre Henry; one in Cologne, directed by Herbert Eimert with principal achievements being made by Karlheinz Stockhausen; and one at Columbia University in New York, directed by Vladimir Ussachevsky and Otto Luening)—now there are virtually hundreds all over the world. In the early days, each studio had its own approach to sound construction. The early French works relied on organic constructions of recorded sounds. These methods were rejected by the Germans who established a more purist approach in which they started with sine tones and built up layers using new pitch relationships not possible on conventional instruments. In America, both of these approaches were incorporated into a broader spectrum of styles that included conventional instrumental sounds, leading to the coexistence of tape and instruments. Examples of work from this period are Henry's "Astrologie" ('51), Stockhausen's "Studie II" ('54), and Ussachevsky's "Piece for Tape Recorder" ('54).

● The Producers

The music producer has also had a great deal to do with the increase of electronics used in today's pop music. Some of the earlier individuals like Brian Eno and John Cale came from more serious academic backgrounds where they were exposed to music by the new breed of classical composers like Cage, Stockhausen, Berio, Kagel and Young, and brought with them into the studio a strange aesthetic for processed sound that has resulted in drastic transformations of performing artists' sounds on record from their live efforts. Cale's work with Nico and Eno's work with Cale, Ultravox, Genesis, as well as his own efforts, are prime examples. Some of these techniques have even been kept and used in live performances after being recorded on disco.

● Synthe-rock

Among the earliest examples of electronics used in rock or popular music were The Chipmunks, in "The Chipmunk Song" ('58), The Beatles' Sergeant Pepper's Lonely Hearts Club Band, Pink Floyds' "See Emily Play" from The Piper at the Gates of Dawn, The Beach Boys' use of the Theremin in "Good Vibrations," and the Rolling Stones' use of reversed piano in "2000 Light Years From Home" from the By Their Satanic Majesties Request—not to mention works by The Grateful Dead, and of course, Frank Zappa and his group The Mothers of Invention. Zappa, perhaps the most serious composer of the early rock genre, let his influences be known and even went so far as to ask well-respected impresario Cathy Berberian to appear in his "200 Motels." So, perhaps the age of psychedelia really marked the first heavy use of electronics, later to achieve finally spaces in the pop era.

Some of the most unusual contemporary synthesized music is the dance-oriented "rock-electronic" coming primarily from the U.S.A. and England. Among the English groups are musicians of classical, "art" rock and folk rock backgrounds who are using fresh ideas that have resulted from transforming the new technologies and popular forms. Some of these new groups have experimented with rhythmically-pulsed electronic bursts and blends. Perhaps the strangest and darkest group, Throbbing Gristle, has steadily advanced its use of electronic gadgets in performance through the transformation of only one large mixer and P.A. system into a stereo wall of active synthetic controlled sound. Their popularity through their adventurous elitism of electronic violence and bleakness has permitted other artists of similar focus to organize a new cadre of music. Groups and individuals such as The Leather Nun, Monte Cazazza, Thomas Leer and Robert Rental are all breaking existing barriers with their warped sensibilities. Other British groups include Cabaret Voltaire, Experiences, Human League, Orchestral Manoeuvers, Durutti Column, Protex, This Heat, General Strike, and the Flying Lizards. All play a heavily electronic rhythmical music.

Here in the U.S. groups like Tuxedo Moon, Units (S.F.), Ron, Sick Dick and the VW's, Dark Day, 8-people, Suicide, Martin Rev, Implog, Devo, WKGB, Information, etc., are relying upon electronics for Pavlovian rhythms. Other groups like Mars, Teenage Jesus, Mez Chatham, Glenn Branca, Theoretical Girls, DNA, and Barbershopgraze use amplification for the power needed to take ideas and reshape them into sonic revelations.

Germany has also spawned a healthy pop/electronics scene, with Tangerine Dream, Kraftwerk, and Cars France with Metal Urbain and Magma; Holland with the Minny Pops; and Japan with the Plastics.

One reason for this advance in electric eclecticism is the accessibility of keyboard synthesizers. Another is the influence of earlier popular groups such as The Grateful Dead, Roxy Music, Genesis, Soft Machine, solo Eno projects, and perhaps even John Lennon's work after meeting Yoko.

● Future music

The devices now found in recording studios would make some of the first producers of electronic music very jealous. Music that once had to be composed on four tapes or more can now be put out on one, and the bulky knobs and equalizers and the like now fit comfortably around one board which two or four hands can control with ease. With computer memory presently available in the most expensive units, even more hands can be "remembered" during the mixing and processing. With devices such as digital reverb and delay, phase shifters, frequency shifters, harmonizers, various filters, ring modulators, vocoders, flangers, real reverb chambers, tape echo, speed change, reverbing, wave shapers, and electronic switches, producers and musicians now have limitless possibilities to turn the straightest sounds into the most way-out space noises.

How much further can the present technology take us? With the advent of digital recording we can look forward to better systems that use computers to process sounds instantaneously. Soon, the only limitation will be the speed of the computer in conducting the massive calculations necessary for any sort of high-frequency musical sound. (A complex sound in stereo would require about 80,000 pieces of information—in the form of numbers—for just one second.)

With the recent developments in microprocessors, the home mini-computer has become yet another tool of the composer. In fact, the non-computer, too, can now experiment with the new devices and get sonic rewards. And for the non-musical, consider the work of musician Laurie Spiegel, who has plans to market a microchip containing a program of her music, instead of a record or tape—just plug into your home computer system, get up, and dance to the beep.

Top Ten Picks

Synthe-sound fave raves of Slick Dick and the VW's

Harold Budd, The Oak of Golden Dreams, Advance.
Fripp and Eno, No Pussyfooting, Antilles.
Philip Glass, Einstein on the Beach, Tomato.
Minamegatu, Wings of the Delirious Dancer, Finnadar.
Minny Pops, Drastic Measures, Drastic Movement, Plures.
Tony Oxley, February Papers, Incus.
Reich, Maxfield and Oliveros, New Sounds in Electronic Music, Odyssey.
Karlheinz Stockhausen, Song of the Youths, Deutsche Gramophone.
Edgar Varese, Music of Varese, Angel.
Michel Waisvisz, Crackle, S.A.J.

1952 A machine-washable, with-no-pressing steer-sucker suit of 60% Orlon and 40% cotton is introduced—the term "Wash and Wear" is coined. 1953 "Saran Wrap" and "HandWrap" plastic films are introduced by Dow Chemical. DuPont begins work with Teflon. 1954 Orlon and nylon featured in Paris

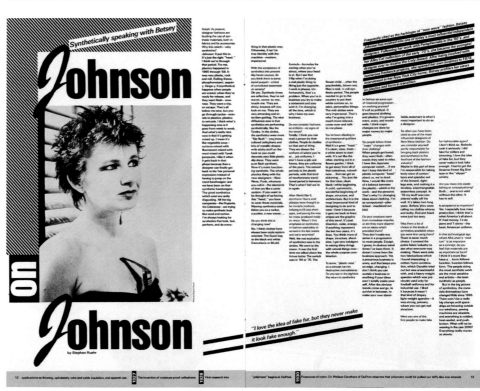

Johnson on Johnson

Synthetically speaking with Betsey Johnson

by Stephen Ruehr

Frequently cited as the harbinger of "new wave" fashion, Betsey Johnson has evolved into one of today's most influential independent designers. Following her work with Paraphernalia in the '60's, she became the youngest designer ever to receive the Coty Award. After being involved with numerous freelance projects, she opened her own business in 1978. Interviewed in her New York City home, Betsey proffers her views on plastics and form in transition.

Fetish: At present, designer fashions are touting the use of synthetic materials, both in fabrics and for accessories. Why this interest—why synthetics?

Johnson: It just fits in. It's just the right "head." I think we're through that period. For me, plastics happened in 1985 through '68. It was very plastic, rock and roll, Rolling Stone, phosphorescent, sequin-y, fringe-y. It (synthetics) happens when people are scared; when they're ready for release, and they want flash—newness. They want a trip, an escape. That's a bit below me now, but you go through cycles—natural-ists to plastics, plastics to naturals. I think what's happening now is it goes from weak to weak. And what's really nice now is that it's getting mixed up. I mean it's like vegetable soup—cottons mixed with fluorescent mixed with wool mixed with Tyvek jumpsuits. I like it when it gets back in that phase because then a designer can finally get back to his "her personal expression instead of having to jump on the trend bandwagon; and we have been on that synthetic bandwagon. The good synthetics which exist are really disgusting. All the big companies—the Duponts, the Celaneses—are trying to make synthetic look like wool and cotton. I'm always looking for synthetics that look, feel, perform, and do every-thing in that plastic way. Otherwise, it isn't in true identity with the machine—modern, impersonal.

With the acceptance of synthetics into present day haute couture, do you think there is some social purport—a kind of convoluted statement on society?

Oh yes. Synthetic times are reflective, they're not warm, come-to-me, touch-me. They are slinky, bounce-off-me, look-at-me. They are very attracting and attention-getting. The nice difference now is that synthetics are performing synthetically, like the Tyveks. In the sixties, the synthetics were more "flip-flash"—you know, colored cellophanes and bits of metallic shapes with sticky stuff on the back so you could decorate your little plastic slip dress. They were pure flash synthetic. Now it's more fascinating synthetic. The whole plastics thing with the new designers—New Wave, Punk, whatever you call it—the elements of that are like a caste system. If you want to be thought of as having this "head," you have to wear these materials. Wearing synthetics establishes a look now as a rocker, a punker, a new-waver ...

Do you think this is changing now?

No, I think clothes have always been caste system oriented. The Gucci bag to the black and white Danceteria or Mudd

formula—formulas for starting when you're about, where your head is at. But I see that I fall right into a real plastic thing to liking just the opposite. I work in phases. Unfortunately, that's a problem. When you're in business you try to make a statement and stay with it. I'm changing all the time, which is why I have my own business.

Do you consider fashions as artifacts—as signs of the times?

Totally. I think you can read a person by their clothes. People do studies on that sort of thing. They are always the uniform of where you're at ... job uniforms, I don't have a job uniform, I don't have a uniform of the years. The natural periods to the plastic periods, with that kind of marching—tran-sitional period in between. That's what I feel we're in again.

After World War II, synthetic fibers and plastics were thought to be miracle products, helping to fill vast short-ages, and paving the way for mass-produced ready-to-wear. Wasn't this emphasis on synthetics in fashion ostensibly re-versed in the late sixties and early seventies? Well, the real explosion of synthetics was in the sixties. In the next to the sixties it was thought to be replaced by anything in this big plastic time. And that filtered up into what people in the real world, and not really designed ... the whole surprise combination.

To some, "plastic-ness" as a concept carries destructive connotations. Do you see in the eighties the return to synthetics

flower child ... after the psychedelic, blown out, Mac's rock-'n-roll syn-thetic period. The people needed to go to the country to put their white cottons on, to relax, personalize things. The mid-sixties were very impersonal. That's why I'm going into a much more relaxed, come-over-and-talk-to-me phase.

You've been alluding to the impersonal qualities of synthetics. Well it's a great "head." It's clean, clear, fresh—a white sheen to start with. It's not like the other, sterling-out in a flower garden. I think to get away from all of that contrivance, natural-ness ... that can get so sickening ... You just die for that clear, clean black-'white beginning. A cold, optimistic, wonderful beginning of shape, structure, and architecture. But it is the most impersonal kind of designing to do and to wear. I love it because it gets me back in lines; it's the purest kind of shape, structure, design. If anything important to me in this life—that my synthetic clothes are very come-to-me, mild-to-me—stripes are the graphic of this trend. It's just direction, order, energy. If anything represents the last two years, it's lines. You think more of shape, structure, direc-tion. I get very indulgent in mixing shiny things with natural things now—the whole surprise com-bination.

To some, "plastic-ness" as a concept carries destructive connotations. Do you see in the eighties the return to synthetics

in fashion as some sort of historical progression, an evolving process? It's all so political. It goes beyond clothing and plastics. It's govern-ment, scary, and world-wide. I think major changes are done by major money by major people.

Do people follow these "major" changes with their clothing? When people get bored, they want flash—after-words they need to retire. I have this Japanese computer watch ... if we don't keep this kind of plastic computer "head" about us, we're dead. Now, I would like more of a balance between the plastic—which is the work—and the personal. That's why I'm changing ideas about clothing. I'm so computer-ized—plas-ticked—machined out there ...

Do your creations stem from immediate impulse, or are they more depend-ent on ideas which provoke them? They don't make any sense in a progression to most people. Except, I guess, in obvious trend times. I've been there. It doesn't come from the business approach. Yet, a precarious business is scary, and that keeps you on edge, changing. I don't think you can sustain a business or anything if your ideas aren't totally stable your-self. After the obvious trends come and go, to survive in between, to make your own identi-

fiable statement is what's most important to do as a designer.

So often you have been cited as one of the most influential designers of New Wave fashion. Do you consider yourself partly responsible for bringing back plastics and synthetics to the forefront of the fashion industry? Maybe in this part of time I'm responsible for taking body wear of cotton/lycra and spandex out of the leotard, tights-legs area, and making it a timeless, interchangeable, seasonless concept. In '78 my stuff was con-sidered really off the wall. It's taken two long years. Before, they were calling my clothing whorey and tacky. Find and black were just too sexy.

Was there a lot of choice in the kinds of synthetics available when you were first using them? There is never much choice. I covered the entire fabric industry to see what everyone was making. There were only two fabrications which I found interesting: a cotton/lycra combina-tion, which Danskin tried out but was unsuccessful with, and a heavy-weight spandex which was per-viously used only for football uniforms and for industrial use. I liked it because it wasn't like that kind of drapey, light-weight spandex—it was strong, primary, where you can get real structure.

Were you one of the first people to make false

eyelashes or fun fur—fashionable again? I don't think so. Nobody took it seriously. I did false fur clothes and trimming. I love the idea of fake fur, but they never make it look fake enough. I had to get the Sesame Street Big Bird type or the "slipper" type.

Are you more into estab-lishing or conceptualizing? Both ... one is not valid without the other. It has to sell.

Is acceptance so important? Yes. I especially love mass production. I think that's what America is all about. If I had money, I'd do jeans and T-shirts—the basic American uniform.

In this technological age where McLuhan's "med-ium" is so important as a concept, do you feel that materials are as important as form? There isn't a more Bau-haus-y ... form follows function, function follows form. The people doing the most synthetic work are the most sensitive and artistic—the least visually used only for football and industrial. But in the big picture of synthetics, the mate-rials themselves have changed little since 1985. There won't be a really big change until space-ships are hovering outside our windows, sewing machines are obsolete, and everything is molded, heat-sealed, and push-button. What will we be wearing in the year 2000? Everything really moves so slowly.

"I love the idea of fake fur, but they never make it look fake enough."

applications as flooring, upholstery, wire and cable insulation, and apparel use. 1927 The invention of moisture-proof cellophane. 1928 First research into "polymers" begins at DuPont. 1930 Forerunner of nylon. Dr. Wallace Carothers of DuPont observes that polymers could be pulled out taffy-like into strands

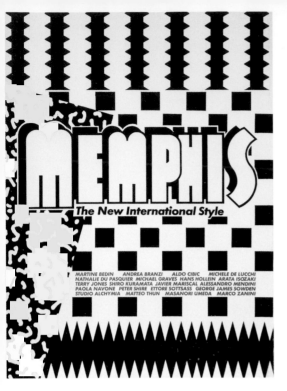

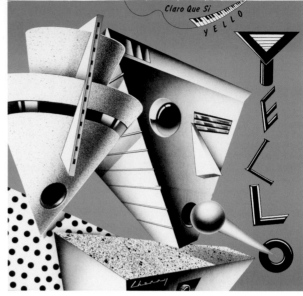

**Designer unknown. Memphis: The New
International Style,** book cover, Electa,
Italy, 1981

[Right] **Jim Cherry. Claro Que Si**
by Yello, album cover, Vertigo, West
Germany, 1981

simply the transmission of information ... Communication always
calls for an exchange of fluids and tensions, for a provocation, and
a challenge. Memphis does not claim to know what people "need,"
but it runs the risk of guessing what people "want".'[19]

Memphis graphics spoke in the same provisional, polyglot
style as the furniture and objects. The cover of the first Memphis
catalogue (1981) presents a jagged collision of sheets of pattern
and Memphis logos are similarly patterned, angular and block-like,
anticipating the geometrical typefaces drawn by Neville Brody
for *The Face*.

It was not surprising then that the startling forms and
imagery of postmodern architecture and furniture design should
inspire graphic commentary from designers and image-makers.
In a 1981 album cover design for the Dadaist Swiss electronic pop
group Yello, provisionality is the guiding theme. Jim Cherry's
sleeve shows two peculiar, synthetic figures, possibly intended
to be members of the band, constructed from a loose collection of
elements that reference modern architecture, domestic appliances
and the world of consumer luxury. One figure's conical head has
a narrow modernist window slit where its eyes would be and a
projecting partition for a nose; the other's left eye looks like a
ventilation panel. Both are decorated with Memphis-like areas
of pattern or texture and the typography of the group's name is
a heterogeneous mix of styles. The cover's mood is retro, though

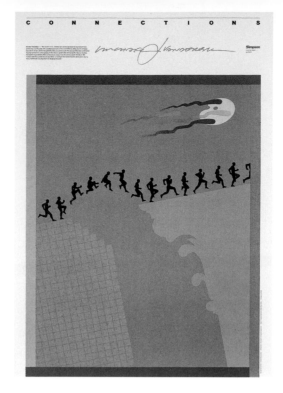

Michael Vanderbyl. Connections,
promotional poster, Simpson Paper,
USA, 1983

it avoids specific quotation, while suggesting that in the playground of consumer culture almost anything has the potential to be plucked from its original context and used as material for semiotic manipulation and bricolage.

In San Francisco, Michael Vanderbyl, a leading member of the Californian new wave, created a number of pieces in response to new tendencies in architecture and design. In a 1983 promotional poster for Simpson Paper, a stream of figures leaps from a modernist skyscraper symbolized by a grid, across a void, and on to the top of a classical column – a clear, if somewhat literal, appeal to the value of pre-modern cultural forms. The decoratively exposed grid recurs in a 1983 poster for the American Institute of Architects, to announce a series of lectures on the theme of the city, where it assumes the outline of a skyscraper skyline surrounded by open, organic space. The postmodern city can seemingly exist in harmonious balance with the surrounding landscape only so long as clear limits to growth – symbolized by a warning sign stamped across the open area – are observed. In a series of promotional mailers for Simpson Paper, Vanderbyl celebrated the work of fashion designer Issey Miyake, architect Michael Graves, and the Memphis group. The Memphis mailer, designed in 1985, indicates the degree to which the new wave's once controversial stylistic innovations had by that time achieved acceptability for commercial clients. Memphis-style texture within the word 'Innovation' helps to give

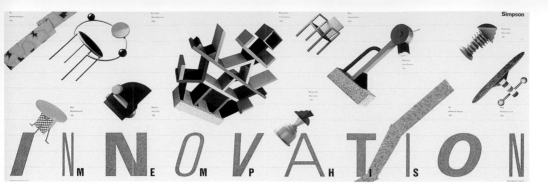

Simpson

Michael Vanderbyl. Innovation,
promotional mailer about Memphis,
Simpson Paper, USA, 1985

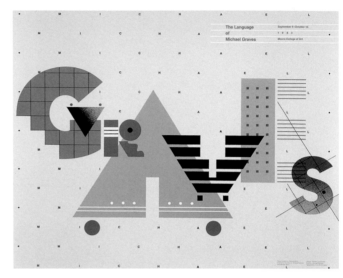

The Language
of
Michael Graves

September 9–October 15
1 9 8 3
Moore College of Art

William Longhauser. The Language
of Michael Graves, exhibition
poster, USA, 1983

cohesion to the widely spaced letters rendered in alternating styles
and weights, and the letterspacing finds structural reinforcement
in the diagonally spaced catalogue of Memphis furniture and
objects. A similarly exuberant response to the formal possibilities
of postmodern architecture and design can be seen in a 1983 poster
by American designer William Longhauser for a Michael Graves
exhibition. Each letter of Graves' surname refers to some aspect
of his architectural language, most notably the 'V' modelled on the
Portland building's oversized, painted keystone. As if this powerful
expression of acclaim were not enough, the growing cult of the
postmodern architectural superstar can be gauged by the fetishistic
use of Graves' first name to compose a repetitive grid of dots.

In Britain, postmodern tendencies in graphic design took
a different form. Where American critics were concerned from
the movement's earliest days to establish a category of design that
could be labelled 'new wave' or 'postmodern', in Britain there were
no attempts at this stage to define the existence of a new wave in
reaction to modernism.[20] This was probably because modernism had
never been the dominant force in British graphic design that it was

in Europe, or that it was, in a more corporate sense, in the United States. Much more than in the US, Britain's new wave was identified with youth culture and popular music and these designers tended to position themselves outside of design's professional mainstream, a quest for identity that could be read as a postmodern gesture in itself. While many designers, using a conceptual approach established in the 1960s, professed to produce communications that could speak univocally to all viewers, some of the most influential British designers of the late 1970s and early 1980s chose to address audiences close to their own concerns. Graphic design was in this fundamental sense an aspect of subculture, a creative tool by which young people communicated among themselves.[21] Their designs were not intended to be meaningful for those on the outside, including designers positioned in the mainstream, and the design profession was consequently slow at first to acknowledge the significance of work that seemed frivolous and marginal to the concerns of visual communication as an ever-expanding business. Nor was this work especially visible to American designers, unless they were music fans. Although some Americans read *The Face*, Neville Brody's large body of work did not become widely known in the US until the late 1980s when *The Graphic Language of Neville Brody* was published. The output of another significant designer, Peter Saville, has never featured in surveys of postmodern design by American writers, even though it is more fully postmodern, in a cultural sense, than much of the decorative work routinely cited as exemplifying early American postmodernism.[22]

If these British designers did come to be termed a 'new wave', it was largely by association. The appellation belonged, in the first instance, to the style of rock music that emerged in the late 1970s after punk rock (see chapter 2 for a consideration of punk graphics) and the key figures – Barney Bubbles, Saville, Brody and Malcolm Garrett – all produced designs for new wave musicians. A song book for Ian Dury designed by Bubbles in 1979 suggests the degree to which Bubbles was aware of international design trends. One version of the book's cover overlays a damaged grid with an informal, ink-drawn portrait of Dury complete with punkish splotches and squiggles, an image close in spirit and style

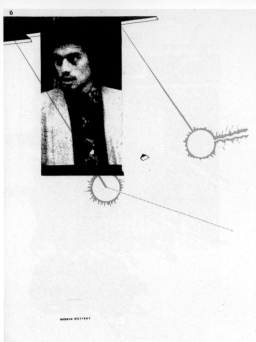

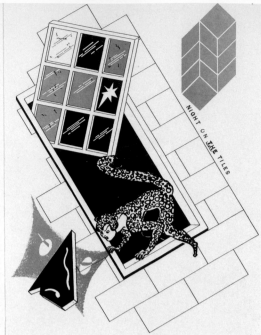

Barney Bubbles. The Ian Dury Songbook,
spread, Wise Publications, UK, 1979

to 'Swiss Punk', the label sometimes applied to Weingart's late 1970s
posters and to designs by Friedman from the same period. Inside,
Bubbles provides a series of enigmatic portraits of individual band
members, which combine surrealistic image-games with a dynamic
command of graphic space. Only Greiman at this stage produced
designs so heavily charged with subjective symbolism.

For the most part, however, British new wave design bore
little resemblance to parallel developments in the US. The work
produced by these designers followed no consistent pattern. It was
eclectic in inspiration and pluralistic in its application of style.
If it was sometimes a response to 'pioneering' modernism, this
manifested itself more as historicism and homage than as a desire
to subvert what later modernism had become. Sometimes it was
hard to pin down specific visual sources for British new wave
designs, but this only served to emphasize their break from graphic
communication's prevailing norms and tropes. Malcolm Garrett's
cover for Magazine's album *The Correct Use of Soap* (1980) combines
conventional typographic and decorative elements – serif typefaces,
box rules, two ellipses – to form a symmetrical device as sharply
defined in appearance as it is inscrutable in purpose. It is much
too elaborate to be called a logo, yet it has the air of being a sign
intended to encode and express the essence of its contents. In what
way does this device relate to 'the correct use of soap'? The question
is clearly unanswerable. The cover says something about the
uncompromising personality of the band, but it also asserts the
designer's freedom to 'make a statement' using his own tools,

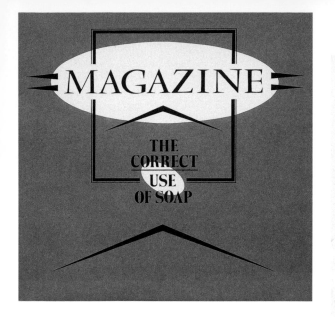

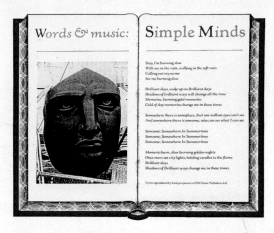

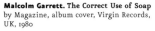

Malcolm Garrett. The Correct Use of Soap
by Magazine, album cover, Virgin Records,
UK, 1980

[Right] **Malcolm Garrett. Someone
Somewhere (In Summertime)** by Simple
Minds, 12-inch single cover, Virgin Records,
UK, 1982

on his own terms. Garrett often cited André Breton and one might
read this strange sleeve as a form of typographic surrealism.

Even when the graphic style employed was radically
different, this quality of strangeness remained. Early releases by
the British band Simple Minds had a hard, precise, robotic beat
and Garrett reflected this mood in cover designs consisting largely
of abstract shapes. When the band's sound became more expansive
and lyrical, he changed direction. For the title of a 12-inch single,
Someone Somewhere (In Summertime) (1982), he used an ornamental
typeface with script-like terminals, which evokes medieval
illuminated manuscripts. Unusually, the lyrics are presented
on the front cover within the frame of a book page, though there
is no attempt to make this look realistic. The pale background
approximates to the texture of parchment, the book's typography
clashes with the title below, and the photograph has the crude
grain – exacerbated by the use of harsh colour – of an old text
book image. In short, the design fulfils all the requirements of
Jencksian postmodernism: it is hybrid, double-coded and
represents a partial return to tradition, though its disjunctive
quality ensures that it can only be read as the product of a
playful, contemporary design sensibility.

In the work of Peter Saville, early British postmodern
design found its most sensitively attuned and rigorously reductive
exponent. Where Garrett and Brody, like Weingart and Greiman,
tended to assert the presence of design, to supercharge their
work with expressive devices and compel viewers to pay attention,

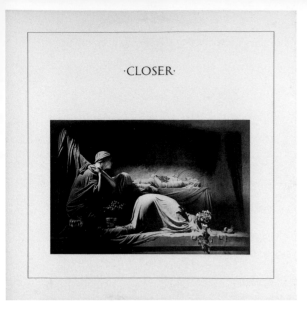

Peter Saville and Martyn Atkins. Closer
by Joy Division, album cover and inner
sleeve, Factory Records, UK, 1980.
Photograph by Bernard Pierre Wolff

Saville achieved the same effect by subtraction. He was an
instinctive rather than theoretical postmodernist who understood
the new cultural mood from his first sight, in 1978, of Philip
Johnson's proposals for the AT&T building, a postmodern New York
skyscraper with a broken classical pediment for a crown. 'Within
12 months, neo-classicism and the influence of architectural
postmodernism were everywhere,' Saville recalls. 'People in
New York were buying columns to put in their apartments.
My contribution was the graphic equivalent. It was always an
emotive feeling and after a year or so I began to trust in my
senses.'[23] No matter how arbitrary Saville's intimations and
borrowings might have seemed, they often struck a chord. In 1980,
for the cover of Closer by the doom-laden Manchester rock band Joy
Division, Saville and his collaborator Martyn Atkins used the bare
minimum of elements. The predominant feature of both 12-inch
sleeve and inner sleeve is whiteness. Each of the four surfaces
carries the same elementary frame constructed from a single rule.
The placement of type inside this frame and the lapidary type style
itself is likewise consistent on all four surfaces. The only image,
positioned on the cover, is a black and white photograph by Bernard
Pierre Wolff, showing four figures in robes mourning a dead man. It
is not clear whether this represents Christ or someone else and the
image is ambiguous in an even more fundamental sense. Does the
photograph show a sculpture recessed in a niche, or a painting? The
scene is lit in such a way that it could be either. Here again, the

design is a hybrid. Its typographic manner is revivalist, its imagery is a neo-classical quotation, its atmosphere is historicist, but its effect comes from the fact that none of these constituent elements would normally find use in combination on a rock album cover. Saville's postmodern devices frame and memorialize the content – music of exceptional emotional power – in a way that was entirely unfamiliar at the time.

These record covers were created at a moment when design was beginning to assume increasing importance in consumer society. Their emphasis on sometimes quite luxurious visual values anticipates the coming decade's economic boom, in which the increasing democratization of design, and a view of design as hedonistic pleasure, would play a central role. Designers were visual interpreters of the emerging mood and they made the assumption that their audiences were sufficiently literate, in a visual sense, to decipher and enjoy a broad range of graphic signals that were often extremely subtle. It may be that, precisely because it was so successful in capturing attention, early postmodern design carried the spores of its own cooption and failure. From the outset, it embodied an implied critique of design's norms, values and limitations. As the 1980s unfolded, designers began to apply postmodern theory to a more self-conscious deconstruction of design's inbuilt assumptions and of its persuasive power as public communication.

2

Deconstruction

From the 1960s onwards, there are many examples of graphic design created by non-designers ignorant of the rules of professional craft; self-taught form-makers who effectively made things up as they went along. Such work is not usually allowed into surveys and histories of design, which are generally based on professional understandings of what constitutes good practice. The profession's aim, expressed through its organizations and in its publications, has been to assert the validity and necessity of its methods as a way of ensuring continuing work for its members. In the postmodern period, restrictive, rule-bound thinking and 'totalizing' tendencies of any kind have been challenged by thinkers in many disciplines. Writing about scientific method, the philosopher of science Paul Feyerabend concludes that 'The only principle that does not inhibit progress is: *anything goes.*'[1] Deviations and errors, he suggests, are essential preconditions of progress; from sloppiness and chaos arise the theories on which the growth of knowledge and scientific advance depend. More generally, postmodern theorists have repeatedly questioned the boundaries between high (valuable) and low (inferior) forms of culture, pointing out the ease with which audiences move between different types of cultural experience – from chart pop to classical music – without pausing to wonder whether this is in some way unacceptable. In such a climate, it becomes increasingly difficult to defend the idea that there are right ways and wrong ways of going about visual communication.

In the 1970s and early 1980s, graphic artists associated with punk rock mounted a sustained assault on professional design's orderly methods and polite conventions, revelling in deviation and chaos and refusing to acknowledge any such category as 'error'. Jamie Reid was a key figure in this movement and his anti-design

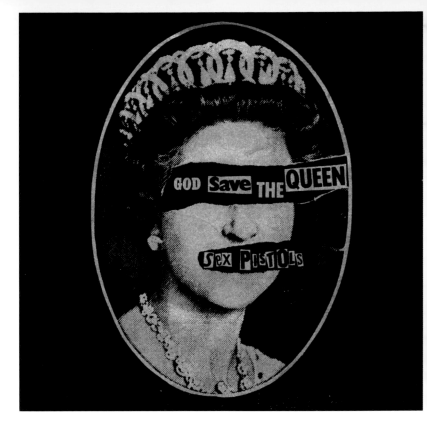

inventions came to define the graphic look of punk, as its angry, musical insurrection took hold overseas. In the mid-1960s, Reid studied painting at Croydon Art School, south London, where he met Malcolm McLaren, who was later to manage the Sex Pistols. In the early 1970s, still based in Croydon, he undertook the graphics for six issues of *Suburban Press*, a community magazine that mixed texts by the Situationists, an international radical movement which had made an incisive critique of modern society, with muck-raking stories about local politics and council corruption. Reid learned many techniques by experimenting with a Multilith 1250 office duplicator. He found the Situationists' theoretical texts verbose and sought ways to simplify these ideas into aggressive graphic form. Like the designers and artists of the 1960s underground press, he ransacked articles and scissored headlines from establishment newspapers and attempted to *détourne* the media – to 'turn it back on itself' – by applying its communications in new contexts. He created a series of stickers printed on fluorescent paper in the style of sales promotions, announcing 'Save petrol, burn cars' and 'Special Offer. This store welcomes shoplifters', which was plastered over shops on Oxford Street, London.

McLaren's invitation in 1976 to become involved with the Sex Pistols, which became the very archetype of a punk rock band,

Jamie Reid. Never Mind the Bollocks
Here's the Sex Pistols by the Sex Pistols,
album cover, Virgin Records, UK, 1977

presented Reid with an opportunity to apply these ideas to a much
more visible public project. On the picture sleeve for the single *God
Save the Queen*, released in May 1977 to mark the British monarch's
silver jubilee celebrations, he masked the Queen's face with rough
strips torn across her eyes and mouth to form voids that carry the
title and band name in cut-up, 'ransom note' lettering. The cover
of the Sex Pistols' first album, *Never Mind the Bollocks Here's the Sex
Pistols* (1977), delivered its verbal affront – considerable, at the time –
in crude, butcher block typography on an acidic yellow background
that was the antithesis of harmonious, tasteful, professional design
and would have been viewed as an unpardonable æsthetic offence
by many practising designers. The song titles, pieced together from
found letters in the now familiar anarchic style, were scattered
randomly across the back of the sleeve. Reid continued in this vein
through the band's subsequent record releases, stickers, tour posters
and promotional materials for the Sex Pistols' film, *The Great Rock 'n'
Roll Swindle*. 'We wanted to make [the audience] think for themselves,
always with that element of questioning the status quo and what is
considered normal,' he explained.[2]

Reid was an artist improvising with graphic techniques
for political purposes, rather than a paid-up member of the
design profession, and this detachment from ordinary professional
assumptions and concerns was typical of punk's amateur designers
and image-makers. In the US, in the late 1970s and early 1980s,
punk scenes thrived in cities such as Los Angeles, Seattle, New York
and Boston, and for these underground communities, street posters
played a critical role. 'For the nascent, developing punk scene –
isolated from the media and the mainstream promoters – the street
poster was the only means of announcing a show. It was *the* medium
of communication, a punk community billboard back in the days
when even college radio wouldn't play the music,' recalls Robert
Newman, a Seattle writer and punk.[3] Posters by band members and
friends were Xeroxed, 'instant printed' or silkscreened in garages
and basements, then flyposted on telephone poles and walls. As
Newman notes, these scratchy images, an urban folk art with a
sinister edge, reflected a belief that anyone could do it and that any
graphic style or level of skill was acceptable. Fine artist Frank Edie's

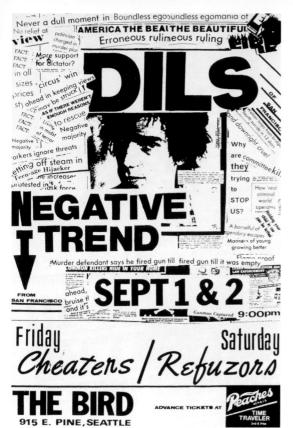

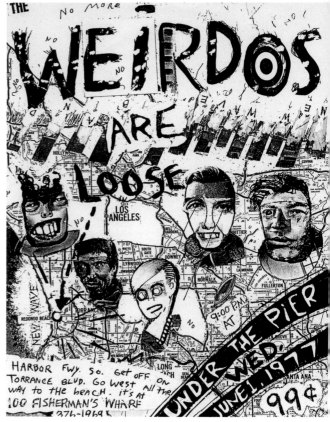

Frank Edie. Concert poster, USA, 1978

[Right] **Cliff Roman.** The Weirdos are Loose, concert poster, USA, 1977

largely typographic poster for The Dils, Negative Trend and other groups, created for The Bird club in 1978, is built from an intricate jigsaw of frequently violent text fragments clipped from newspapers to form an agitated alphabetic backdrop from which the main gig details emerge with powerful clarity. Words slide together and break apart, but a high degree of graphic organization underpins the apparent chaos. The same spiky tension between control and disorder can be seen in a 1977 concert poster by Cliff Roman, a student at California Institute of the Arts and member of The Weirdos. Distorted collage portraits of the group and urgent, hand-drawn lettering – a cheap solution often used by punks – erupt from the Los Angeles street map. The device serves a practical purpose, showing people where to go, while declaring ('The Weirdos are loose …') the presence in the city of an almost combustible punk spirit.

Punk design in its rawest forms was barely recognized by the professional mainstream at this point, let alone accepted as a valid form of design, but by the start of the 1980s some designers were making sustained use of similar devices and strategies. In 1980, Terry Jones, former art director of British *Vogue* and designer of one of the first books about punk, *Not Another Punk Book* (1977), launched his own magazine, *i-D*, to document trends in popular culture and

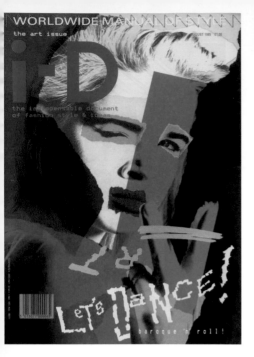

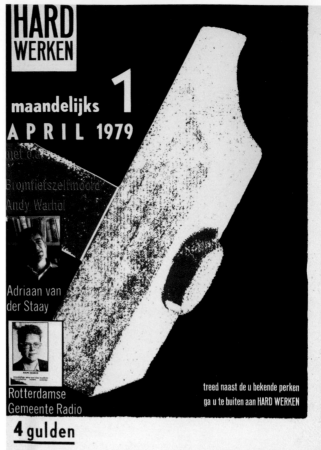

Terry Jones. **i-D**, no. 28, magazine cover, UK, 1985. Photograph by Nick Knight

[Right] **Hard Werken. Hard Werken**, no. 1, magazine cover, The Netherlands, 1979

styles of street fashion. Jones coined the term 'instant design' to describe his restless, speedy, journalistic way of working and, in a 'manual' about his career published in 1990, he catalogues the graphic techniques used to achieve these rapid transcriptions of the passing scene: handmarks made with stick, pencil, pen or brush; stencils and rubber stamps; manual and electric typewriters; computer lettering (at this point still crude and 'low-tech'); montage; photocopying; blocks containing type or logos; and print effects, often developed from mistakes. In the course of the 1980s, all of these devices were used in *i-D*, which went through many changes of graphic style, paper and page size. 'There was a stage when everything was so æsthetically beautiful,' Jones said in 1988. 'What I'm going through now is an anti-style phase. And I think we've got some way to go with the anti-style, the anti-layout and the anti-art before it gets assimilated.'[4]

    In Rotterdam, similar ideas were explored in the magazine *Hard Werken* ('hard work'), which between 1979 and 1982 published ten large-format issues. Its editors were also responsible for its design and by 1980 several members of the team had decided to band together to

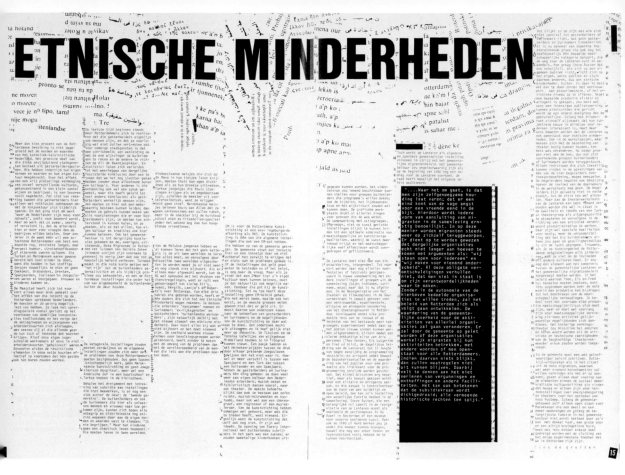

Hard Werken. Hard Werken, no. 3, magazine spread, The Netherlands, 1979

form the Hard Werken Association, among them Rick Vermeulen and Tom van den Haspel (both designers) and Henk Elenga and Gerard Hadders (originally trained as fine artists). They were joined in 1983 by Willem Kars, who had run the graphic workshop where *Hard Werken* magazine began life. Hard Werken, like Terry Jones, occupied a space much closer to mainstream perception than the first wave of punks. They consciously rejected the functionalist tradition, exemplified by Wim Crouwel and Total Design, which had ossified into unadventurous dogma in less supple hands, and their raucously eclectic, supposedly 'anti-typographical' manner was viewed with deep suspicion by more classically inclined colleagues, who labelled it 'ugly'.

'We don't have a collective style,' Hard Werken explained. 'Some of us work intuitively, others more deliberately and controlled, but we're all different. A lot can be used, though. In that sense we are fairly aggressive. It looks as if we combine every conceivable colour and typeface. On the magazine we don't bother very much about sticking to the rules, or about what is proper. Nor are we concerned with functionality or legibility, but rather with the total picture, even if that picture is illegible at times …'[5]

In its first phase, from 1980 to 1985, working mainly for clients in the cultural sector – arts organizations, theatres and publishers – Hard Werken produced some of the most challenging designs of the period. A poster by Van den Haspel for 'The Year of Japanese Film' (1981) anticipates by several years the deconstructed design of the late 1980s. Its free-floating typographic elements and irregularly shaped zones of texture form loose, provisional groupings that suggest instability and flux and seem to have only the most tangential, and certainly non-literal, relationship to the films. However, Hard Werken's inventions, though subjective and informed by ironic humour, did not represent any stated ideology or theoretical position and the group's rule-defying experimental designs coexisted from the outset with more conventional approaches to design, which eventually predominated as Hard Werken mutated into a commercial design group before finally, in the mid-1990s, changing its name. The deviations were not, for its founders, a 'precondition of progress', though their early experiments would continue to attract younger designers for some years. Nor was punk, for the most part, a clearly formulated attack on the professional limits of design. Punk treated visual form with the same freedom as punk music, as part of the same milieu, but the audience for these gestures was society in the broadest sense, rather than designers, though young designers were often members of the audience.

With the tendency termed 'deconstructionist' (and sometimes, confusingly, 'deconstructivist') design, the conventions of professional graphic design, both modernist and eclectic, were subjected to deliberate interrogation, destabilized and repudiated. Deconstructionist designers were fully aware of what design had been, in a historical sense, and of the prescribed forms that conventional opinion believed it should take in the present. However, for reasons that will become clear, the term 'deconstructionist' is problematic in a number of ways when it comes to graphic design. Deconstruction was never a full-blown movement or a coherent, clearly defined 'ism' – like Constructivism or Surrealism – in the sense of having adherents who described themselves as deconstructionists, held meetings, organized exhibitions and issued statements announcing their convictions

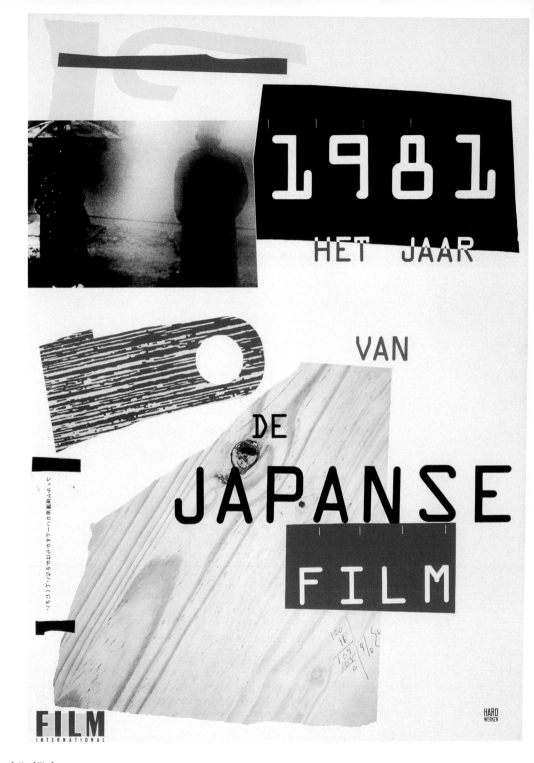

Tom van den Haspel, Hard Werken.
The Year of Japanese Film, film
festival poster, The Netherlands, 1981

and plans. Few of the designers who worked in a 'deconstructionist' way made any direct reference to deconstruction in its theoretical sense, or displayed any close knowledge of key deconstructionist thinkers and texts. If deconstruction was seen as anything at all by most designers, it was as a transiently fashionable, lamentably misguided style, and the small number of designers and critics who did understand deconstruction, or believed in its possibilities for graphic communication, were quick to point out the inadequacy of this view.

Even within philosophical and theoretical circles, deconstruction remains a concept every bit as controversial as postmodernism and the relationship between the two is also open to question. A consideration of such matters falls outside the scope of this book, but it should be borne in mind that deconstruction is an enterprise in which it would be unwise to claim any fixed or final definitions, since the method sets out, with the utmost scepticism and rigour, to interrogate such certainties. The term 'deconstruction' was introduced by the French philosopher Jacques Derrida in his book *On Grammatology*, published in 1967 and translated into English in 1976, and in the following decade, Derrida's ideas had an enormous impact in the universities on the teaching of humanities – to the dismay of those who contested them.[6] *On Grammatology*'s discussion of writing as a distinctive form of representation makes it probably Derrida's single most significant text for graphic designers, since typography and design, as material processes, fall within its concerns.[7] The literary critic Jonathan Culler suggests that we understand deconstruction's essential project as a critique of the hierarchical oppositions that have traditionally structured Western thought. Among these are inside|outside, mind|body, speech|writing, presence|absence, nature|culture and form|meaning. These oppositions are not natural and inevitable, as we tend to assume, but cultural constructions produced by discourses that depend on our taking them for granted. Deconstruction's purpose is not to destroy these categories but to dismantle and 'reinscribe' them – to change their structure and make them function differently.[8] As literary critic Christopher Norris puts it, the deconstructive method 'seeks to undo both

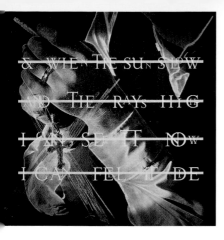

Barnbrook Design. Heathen by David Bowie, CD booklet page, ISO Records, UK, 2002. Photograph by Markus Klinko

a given order of priorities *and* the very system of conceptual opposition that makes that order possible'.[9] Some basic assumptions of deconstructionist thought are that linguistic meaning is unstable and indeterminate; that, for this reason, no method of analysis, not even philosophy (always seen as privileged category), can lay claim to ultimate authority when it comes to textual interpretation; and that interpretation is consequently closer to game-playing than to analysis, as we have traditionally understood the term.[10] In a much-quoted phrase, Derrida went so far as to say, 'There is nothing outside the text.' He coined the word *différance*, combining the French verbs for 'to differ' and 'to defer', to suggest the way that language depends on the play of differences between one word and another, while meaning itself is always deferred (*différance*'s elusive meaning graphically illustrates the point). The purpose of such devices was to prevent conceptual closure, or the reduction of his texts to an ultimate meaning. All of these ideas can be seen at work in postmodern graphic design and Derridean concepts such as *sous rature* – the tactic of putting an idea 'under erasure' by crossing it out, in order to alert the reader not to accept it at face value – have found their way into graphic practice.

It was the 'Deconstructivist Architecture' exhibition held from June to August 1988 at the Museum of Modern Art (MoMA), New York, and its catalogue, that probably did most to introduce deconstruction to graphic designers. Curated by Philip Johnson, with the assistance of Mark Wigley, the exhibition featured architectural projects by Frank Gehry, Daniel Libeskind, Rem Koolhaas, Peter Eisenman, Zaha Hadid, Coop Himmelblau and Bernard Tschumi. What distinguished and linked their work, argued Wigley, was a sensibility in which 'the dream of pure form has been disturbed. Form has become contaminated.'[11] Deconstructive architecture, he explained, does not dismantle buildings, rather it locates the inherent dilemmas within them, exposing the 'symptoms of a repressed impurity'. Deconstructivists pick up where an earlier generation, the Russian Constructivists, left off. In the 1910s and 1920s, avant-garde artists such as Tatlin and Rodchenko proposed radical structures, based on unstable geometric forms, but they never realized them as buildings.

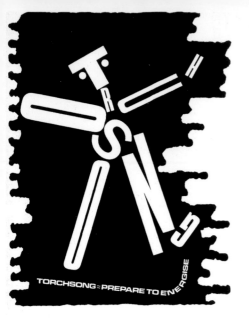

Neville Brody. Magazine advertisement for Torchsong, UK, 1984

Deconstructivism does not want to demolish, decompose or destroy a building's structure by attacking it from the outside. Such a strategy produces a decorative 'æsthetic of danger', but no sense of genuine, concrete threat. Instead, deconstructivism seeks to disrupt, dislocate and deviate by incorporating a disturbance into the building's internal structure. Wigley pointed out that these projects did not share a single style or æsthetic direction, but he also stated that, in his view, they did not derive from the mode of philosophy known as deconstruction and should not be seen as applications of deconstructive theory. Yet, just a few months earlier, the first International Symposium on Deconstruction, at the Tate Gallery, London, had opened with a specially recorded video interview with Derrida by Christopher Norris that made the connections between theory and architecture an explicit point of departure. Eisenman and Tschumi, the two most theoretically aware architects among Johnson and Wigley's seven at MoMA, both disagreed with Wigley's idea of deconstruction in architecture as non-Derridean.[12]

It was hardly surprising, given these differences of interpretation in the architecture camp, that graphic design's borrowing of the label 'deconstruction' lacked focus and rigour. In 1990, in the article 'De-constructing Typography', one of the first published discussions, design historian Philip Meggs uses the term 'deconstructivist' in relation to design and typography, even though the developments he describes do not relate to Constructivism in the way that architectural examples had been shown to do by Johnson and Wigley. This misleading usage would persist for several years and still sometimes occurs. Taking the word 'deconstruction' at face value, Meggs defines it as 'taking the integrated whole apart, or destroying the underlying order that holds a graphic design together'.[13] This reduces visual deconstruction to dismantling, the interpretation that Wigley had been at pains to avoid, and neglects the sense of a disruption or deviation arising from within an architectural (or typographic) structure. Nor does it really explain all the examples that Meggs discusses. In Neville Brody's ad for Torchsong, the letters of 'Torchsong' have been scrambled to form a typographic personage.

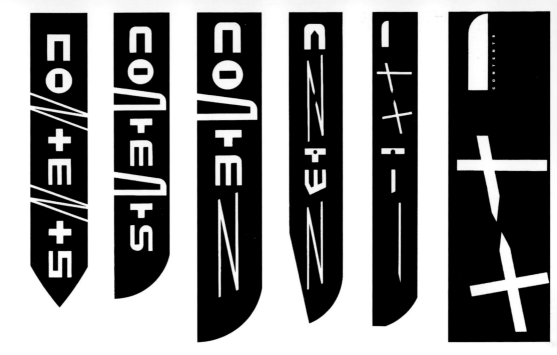

Neville Brody. The Face, nos. 50–55, progressive breakdown of magazine contents page logo, UK, 1984

This may not be traditional, linear typography, but it is still a form of æsthetic order and results in 'a vigorous structure', as Meggs notes, not chaos. The 'underlying order' has not been destroyed by this process so much as dynamically rearranged. However, in 1984, in a series of six designs, Brody subjected the word 'contents', on *The Face* magazine's contents page, to a process of progressive degeneration, month by month, until the letters became an illegible collection of abstract marks. By the early 1990s, the issue of legibility would be one of the main points of concern in discussion about deconstructionist tendencies in design.

In another early article, also published in 1990 in the United States, the designers Chuck Byrne and Martha Witte base their definition of deconstruction in design on a more critically aware sense of deconstruction's origins in theory. For them, the word refers to 'the breaking down of something (an idea, a precept, a word, a value) in order to "decode" its parts in such a way that these act as "informers" on the thing, or on any assumptions or convictions we have regarding it'.[14] Their emphasis on meaning is a significant step on from the notion that deconstruction is simply taking things apart in the hope of 'reinventing' form and 'revitalizing print media'.[15] They suggest that typographic design, with its basis in words and text, is probably the most logical visual extension of deconstruction and they go on to argue that 'when the deconstructionist approach is applied to design, each layer, through the use of language and image, is an intentional performer in a deliberately playful game wherein the viewer can discover

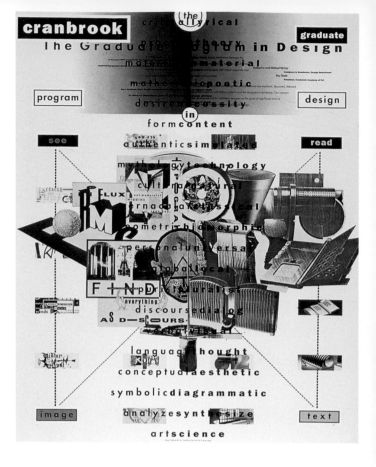

Katherine McCoy. The Graduate Program in Design, poster, Cranbrook Academy of Art, USA, 1989

and experience the hidden complexities of language.'[16] Where early critics of deconstructionist design tended to reject its devices as little more than the application of superfluous complexity and extraneous style, Byrne and Witte advance the view that, on the contrary, these devices potentially act to clarify or develop aspects of a communication that uniform, modernist treatments sometimes obscure.

From the late 1980s, such approaches were most strongly identified with the design department at Cranbrook Academy of Art, where Katherine McCoy and her husband Michael McCoy had been co-chairs since 1971. In 1990, the book *Cranbrook Design: The New Discourse* was published to accompany an exhibition of the same name shown first at Cranbrook Academy of Art Museum (November 1990), then at Steelcase Design Partnership in New York (January 1991). Its design by Katherine McCoy, P. Scott Makela and Mary Lou Kroh offered a striking and then highly unusual example of deconstructive tactics in action. A vertical fault line runs through each of the essays, splitting the text into two columns separated by a narrow gully. The right-hand column is set a millimetre below the left so that the reader's eye, as it travels along the line, must not only jump the text

KATHERINE mcCoy
MICHAEL mcCoy

Art science

Nothing pulls you into the territory between art and science quite so quickly as design. It is the borderline where contradictions and tensions exist between the quantifiable and the poetic. It is the field between desire and necessity. Designers thrive in those conditions, moving between land and water. A typical critique at Cranbrook can easily move in a matter of minutes between

Mathematic poetic

a discussion of the object as a validation of being to the precise mechanical proposal for actuating the object. The discussion moves from Heidegger to the "strange material of the week" or from Lyotard to printing technologies without missing a beat. The free flow of ideas, and the leaps from the technical to the mythical, stem from the attempt to maintain a studio plat-

Desire necessity

form that supports each student's search to find his or her own voice as a designer. The studio is a hothouse that enables students

the new

and faculty to encounter their own visions of the world and act on them — a process that is at times chaotic, conflicting, and occasionally inspiring.

Watching the process of students absorbing new ideas and influences, and the incredible range of interpretations of those ideas into design, is

Mythology technology

an annual experience that is always amazing. In recent years, for example, the de-

discourse

partment has had the experience of watching wood craftsmen metamorphose into high technologists, and graphic designers into software humanists. Yet it all seems consistent. They are bringing a very personal vision to an area that desperately needs it. The messiness of human experi-

Purist pluralist

ence is warming up the cold precision of technology to make it livable, and lived in.

Unlike the Bauhaus, Cranbrook never embraced a singular teaching method or philosophy, other than Saarinen's exhortation to each student to find his or her own way, in the company of other artists and designers who were engaged in the same search. The energy at Cranbrook seems to come from the fact of

Individual communal

the mutual search, although not the mutual conclusion. If design is about life, why shouldn't it have all the complexity, variety, contradiction, and sublimity of life?

Much of the work done at Cranbrook has been dedicated to changing the status quo. It is polemical, calculated to ruffle designers' feathers. And

Dangerous rigorous

Katherine McCoy, P. Scott Makela and Mary Lou Kroh. Cranbrook Design: The New Discourse, book page, Rizzoli, USA, 1990

gap, but step down to the lower level. In a poster for the Cranbrook graduate programme, created in 1989, Katherine McCoy had used a series of Derridean oppositions – 'art|science', 'mythology|technology', 'purist|pluralist', 'vernacular|classical' – to structure the composition around a central spine. In the McCoys' essay exploring aspects of the 'new discourse' at Cranbrook, the designers insert these paired concepts into the text between the widely spaced lines, forming both an unexpected interference and an alternative reading path. The McCoys describe the uses of theory at the academy:

'The emerging ideas emphasized the construction of meaning between the audience and the graphic design piece, a visual transaction that parallels verbal communication. Building on the linguistic theories of semiotics but rejecting the faith in the scientifically predictable transmission of meaning, these ideas began to have an impact on the students' graphic design work. New experiments explored the relationships of text and image and processes of reading and seeing, with texts and images meant to be read in detail, their meanings decoded. Students began to deconstruct the dynamics of visual language and understand it as a filter that inescapably manipulates the audience's response.'[17]

Deconstruction   51

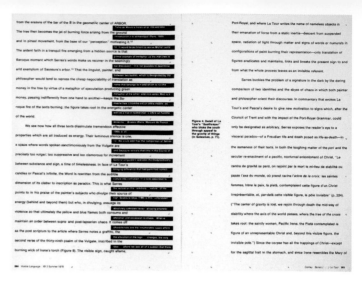

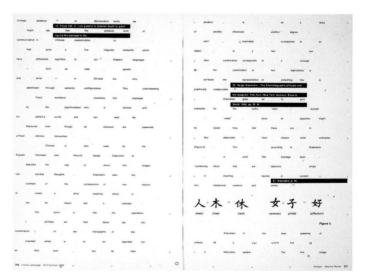

Cranbrook Academy of Art students. Visible **Language,** spreads from 'French Currents of the Letter' issue, USA, 1978

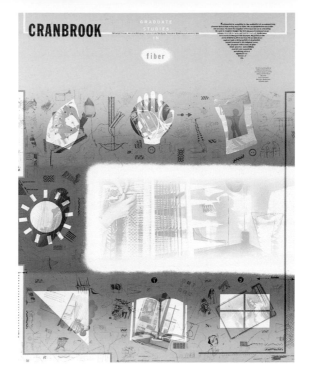

Jeffery Keedy. Graduate Studies in Fiber, poster, Cranbrook Academy of Art, USA, 1984

These experiments were already under way by 1978, when several students, under the direction of Katherine McCoy and Daniel Libeskind (head of architecture at Cranbrook), designed 'French Currents of the Letter', an issue of the journal *Visible Language* devoted to poststructuralist literary theory. As the reader proceeds through the eight essays, standard book conventions are progressively undermined. The text column expands to fill the inner margins, interlinear space increases, word spaces inflate until the text explodes into particles, and footnotes, usually confined to a subsidiary role, slide across into the body of the text. The intention was to highlight the physicality of the printed word's presentation and to establish new non-linear connections between words, opening the possibility of alternative ways of reading.

By the mid-1980s, the students were actively involved in determining the direction of these investigations and critical theory was assuming increasing significance. Jeffery Keedy, a Master of Fine Arts student at the academy from 1983 to 1985, occupied a significant position in these developments. Under the influence of Hal Foster's *The Anti-Æsthetic* (1983) and the writings of Roland Barthes, Keedy began to seek ways of exploring design as a cultural practice closely connected to the themes of popular culture so skilfully deconstructed by Barthes, rather than as a focused, professional, problem-solving tool. A 1984 poster for Cranbrook's fibre studies programme was a calculated exercise in, as Keedy put it, 'doing everything wrong'. There is no strict

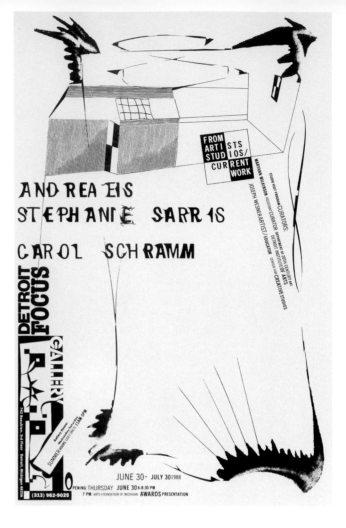

Edward Fella. Exhibition poster, Detroit Focus Gallery, USA, 1988

hierarchy of information or unified message. Instead, quirky details from student sketchbooks are distributed haphazardly across its surface to convey the pulse and flux of the creative process and this intricately layered visual field cannot be absorbed at a single glance. The pursuit of theory continued through the 1980s, as designers such as Andrew Blauvelt, David Frej, Allen Hori and Edward Fella joined the school. While McCoy did much to distil her students' concerns and to act as their public face in her conference appearances and writings, it was not without a certain amount of resistance on her own part and a reluctance to succumb entirely to poststructuralism's assault on established values.

For Keedy and Fella, the pressing task was to challenge the rigid thinking, worn-out visual schemas and sterile corporate applications of modernism in America. Keedy rejected modernism's utopian vision as bankrupt and resisted what he saw as an obsession with regularity and clarity in design. He stressed the personal

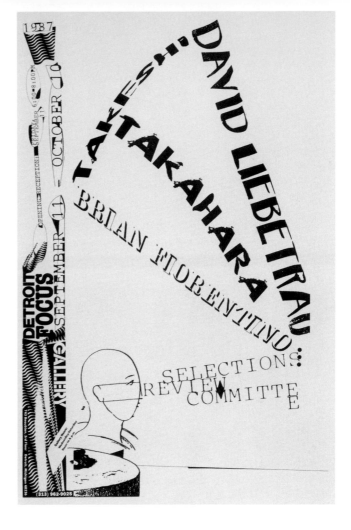

Edward Fella. Exhibition poster,
Detroit Focus Gallery, USA, 1987

nature of his approach and, like McCoy, insisted on the human value
of ambiguity for audiences who were fully capable of negotiating
these complexities. Where graphic design is concerned, he
remarked, 'You don't really need a lot of rules to protect the general
public.'[18] In a conversation published in *Emigre* magazine – virtually
a house journal for deconstructionist design in the early 1990s –
Keedy and Fella discussed the impulses that informed the practice
that Fella termed 'anti-mastery'. Fella complained that design
was becoming smarter and slicker and expressed the view that the
moment had arrived when this 'conceit' must be punctured. His
own response was to base his designs on principles of inconsistency
and irregularity, as seen in late 1980s projects for clients such as the
Detroit Focus Gallery. 'In fact, the irregularity is rigorously thought
out, based loosely on deconstruction,' he said. 'If deconstruction
is a way of exposing the glue that holds together western culture,
I thought, "What is it that holds together typography? It's space."'[19]

Template Gothic

ABCDEFGHIJKLM
NOPQRSTUVWXYZ
abcdefghijklmnop
qrstuvwxyz AND &№
ÆæfiO123456789

Barry Deck. Typeface for Emigre,
USA, c.1990

The goal in typography has always been to control and regularize the use of space – between individual letters, words and lines, between kinds of typographic material (title, main text, subheading, caption), between the text and the page's edge. Fella treated these spaces in a totally elastic way. In a poster for Andrea Eis and other artists (1988), there is no consistency in the spacing within and between the names and the irregularity is pushed further by Fella's distortion of a sanserif typeface with his own hand-drawn thickenings, curves and tails, so that each character is different. Even in the smaller, purely functional typographic elements, there are continuous size changes and a constant flouting of the typographic baseline. At first sight, to many designers coming across Fella's work at the time, his designs could appear random and incompetent, as though their creator were ignorant of every rule governing 'good' typography. His effects were, however, knowing and self-reflexive. He had worked for 30 years as a commercial artist before deciding to become a student at Cranbrook and, as intellectual inspiration, he cited Barthes, the novelist Vladimir Nabokov, semiotics, structuralism, literary criticism and poetics. (Talking to Keedy, Fella quoted Hard Werken: 'A lot can be used.') His well-practised hand-skills meant that he was in no hurry to take up the computer and he bypassed the early bitmap phase, while recognizing – as soon proved to be the case – that his fluidly transformative æsthetic was entirely compatible with the open realm of digital space.

Fella had a marked influence on a generation of designers, both in the United States and elsewhere. This began at Cranbrook, which he often visited before becoming a student, and continued after he graduated when he joined the design faculty at California Institute of the Arts (CalArts) in 1987. By 1990, his experiments were beginning to be publicized more widely and this work continued throughout the decade, in the form of posters to announce lectures by visiting artists – often produced after the event – as well as his own lectures at other institutions. Keedy, who was also teaching at CalArts, acknowledged this influence and a series of programmes created for Los Angeles Contemporary Exhibitions (LACE) from 1988 to 1990 explore the ideas of pastiche, cultural gluttony and the 'anti-

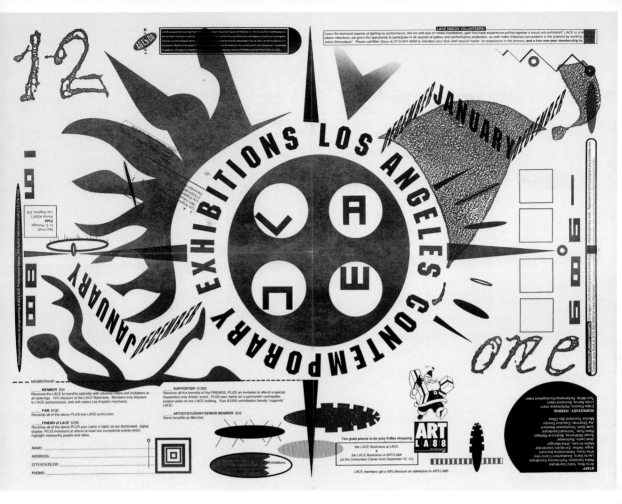

Jeffery Keedy. Event programme,
Los Angeles Contemporary
Exhibitions, USA, 1988

æsthetic' with an aggressive, though intellectually systematic,
disregard for conventional graphic decorum reminiscent of the
rule-breaking mutations in Fella's work. Keedy's typeface Keedy
Sans, launched in 1990 by *Emigre Graphics*, flaunts Fella-esque
inconsistencies in its spacing, while the terminals of the characters
are rounded in some cases and sliced at an angle in others, making
it feel simultaneously soft and sharp – it was advertised in *Emigre*
with the slogan 'Wilfully contradict expectation'. 'It was a typically
postmodern strategy for a work to call attention to the flaws
and artifice on its own construction,' Keedy explained.[20] A similar
strategy can be observed in CalArts graduate Barry Deck's Template
Gothic – another typeface project with an acknowledged debt to
Fella – which, as Deck noted, was intentionally imperfect to reflect
the 'imperfect language of an imperfect world'.[21] It became one
of the defining typefaces of the new decade.

If deconstructionist design in the 1980s was a semi-
underground, seemingly rather subversive activity, carried out

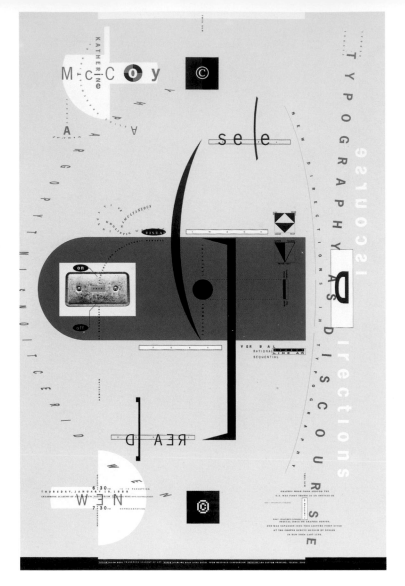

Allen Hori. Typography as Discourse,
event poster, American Institute of
Graphic Arts, USA, 1989

in the insulated 'hothouses' of the academy and viewed by
professionals with deep suspicion, in the early 1990s deconstruction
was primed for popular assimilation. In Europe, one of the channels
by which this would occur had been opened in 1985 when Katherine
McCoy asked Gert Dumbar, Dutch founder of Studio Dumbar, to
lecture at Cranbrook. Dumbar did not share the students' theoretical
agenda, but he was interested in their inventive and expressive
approach to form and, from the mid-1980s onwards, a stream of
Cranbrook students – among them Jan Jancourt, Edward McDonald,
David Frej, Robert Nakata, Allen Hori and Martin Venezky –
became interns at Dumbar's base in The Hague, where their work
helped to redirect the studio's output, especially for cultural clients.

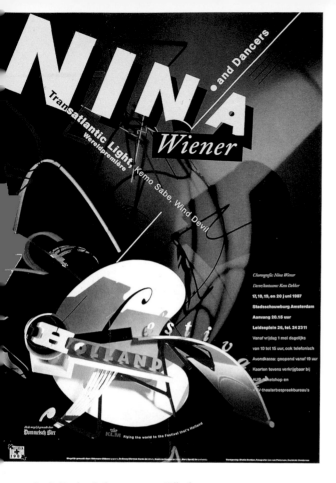

Studio Dumbar. Performance poster, Holland Festival, The Netherlands, 1987. Photograph by Lex van Pieterson

[Right] **Why Not Associates. Next Directory,** catalogue cover, front and back, Next, UK, 1991. Photography by Why Not Associates and Rocco Redondo

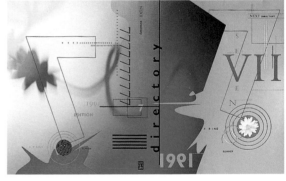

From 1985 to 1987, Dumbar was professor of graphic design at the Royal College of Art in London, where he had a marked impact on a number of students, most notably David Ellis and Andrew Altmann, who, on graduation in 1987, formed Why Not Associates. Where Cranbrook design had been steeped in theory and sometimes made these ideas the subject matter of the design – as in Allen Hori's 'Typography as Discourse' poster (1989) – Why Not's commercial projects of the late 1980s and early 1990s employed superficially similar visual devices for largely æsthetic effect. In a directory cover for the Next clothing company, the typographic elements float at random in an indeterminate, partly photographic, pictorial space. The second half of the date, 1991, is flipped to form a

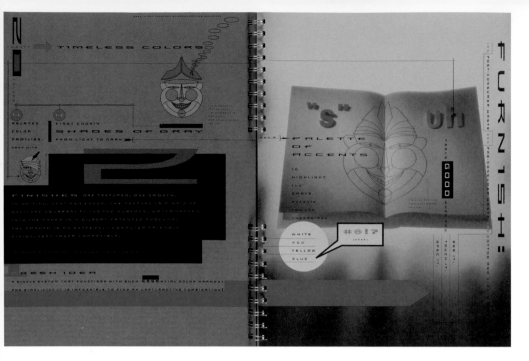

Rick Valicenti and Michael Pappas, Thirst.
Brochure for Esse paper range, spread,
Gilbert Paper, USA, 1990

mirror image (this happens three times) and the catalogue number,
7, is rendered as a word, a number and a roman numeral on the
front alone and is then repeated many times on the back. Some
kind of 'deconstruction' of these few simple components has been
performed, but the effect is decorative rather than revelatory in
its spinning of visual seduction from such slender textual threads.

 In Chicago, as the 1990s began, Rick Valicenti and his
company Thirst, were among the most prominent early American
disseminators of the deconstructionist 'style' as it was rapidly
coming to be perceived. Until 1988, when he decided to change
direction, Valicenti produced slick corporate design for Chicago's
financial institutions, which rarely departed from formula.
His aim with Thirst was to offer 'art with a function' that
fully acknowledged the design process and pushed his own self-
expression to the fore. In a 1990 brochure for the paper company
Gilbert, a regular Thirst client, the organization of information
is bitty, agitated and non-linear, with many focal points. Lateral
devices such as arrowed rules and blocks of colour encourage
horizontal scanning across the entire spread and information must
be extracted piecemeal, in no particular order. On another spread,
devoted to Elvis Presley, news about posthumous sightings of the
'king' is presented in irregular text boxes filled with a jumble
of type styles and sizes. As with Why Not, the aim was to use
'excessive' design as a way of engaging and entertaining the
viewer. When a colleague, Paula Scher, suggested to Valicenti that
all his work was about Dada, Valicenti responded self-referentially

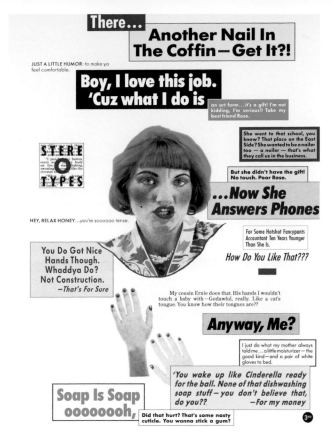

Rick Valicenti, Thirst. Stereotypes, insert for **Step-by-Step** magazine, USA, 1990. Photography by Tony Klassen

by designing a four-page magazine insert, aimed at fellow designers, specified in a way that encouraged the typesetter, a non-designer, to make all the critical decisions about type.

It was David Carson, however, more than any other designer, who, in the early 1990s, was most active and effective in popularizing these approaches. For many young designers, his work as art director of *Ray Gun* magazine from 1992 to 1995, supported by lectures and workshops around the world, provided an introduction to experimental design – one so overwhelming for some viewers that it tended to obscure his work's relationship to earlier experiments. *Ray Gun* also delivered the first experience of this type of design to many non-designers, especially outside the US, and it was often assumed, in media coverage, that Carson's approach was entirely without precedent. Certainly, the success of *Ray Gun*'s design as a hip signifier of 'Generation X' youth culture encouraged the deconstructed style's rapid take-up up by corporate advertising and Carson himself created ads for Pepsi-Cola, Nike and, later, Microsoft.[22] By 1997, a British newspaper was hailing him, in a headline, as 'A Hero of Deconstruction'.[23]

In Carson's body of work, the rule-breaking impulse seen in punk and deconstruction became the central idea. No convention was too unassuming to challenge and any structural principle could be disregarded in the cause of expressive design. In his first book, *The End of Print* (1995), he describes his way of working as a 'loose, intuitive, no-formal-training kind of approach'. He goes on to explain: 'Maybe at some subconscious level things are done to upset somebody – part of me continues to see no valid reason for many of the accepted rules of design. Perhaps that is why I have not bought into many of the accepted rules … I'm not anti-school, but when I became interested in design I really didn't know what those rules were and so I just became fascinated by exploring the look and feel of the subject.'[24] Echoing designers from Cranbrook and CalArts, Carson argues that the rationalism of grid systems and other kinds of typographic formatting is 'horribly irrational' as a response to the complexity of the contemporary world.

Carson's repudiation of design and editorial conventions began in earnest at *Beach Culture* magazine, where, in 1991, he first abandoned page numbers. On the fifth issue's contents page, the now role-less numerals become ingredients in a thick stew of typographic matter, with no definite top or bottom, which also attempts to generate interest from the 'worst typeface at hand'.[25] At *Ray Gun*, typographic material was treated with an even more painterly and emotive degree of freedom. In a feature on a band called Deconstruction, published in 1994, the columns are carved into irregular shapes, angled fracture lines run through the text, forced justification is used to space out the last line of each paragraph and one of the columns is pushed out to the edge of the page, so that the page trim (never totally predictable) cuts off some of the letters. The second half of the final paragraph, beginning mid-sentence, is placed at the start of the article. Carson's word pictures were often evocative. On the opening spread of an interview with the reclusive British rock star Morrissey, titled 'The Loneliest Monk', a pull-quote from the piece – 'I have no interest in any aspect of whordom [sic]' – is broken into three irregular type-clusters which revolve around a photo of the singer, who is about to move out of shot, returning the viewer to the image. At other times, in a challenge to fixed editorial hierarchies still unthinkable in most publications, though never far from the surface in 1990s postmodern design, Carson interposed himself unavoidably between reader and story. In one famous case, he replaced a feature about the singer Bryan Ferry with two columns of unreadable dingbats (the text was printed in full, for those who cared, at the back of the magazine). The assumption with all these devices was that readers would readily enter into the process of disentangling, deciphering or dismissing the text. At a time when young people were reading less, Carson suggested (as did many others at the time) that such devices were necessary to compete with other media attractions and that material designed to this degree might be better absorbed and remembered, if the reader had to work at it. Many letters from readers did seem to bear this out, at least in the case of *Ray Gun*, though the argument is at odds with the suggestion by Carson and others that much of the writing in the magazine was not worth reading in the first place, and its application in more general reading contexts was disputed by critics (see chapter 6).

While *Ray Gun*'s art director and cast of young designers employed graphic devices that bore a resemblance to earlier deconstructionist work, the magazine's success signalled the emergence of a new graphic style – grunge – that in some ways looked back even further, to punk's torn edges and dirty graphics, just as the grunge rock of the early 1990s partly rekindled the spirit of punk rock. Grunge, like punk, was energetic, disrespectful, angry (or perhaps just angry-seeming) and subcultural in origin, though this could not last. 'The "Clean Grid of Modernity" has been formally rejected by the nihilism of Industrial Youth Culture,' wrote Joshua Berger, art director of *Plazm*, published in Portland, Oregon, and second only to *Ray Gun* as a product of the grunge sensibility.[26] Typefaces by American companies such as Plazm Fonts (an offshoot of the magazine) and House Industries display ravaged outlines and decayed, crumbling edges, where chunks appear to be missing. Elliott Earls' dysfunctional trio of typefaces – Dysphasia, Dysplasia and Dyslexia – sprout strange, unseemly excrescences. Luc(as) de Groot's font, Jesus Loves Your Sister, spurts liquid trails from every available surface. The essential difference between 1970s punk and 1990s grunge was one of technology. Punk graphics were made cheaply by hand, with biros, photocopies, found type, scissors and

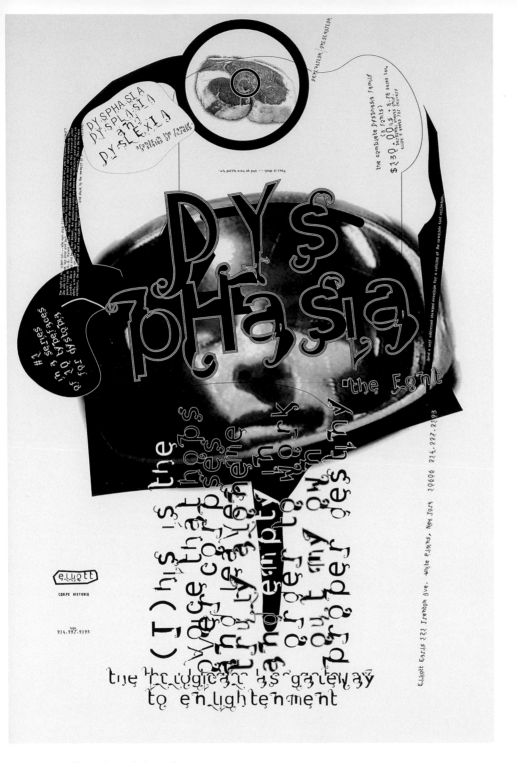

Elliott Earls. Dysphasia, typeface
family poster, USA, 1995

EROSIVE

ABCDEFGHIJKLM
NOPQRSTUVWXYZ
0123456789 PLAZM FONTS ?'
(A)(©)(R)&['?/+§%!()

Condemd House

ABCDEFGHIJKLMNOPQR
STUVWXYZabcdefghijklmn
opqrstuvwxyz0123456789

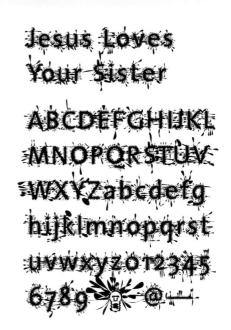

Jesus Loves
Your Sister
ABCDEFGHIJKL
MNOPQRSTUV
WXYZabcdefg
hijklmnopqrst
uvwxyz0123456789 @

paste. Grunge, despite its degraded, broken, untechnological
appearance, was a product of powerful digital tools that potentially
allowed anyone with the talent and inclination to knock up a
typeface in a day. Yet, as type designer Tobias Frere-Jones observed,
one reason for the development of this style at the moment when
the computer could render everything with seamless perfection
was that it allowed designers to offer something that ordinary
computer users, working with predetermined templates, could
not achieve: aggressively artistic individuality. 'For designers who
want a non-Modernist and individual portfolio, grunge becomes
a seductive method of self-identity.'[27]

By the late 1990s, grunge had long since shed its initial
transgressive charge. As the American critic Jon Wiener observed
in 1997, deconstruction had 'gone pop'. A database search revealed
that the word or a variant had appeared in almost 7,000 articles
over the previous two years, from *Entertainment Weekly* to *The New York
Times*, from *Playboy* to *Sports Illustrated*.[28] In everyday journalistic
parlance, deconstruction had become a trendy synonym for
'analysis' or 'explanation' and sometimes for 'taking things apart'
or even 'destruction'. In design, by the mid-1990s, deconstruction
was understood – if it was understood at all – in much the same
way, to the consternation of those who had, a decade earlier,
attached high hopes to its critical possibilities for design.
As Katherine McCoy noted: 'One of the regrettable things about

the term is that people who haven't read about it very deeply conclude that it is just about form and, more than that, that it is about the disassembling of visual language. That is part of the process, but I am interested in the idea of deconstructing the relationship of written and visual language to understand the dynamics and intentions of communication.'[29] The aim was never to develop a new graphic style – the style that became grunge. It was to discover from the process of analysis new ways of encouraging the audience's participation and to 'open up' meaning so that audiences could be involved in its construction and interpretation.

Yet it could be argued that something like this is exactly what occurred. Open-endedness and freedom of personal interpretation were often used as rationales to explain how *Ray Gun* and similar projects engaged their audiences. As Ellen Lupton and Abbott Miller remark: 'Post-structuralism's emphasis on the openness of meaning has been incorporated by many designers into a romantic theory of self-expression: as the argument goes, because signification is not fixed in material forms, designers and readers share in the spontaneous creation of meaning. Interpretations are private and personal, generated by the unique sensibilities of makers and readers.'[30] Such a view can be used to justify almost anything and, in practice, often effaces rather than facilitates critical thinking. In their book *Design Writing Research* (1996), Lupton and Miller suggest that we see the production of meaning not as a private matter but as structured by external codes in language, education, media and custom within which an individual must operate. From this basis, they argue for a much more focused application of deconstruction and a return to the ideas set out by Derrida in *On Grammatology*, *The Truth in Painting* and other texts. Instead of consigning deconstruction to a brief moment in the late 1980s and early 1990s, they see it as part of the continuing development of design and typography as modes of representation. They suggest that a study of typography and writing informed by deconstruction would examine graphic structures that 'dramatize the intrusion of visual form into verbal content, the invasion of "ideas" by graphic marks, gaps, and differences'.[31] By 'reshuffling and reinhabiting' the normative structures of mass media, design could be used as a critical tool to 'expose and revise' the mechanics of representation.

At such moments, Lupton and Miller appear to hint at a more politically engaged form of design – what, otherwise, is the purpose of this reinhabiting and revision? – but the abstractions of their terminology leave questions of personal commitment and politics unclear for even the sympathetic reader. Who will undertake these revisions, in what circumstances, with what motivations and to what end? In the postmodern period, many designers have struggled critically and productively with issues of engagement and resistance, without any need for direct reference to deconstruction (chapter 6 will return to this theme). It must be clear that, while some designers with a theoretical cast of mind will continue to find uses for deconstruction's difficult source texts, a wider application of these theories in design seems unlikely, even now that deconstruction has run its course as a style. The number of significant design projects that can be related in a direct way to deconstruction as a philosophical enterprise remains small and the few notable examples, such as Derrida's *Glas* (English edition, 1986) or Mark C. Taylor's *Hiding* (1997), tend to feature the close involvement of the theorist|writer and have a complexity in their relationship of content and form that highlights the superficiality of projects that treat deconstruction as nothing more than a fashionably distressed style. More than a decade after its publication, Avital Ronell's *The Telephone Book* (1989), a deconstruction of 'phonocentrism' – a pun on Derrida's term for the privileging of speech over writing – remains a bizarre landmark, the *Ulysses* of deconstructive typography. Designed by Richard Eckersley (designer of *Glas*), the book reconsiders the telephone in historical, literary and psychoanalytical terms. It opens with a joint statement from its 'textual operators':

'Your mission, should you choose to accept it, is to learn how to read with your ears. In addition to listening for the telephone, you are being asked to tune your ears to noise frequencies, to anticoding, to the inflated reserves of random indeterminateness. ... At first you may find the way the book runs to be disturbing, but we have had to

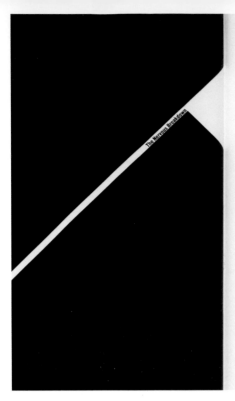

The Nervous Breakdown

We have to cut the shit.

Or perhaps you have not understood. It is no longer a question of adducing causes to the telephone, assigning its place, and recognizing in it a mere double and phantom of an organ (like Woman, reduced to the phantom of a missing organ). This would be much, and much that is engaging: the phone as a missing mouth, displaced genital, a mother's deaf ear or any number of M.I.A.–organs such as the partial object-ear transmitting and suturing the themes of *Blue Velvet*. Put through the body-slicing machine, the telephone will have become an organ without body. But "without body"—what is this? The ear, eye, even skin, have been divested of authority as they acquire technical extension and amplification in media. [69] All this belongs to our subject. But the radicality of the transaction takes place to the extent that technology has broken into the body (every body: this includes the body politic and its internal organs, i.e., the security organs of state). The somaticizations that a neurotic might chart are little compared with the electric currents running through the schizonoiac body. Hitting the lights on Reich's contention, we read: "With respect to their experiencing of life, the neurotic patient and the perverted individual are to the schizophrenics as the petty thief is to the daring safecracker." [70] The schizophrenic gives us exemplary access to the fundamental shifts in affectivity and corporeal organization produced and commanded by technology, in part because the schizophrenic inhabits these other territorialities, "more artificial still and more lunar than that of Oedipus." [71] In the

O mouth!

at the moment" (*W*, 120). At this point, Heidegger appears to rely on a communality of sense, a *sensus communis*, or an essential consensus, into which the unpresent tense of schizophrenic discourse could not, admittedly, be happily entered. However, even in this convocation of something like a contractual agreement of sense, a common contextuality and steadiness of address, Heidegger amends the speaking to include, as an address, the human and the thingly: "That includes fellow men and things, namely, everything that conditions things and determines men. All this is addressed in word, each in its own way, and therefore spoken about and discussed in such a way that the speakers speak to and with one another and to themselves. All the while, what is spoken remains many-sided. Often it is no more than what has been spoken explicitly, and either fades quickly away or else is somehow preserved. What is spoken can have passed by, but it also can have arrived long ago as that which is granted, by which somebody is addressed" (*W*, 120). **The Laingian** reading of Heidegger establishes a dimension which appears to set objections to schizophrenogenic modes of address, to the distortions of the place of sender and recipient toward which Heidegger's thinking may appear to harbor intolerance. Nonetheless even in these passages, the temporal rendering of that which is spoken in addition to the incomparable inclusion of thingly speakers already complicate any itinerary that would seek reliably to reroute schizophrenic Saying from a more normative grasp of language. But the material with which to seek presence of person in the speaking cannot be securely retrieved from any Heideggerian path of language. In "The Way to Language," Heidegger continues in this way, averting the dangers of the straight and narrow:

Everything spoken stems in a variety always from the un-spoken, whether this be something not yet spoken, or whether it be what must re-main unspoken in the sense that it is beyond the reach of speaking. Thus, that which is spoken in various ways be-gins to appear as if it were cut off from speaking and the speakers; and did not belong to them, while in fact it is they alone who, in speaking and to the speakers whatever is in what way they stay within what is spoken of the un-spoken. (*W*, 120; italics ad.)

Not long after this reading, which in part corresponds to the descriptive analysis of schizophrenic utterance in Laingian, Heidegger offers to accentuate the cutting. Analyzing the sign in terms of *secare*, "to cut," he returns to the decisive disconnectedness in all language tracings. The speaking which appears as if disconnected from speaking and the speakers cannot therefore be used to explicate an essential dimension, gleaned from Heidegger, of schizophrenia in its most advanced stages of psychosis—unless, of course, Heidegger were himself to be implicated in the unfolding of a schizophrenogenic understanding of language. This would be going very far, on the other way to language, whose essential signpost reads "Wrong Way, Do Not Enter." **In another** essay, "The Nature of Language," Heidegger has the following to say on the question, raised so often by the doctors, of not being there:

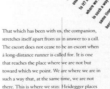

All is way. . . . The way allows us to reach what concerns us, in that which commands or provides for us. To be sure, it is proper to speak of a way only if we will go it, that is, if we are already on the way. To it? Answer: because we are already what concerns us, and from such a way first of all become what we are. We are what we are by pointing to what concerns us. The way allows us to reach what concerns us, because we do not yet properly realize what concerns our nature until this way is reached, where we ourselves are approached. This way gives us in all other ways, different from it, calls for an essort that no one far defined. (*W*, 92–93)

That which has been with us, the companion, stretches itself apart from us in answer to a call. The escort does not cease to be an escort when a long-distance runner is called for. It is one that reaches the place where we are not but toward which we point. We are where we are in such a way that, at the same time, we are not there. This is where we stay. Heidegger places some words after one that is simple, single, and armed with the antennae of a colon, *Answer*: Why do we care to mention this total response unit?

[Opposite] **Richard Eckersley. The Telephone Book** by Avital Ronell, book spreads, University of Nebraska Press, USA, 1989

break up its logic typographically. Like the electronic impulse, it is flooded with signals. To crack open the closural sovereignty of the Book, we have feigned silence and disconnection, suspending the tranquil cadencing of paragraphs and conventional divisions.'[32]

Agitated by moments of noise and silence, *The Telephone Book*'s text is unstable, reforming itself from page to page. Letters collide, blur and ripple as size changes pulse along the line length. Letter spaces increase, word spaces enlarge, gaps open between the lines, then close until the letters touch. Columns expand and contract, assuming temporary new shapes. Undulating fissures form and the text splits apart schizophrenically, doubling itself, before fusing back together a page later. The point of these typographic modulations is not that they offer the reader a set of competing visual amusements, or encouragements to read, or doubtful graphic mnemonics, but that they arise from the text, in a close cooperation between writer, designer and compositor, and serve textual meaning.[33] *The Telephone Book*'s lasting impact derives from the playful intelligence and systematic critical purpose with which it puts 'under erasure' every rule in the book.

3

Appropriation

In 1978, the German electronic music group Kraftwerk released the latest in a series of highly original albums whose austere synthetic melodies and pulsing robotic rhythms would have a lasting influence on the development of dance music. The 12-inch record was titled *Die Mensch-Maschine* ('The Man-Machine') and its front cover announced at first glance that its musical and æsthetic concerns were radically different from most popular music of the time, whether rock, disco or punk. The four band members, wearing identical red shirts and black ties, were framed by diagonal rules and panels of block-like type reminiscent of Russian Constructivist typography of the 1920s, a historical reference confirmed by the use of red, black and white as the main colours. The same slanted composition and typographic manner was used on the back cover, which also featured various geometrical shapes. A credit confirmed that the design by Karl Klefisch had been inspired by the work of El Lissitzky, avant-garde 'constructor' of such works as *About 2* (1922); the back cover was, in fact, a quotation from one of the book's pages. *Die Mensch-Maschine* was not a parody in any direct sense, but two ideas were communicated clearly: that the music, too, was to be understood as 'avant-garde', infused by a spirit of bold artistic exploration; and that it was 'futuristic', anticipating a new world that would be different from everything we know, but in some sense still positive. Nevertheless, the designer and musicians chose to construct an image that was backward-looking, if not quite nostalgic, and whether they intended it or not, the cover could also be read as tongue-in-cheek and humorously camp in its straightfaced seriousness. If Kraftwerk's music was so progressive and new, one might ask, why did it need to be represented by imagery that referred ambiguously to a moment of political failure in the past?

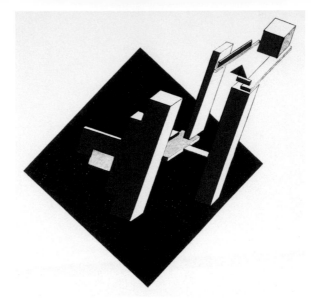

El Lissitzky. About 2, detail of book page, Germany, 1922

The Kraftwerk cover was an early sign of a postmodern phenomenon that rapidly became a trend. In graphic design, it was particularly apparent on record sleeves, a small boom industry at the time and a field that had always allowed a high degree of experimentation, though the trend was by no means confined to this area. Before the 1980s were very far advanced, these years had been dubbed 'the age of plunder' and by the decade's end it was common to see newspaper and magazine articles lamenting it as 'the age of parody'. The literary critic Fredric Jameson, writing in 1983, summarized the prevailing cultural obsession with the past. All the styles and worlds that can be invented by writers and artists have already been invented, he argued, and after 70 or 80 years of classical modernism, the result is exhaustion. 'In a world in which stylistic innovation is no longer possible, all that is left is to imitate dead styles, to speak through the masks and with the voices of the styles in the imaginary museum. But this means that contemporary or postmodernist art is going to be about art itself in a new kind of way; even more, it means that one of its essential messages will involve the necessary failure of art and the æsthetic, the failure of the new, the imprisonment in the past.'[1]

Jameson draws a critical distinction between pastiche and the related phenomenon of parody. Both involve the imitation or mimicry of the mannerisms and tics of other styles. In the case of parody, the aim is to emphasize the peculiarities of the original in a way that mocks them and this applies whether the parody is sympathetic or malicious. The effect depends on a shared sense in the audience that the original is excessive in some way and departs from an accepted norm. However, if as Jameson contends, the idea of the normal has broken down as society has fragmented and if postmodern society is now composed of a multitude of separate groups each speaking a private language or idiolect of its own, then there can be no shared linguistic norm against which a parody can register its comic effect. This is the moment, he argues, at which pastiche appears. Pastiche resembles parody in the way that it puts on the mask of a pre-existing style and in the accuracy of its imitation, but, unlike parody, it has no underlying satirical impulse, or intention to ridicule and deflate its subject. On the contrary, it is a neutral practice. 'Pastiche is blank parody, parody that has lost its sense of humor,' Jameson notes.[2]

Jameson's distinction between parody and pastiche hovers over any attempt to examine the ways in which postmodern graphic design has made use of the histories of design and art. The issue is further complicated by the fact that the designers themselves would, in most cases, certainly not have viewed their own practice in the negative light that Jameson's use of the word 'pastiche' suggests. Nor would their audiences necessarily have agreed that their consumption of these images was as dead-eyed and directionless as terms such as 'neutral' and 'blank' make it sound. Graphic design has always borrowed images and approaches from other fields, especially from fine art and popular culture; visual references of all kinds are an essential feature of the way that it communicates. Are the countless 'appropriations' of the last two decades any different in essence? As we shall see, the issue of appropriation has been the source of considerable debate within design, just as it has within art.

In Britain, in the late 1970s, Barney Bubbles was a crucial figure in the development of postmodern graphic design. He was already an influence on an emerging, younger generation of designers because of his work for the hippie rock group Hawkwind, when in 1976, at the height of punk, he became full-time designer for Stiff Records, set up by Jake Riviera. Bubbles' exceptional facility as a 'new wave' image-maker of the post-punk period was soon evident in his cover for the album *Music for Pleasure* by the Damned (1977), a Kandinsky-like semi-abstract built out of lines, zig-zags, semi-circles, symbols and planes of colour mashed together in a composition that

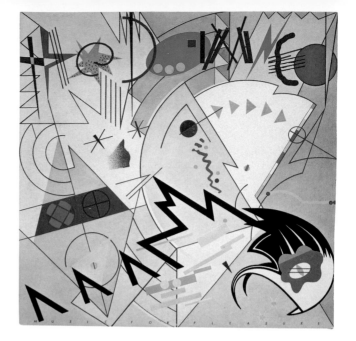

throbs with kinetic energy. The band's name and portraits of the
band members are hidden in the thicket. As with Kraftwerk, the
cover is not exactly a parody – more a tribute that gleefully
embraces its source material – though its humour is the antithesis
of Jameson's blank pastiches. Willing to use anything that seemed
to work, Bubbles was just as likely to base a design on suburban
tastes in interior decoration, as he did with *Do It Yourself* by Ian Dury
and the Blockheads (1979), which came clad in a choice of 52
different wallpapers. His most ambitious sleeve, *Armed Forces* (1979),
for Elvis Costello and the Attractions, is a riotous *mélange* of art
historical allusions to Mondrian, Abstract Expressionism, Op Art
and Pop, fronted by a painting of a herd of elephants in a kitsch
popular style. Five cover flaps can be opened and closed to form
alternative compositions, according to the viewer's whim. Clothing
his own identity in the borrowed garments of fine art, Bubbles,
whose real name was Colin Fulcher, concealed what appears to
be a joky self-portrait, with large red nose, behind the splattered
yellow band details at the heart of the fragmented image.

Younger British designers such as Malcolm Garrett and
Neville Brody were quick to acknowledge Bubbles' influence on
their work. However, for these designers and for Peter Saville,
with whom they are often grouped, historical inspiration came,
even more than it did for Bubbles, not only from postwar art,
but – as with *Die Mensch-Maschine* – from early twentieth-century
modernism in art and design. Herbert Spencer's book *Pioneers of
Modern Typography*, first published in 1969, was a key influence on
this generation, providing short introductions to the work of

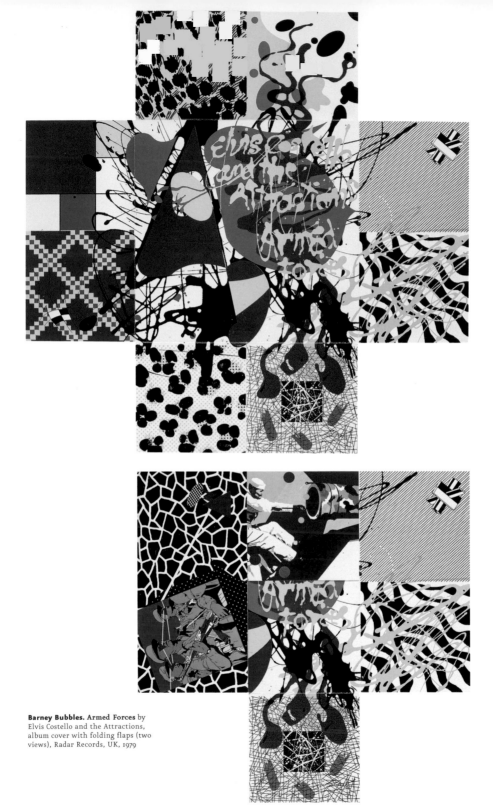

Barney Bubbles. Armed Forces by
Elvis Costello and the Attractions,
album cover with folding flaps (two
views), Radar Records, UK, 1979

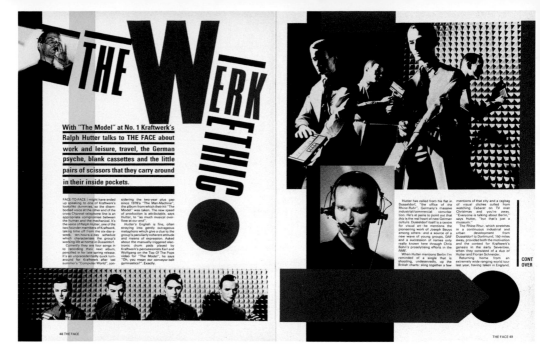

THE FACE 49

[Above] **Neville Brody.** The Face,
no. 23, magazine spread, UK, 1982

[Right] **Malcolm Garrett.** A Different
Kind of Tension by the Buzzcocks,
album cover, EMI Records, UK, 1979.
Photograph by Jill Furmanovsky

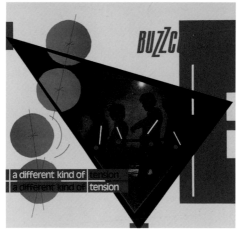

El Lissitzky, Theo van Doesburg, Kurt Schwitters, H.N. Werkman,
Piet Zwart, Paul Schuitema, Alexander Rodchenko, Laszlo Moholy-
Nagy, Herbert Bayer and Jan Tschichold. Malcolm Garrett's cover
for A Different Kind of Tension by the Buzzcocks (1979) interprets
the album title in a cheerful, day-glo graphic with a clear debt
to Lissitzky's 1919 poster Beat the Whites with the Red Wedge (shown
in Spencer's book), in which a red triangle breaks through the
perimeter of a circle. In 1982, when Neville Brody was designer
of The Face, he fashioned the opening spread of a feature about
Kraftwerk in a style that referenced both Die Mensch-Maschine and
its graphic origins in Lissitzky's work. (The same issue also profiled

Garrett, who namechecked the Futurists, the Dadaists, Lissitzky and Tschichold.[3]) This was a period in which ambitious young designers constantly invoked the achievements of modernism's leading lights half a century earlier. Brody was careful, however, to draw a distinction between merely copying the work of the Dadaists or the Constructivists, which he deplored, and deriving more general lessons from their example. 'I looked at it and tried to evaluate the core of what was being done, and why. What I took from it was a sense of dynamism, a sense of humanism and a non-acceptance of traditional rules and values. Once you looked at that, you could then pursue your own response. I have always felt that the last fifty years of design have been recycling these already explored areas.'[4]

In 1990, declaring that 'All art is theft', Garrett coined the term 'Retrievalism' to describe his method. 'We live in a Retrievalist world where the past is a bottomless pit that can be infinitely ransacked. Invention is a myth. We create only from using what already exists. There are no new colours. Retrievalism acknowledges the past, yet detests nostalgia. We must by necessity retrieve from the past to re-invent the future. This is a new Futurist age.'[5] Garrett seems to agree with Jameson's argument that stylistic innovation is no longer possible and that everything has already been invented, yet he insists that postmodern recombinations of the old can still become the building blocks of an authentic cultural moment. What gets overlooked, when the past is treated as a quarry from which useful visual material can be extracted at will, are the changes of meaning – the drainage of meaning – that occurs when visual ideas with specific purposes are applied in new contexts. In Lissitzky's *Red Wedge* poster, the triangle and circle stand for political factions and progressive visual form underscores a progressive political message. The Buzzcocks' sleeve treats similar motifs as super-stylish product packaging that benefits from a historical association with a radical moment, without representing anything of comparable significance, if it represents anything at all.

In a well-illustrated article in *The Face* titled 'The Age of Plunder', published in 1983, the cultural critic Jon Savage launched one of the earliest broadsides (certainly in Britain) against the use and abuse of historical form. Among other examples, Savage showed

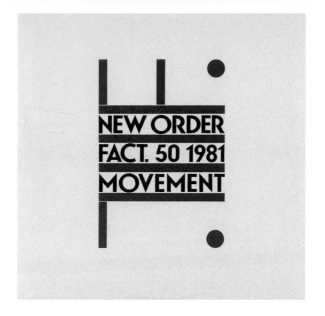

Peter Saville. **Movement** by New Order,
album cover, Factory Records, UK, 1981

Bubbles' *Music for Pleasure* sleeve; a design for *Mechanix* by UFO (1982)
based on a Jean Carlu poster for the US Office of War Information
(1941); and a cover for the single *Ziggy Stardust* by the rock group
Bauhaus (1982) that modified the hugely influential German art
school's famous stylized 'face' logo. Savage took the view that this
visual plunder was a symptom – one of many – of a Thatcherite
political culture in which everything is turned into a disposable
consumer commodity. 'The Past then, is being plundered in Pop
as elsewhere in order to construct a totality that is seamless, that
cannot be broken. It is a characteristic of our age that there is little
sense of community, of any *real* sense of history, as THE PRESENT
is all that matters.'[6] Refashioned in our own image and reduced
to triviality, history's lessons can be ignored.

Two of Savage's most provocative examples were drawn
from Peter Saville's work for the Manchester rock band New Order,
which grew out of the earlier group, Joy Division. In his opening
spread for the article, Neville Brody chose to highlight one of
these cases, the sleeve of *Movement* (1981), by placing it next to its
historical source and alongside the admonitory headline, 'The Age
of Plunder'. To those who had assumed, until this point, that
Saville, as Factory Records' regular designer, had single-handedly
devised this strikingly austere and powerful design, it must have
come as a surprise to learn how closely it was based on a Futurist
poster created in 1932 by Fortunato Depero (the original sleeve did
not credit Depero, although a credit line was later added to the CD
release). A few details had been changed – a vertical rule had been
moved to the left, four lines of type had become three, a second
colour had been introduced – but in its most salient features, it
was the same. The second sleeve, for New Order's *Procession* (1981),

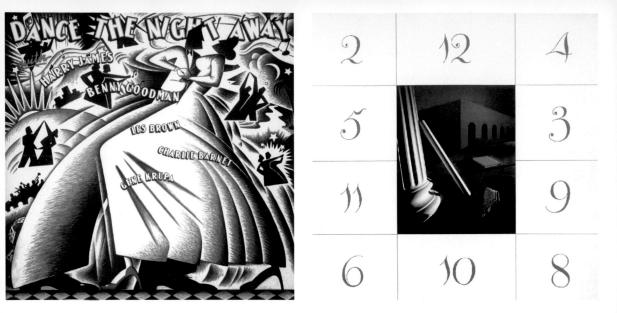

Paula Scher. Dance the Night Away, album
cover, CBS Records, USA, 1980. Illustration
by John O'Leary

[Right] Peter Saville. Thieves Like Us by New
Order, 12-inch single cover, Factory Records,
UK, 1984. Photograph by Trevor Key

was even closer to its source, also a Depero design, this time for
a Futurist publication of 1933; the only substantial difference
was the removal of the title, 'Dinamo Futurista'. Saville's
wholesale quotation of his sources was quite different from
American designer Paula Scher's use of Futurism. For the cover
of *Dance the Night Away* (1980), a compilation of big band recordings
by the likes of Benny Goodman and Gene Krupa, released by CBS
Records (where Scher was an in-house art director), she
commissioned an original illustration in a Futurist style. Scher's
design, incorporating her own typography, was a lively pastiche.
If Saville's designs weren't outright plagiarism, then they had to
be understood as graphic examples of the kind of postmodernist
'appropriation' seen in the art world in the early 1980s, where
works by earlier artists were absorbed and 'recontextualized'
by contemporary artists as new artworks. In one of the more
controversial examples, American artist Sherrie Levine presented
photographs by Edward Weston and Walker Evans as her own,
insisting that by claiming them in this way they became new pieces.
As Saville later explained: 'To me, it was better to quote Futurism
verbatim, for example, than to parody it ineptly – it was a more
honest, more intellectual and in a way more artistic approach.
It was so literal and so obvious that it never crossed my mind
that people would think that I had invented this work.'[7] In
another New Order sleeve for *Thieves Like Us* (1984), Saville created
a convincing-looking facsimile of a Giorgio de Chirico painting.
There was a forensic precision in his appropriations that gave
them a lasting allure as graphic objects, but his work's power
also came from the way that his selections functioned as *ideas* in
relation to the musicians and music they expressed, and the way

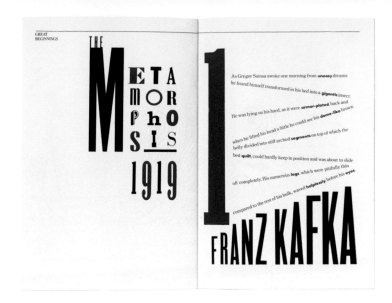

THE METAMORPHOSIS 1919

As Gregor Samsa awoke one morning from **uneasy** dreams he found himself transformed in his bed into a **gigantic** insect.

He was lying on his hard, as it were **armor-plated**, back and when he lifted his head a little he could see his **dome-like** brown belly divided into stiff arched **segments** on top of which the bed **quilt** could hardly keep in position and was about to slide off completely. His numerous **legs**, which were pitifully thin compared to the rest of his bulk, waved **helplessly** before his **eyes**.

1 FRANZ KAFKA

Paula Scher and Terry Koppel. Great
Beginnings, self-promotional book spread,
USA, 1984

that the designs contributed as a series to Factory's identity and mystique as a record label.

In the course of the 1980s, especially in the United States, 'retro' became one of the defining styles of the decade. Paula Scher's understanding of historical form – Futurist, Constructivist, De Stijl, Bauhaus, Art Deco, Pictorial Modernism – and her eclectic ability to reinvent it in the service of her clients made her an influential figure. In 1984, after leaving CBS, Scher started a new firm, Koppel & Scher, with partner Terry Koppel. One of the duo's first projects, a self-promotional brochure that was almost a manifesto, titled *Great Beginnings*, presented the opening lines of literary classics such as Goethe's *Faust*, Kafka's *Metamorphosis* and Thomas Mann's *Magic Mountain* in period styles appropriate to the texts. Other designers such as Louise Fili, art director of Pantheon Books, and Carin Goldberg, also a book jacket designer, produced work that borrowed from historical sources, ranging from the typography of the Vienna Secession to Bauhaus designer Paul Renner. Any historical style was deemed fair game and though the results were often accomplished and commercially astute, the recycling trend looked increasingly problematic to some observers as the decade wore on. In 1990, at a conference on the theme of 'Modernism & Eclecticism' in New York, Tibor Kalman gave a keynote lecture in which he addressed the uses of history in graphic design, good and bad, and a revised version of the text, co-written with J. Abbott Miller and Karrie Jacobs, was subsequently published in *Print* magazine. 'Designers abuse history,' they argue, 'when they use it as a shortcut, a way of giving instant legitimacy to their work and making it commercially successful ... historical reference and down and outright copying have been cheap

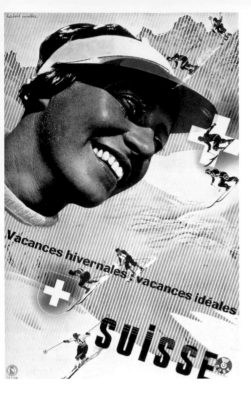

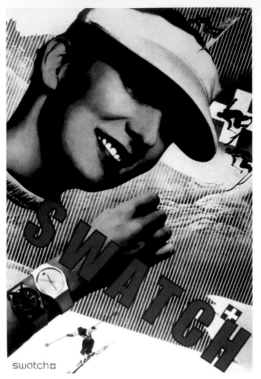

Herbert Matter. Travel poster,
Switzerland, 1934

[Right] **Paula Scher.** Poster for
Swatch watches, USA, 1986

and dependable substitutes for a lack of ideas.'[8] For the writers,
this kind of design was 'jive modernism', feeding off modernism
like a parasite for gains in prestige, style, clients and awards, while
ignoring its underlying politics and philosophy. Like Savage, who
had drawn close links between historicist design and conservative
politics, they argued that jive modernism contributes to a
'prevailing Reaganesque conservatism'.

As one of their principal examples, Kalman, Miller and
Jacobs showed a poster by Paula Scher advertising Swatch watches
(1986) based on a Swiss travel poster designed in 1934 by Herbert
Matter. Scher's poster is neither parody (it has no obvious satirical
intention) nor is it quite pastiche (it isn't a wholly new image in
the general style of Matter). It is closer in visual approach to
Saville's appropriations, but without the attempt to create a third
idea in the imaginative space between image and subject matter.
Where Saville's use of Futurism is metaphorical, encouraging us
to ask what it has to do with New Order's electronic rock, Scher's
selection of source image is literal and descriptive. It shows
something typically Swiss, skiing in the mountains, thereby
identifying the product with exhilarating outdoor pursuits. Scher
takes the main elements of Matter's original image, which had a
broadly economic purpose – to encourage tourism – and re-creates
them, without Saville's fetishistic fidelity to detail, for the simple
purpose of selling Swiss timepieces. The angle of the model's head

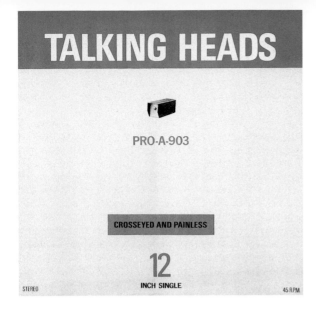

Tibor Kalman, M&Co. Crosseyed and Painless
by Talking Heads, 12-inch single cover, Sire
Records, USA, 1980

is adjusted so that she looks towards the viewer, emphasizing the
watches on her wrist, which replace the Swiss flag, and the word
'Swatch' is twice the size of 'Suisse' (Switzerland) in the original
poster. While there is nothing particularly heinous about the
appropriation – the original hardly embodied any deep
revolutionary intention – Scher's poster continues to provoke
discussion because it so tellingly embodies the assumption,
expressed by Garrett, that the past is a 'bottomless pit' available
for postmodern ransacking by designers.[9]

Kalman's position as critic was in any case complicated by
the use made in his own work of existing source material. In the
1980s, Kalman and his New York design company M&Co became
strongly identified as champions of the 'vernacular' – design
produced by ordinary people rather than professional designers,
such as roadside sign painting, shopfront lettering and posters
announcing social events or items for sale. Vernacular design's
appeal lay in its authenticity, the sense that it was a natural,
unfiltered expression of the way people felt, of their local concerns,
untainted by strategy, marketing imperatives and the slickness and
calculation typical of design's elite professional class. Kalman
admired the 'invisible' quality of vernacular design, the fact that
it is just there, part of the landscape, a form of visual slang, and
the way that it seems to be from another time (often because it is).
'We're interested in vernacular graphics,' he explained, 'because it's
the purest and most honest and most direct form of communication.
We will unabashedly steal from vernacular work.'[10]

An early M&Co design for the 12-inch single *Crosseyed and
Painless* by Talking Heads (1980) was modelled on the flat colours
and deadpan presentational style of a scientific equipment

A.I.G.A.N.Y.

PRESENTS
FRESH DIALOGUE 1986 :

Design without Designers:

OR

HOW I LEARNED TO
STOP LETTERSPACING
AND LOVE THE NON.

TIBOR KALMAN OF M&Co.
LEADS THIS YEAR'S ROMP THROUGH
THE GOOD, THE BAD AND THE ADEQUATE.
FEATURING TEN
YOUNG AND RESTLESS DESIGNERS.
ICONS WILL CRUMBLE.
OPINIONS WILL FLY.
CONVENTIONS WILL BE FLOUTED.
LATECOMERS WILL BE SEATED.
BE THERE OR BE SQUARE.

Who?	Who?	What?
CBS Records Art Director. Insisted that speakers be listed alphabetically.	CHRIS AUSTOPCHUK	Out of the mouths of babes; The teacher learns, the students teach.
Hails from the Buckeye State, and has seen Massimo Vignelli in his underwear.	MICHAEL BIERUT	The client as designer.
Important person at Bonnell Design Associates. Wears glasses.	BILL BONNELL	Will think of something important.
Famous downtown graphic design denizen ('70-'73), presence ('73-'82), personage ('82-).	JO BONNEY	Designing artists.
Couple of white designers sittin' around bitchin'.	DOUBLESPACE	Letterheads: When they're good, they're very, very good. When they're bad, they're fabulous.
Creative Director (not allowed to sign checks) at Drentel Doyle Partners.	STEPHEN DOYLE	Stealing from the bland.
Wears many hats. Teacher, writer, graphic designer, furniture designer, artist, bon vivant.	DAN FRIEDMAN	Modernism gone wild.
Reputed Underboss of the M&Co. Family. Also wears glasses, but just for effect.	ALEXANDER ISLEY	Unseen design.
WJMD seeks fun-loving & well-endowed clients for creative affn, in well-app'd conf. rm. tris. w/ Photo a must. No deadlines, please. Box 9.	TIBOR KALMAN	Will attempt to show portfolio and pass out business cards.
Of Strong Cohen, New Haven. This is Tom's first trip to New York, so let's all be on our best behavior. Thank you.	TOM STRONG	Buildings that talk. (Yes, they really do.)

Tibor Kalman with Alexander Isley, M&Co.
Design without Designers, event invitation,
American Institute of Graphic Arts, USA, 1986

catalogue. In 1986, for an American Institute of Graphic Arts (AIGA) symposium titled 'Design without Designers', M&Co created a set of publicity materials flaunting the kind of clumsily spaced, mismatched typography more likely to issue from a back-street printshop than a national design organization committed to professional standards. The graphics devised by M&Co from 1985 to 1993 for Restaurant Florent, a 24-hour 'diner for the debonair and the dispossessed' in the meatpacking district on Manhattan's West Side, were the studio's most elaborate essay in vernacular style. None of these designs was a wholesale quotation, appropriation or parody of vernacular sources, but each made constant, surprising references to everyday (non)design. For a promotional postcard, M&Co designer Alexander Isley matched icons from the Yellow Pages – of a chair, a truck, a gun, the Bell telephone company logo, a globe and a coffee cup – against location and service details. Other promotional materials showed cut-out photos of a steak or underwear or a comb that brought to mind the artlessly direct publicity shots of an earlier era. In 1985, for an issue of *Print* devoted to graphic parodies, Paula Scher had written and illustrated a feature purporting to reveal how two émigrés, Lubevitch and Moscowitz, were the overlooked originators of delicatessen design. As an example of their innovative 'corporate signing', she showed a sandwich menu board with cheap plastic movable type.[11] Taking the idea a step further, Kalman used movable type in typographically dyslexic print ads for Florent that gloried in wonky alignment, characters upside down and optimistic substitutions – an inverted 'V' for a circumflex accent, a '$' sign for an 'S'.

JUNE
WHEW
HOT
HUMID 74'/.

JUNE 11   RIGHT TO DIE
FVNDRAI$ER
&
APOLLO AMATEUR NITE
TAKE THE A TRAIN
JULY 14 BASTILLE ^FETE
&
TOUJOURS BOUDIN

FLORENT
989 5779

MNCO

Tibor Kalman, M&Co. Print advertisement for
Restaurant Florent, USA, c. 1987

[Right] **Alexander Isley and Tibor Kalman,
M&Co.** Promotional postcard for Restaurant
Florent, USA, 1986

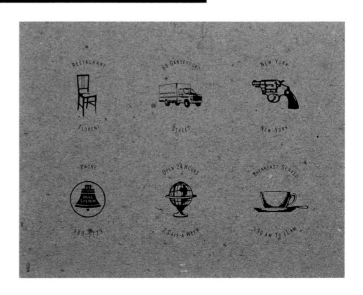

M&Co's work was extremely witty, but its relationship to the vernacular was not without its contradictions. If it was unacceptable to steal ideas from design history, why was it acceptable, even desirable, to 'unabashedly steal' from vernacular sources? Surely a sophisticated metropolitan design firm that made clever use of naïve examples of 'un-design' or 'non-design' came perilously close to the kind of knowingness and calculation that Kalman railed against in other areas of the design profession? Was there not also an unspoken assumption in such borrowings, as visual ideas were transported from low culture (everyday designing) to high culture (professional design), that high was inherently superior? A professional designer receiving the 'Design without Designers' leaflet understood immediately that its typography was 'wrong' and, since it came from the AIGA, that it had been purposely designed to look like it was produced by someone ignorant of the 'rules' of good design. To get the joke was to collude in its mockery of naïve popular sources.[12]

In 1990, some of these issues surfaced in a debate between Kalman and Joe Duffy, head of the Duffy Design Group in Minneapolis, which was published in *Print* magazine.[13] Duffy's work had become famous, in the late 1980s, for a decorative retro style that drew on Pictorial Modernism, Expressionism and Art Deco, as well as the vernacular, to create a warm, nostalgic, reassuring blend that could be applied to food labels (Classico pasta sauce), paper samples (French Paper's Speckletone), product packaging and annual reports. In 1989, Duffy's company joined the Michael Peters Group, then the largest design firm in the world, and this union was announced by a full-page ad in the *Wall Street Journal* aimed at corporate CEOs – 'How two guys with art degrees can do more for your business than a conference room full of MBAs.' Kalman and others took exception to this move, seeing it as the latest step in the inexorable transformation of design into an activity that was primarily about business. Yet their impassioned discussion about historical sources was ultimately inconclusive. In each of the cases raised by Kalman, Duffy argued that there was a logical business reason why the product required nostalgic forms of design to communicate its essential qualities. For instance,

French Paper, founded in 1871, family-owned and based in Niles, Michigan, was one of the smallest paper mills in the US – about as 'down-home and nostalgic', said Duffy, as it was possible to be in the paper industry. Kalman countered by arguing that the essential difference was that M&Co used elements from the past in a new way, while Duffy did nothing new with them. Duffy replied that they were used for exactly the same purpose that M&Co used them for – to communicate – and that the contexts in which they did this were certainly new.

Perhaps the difference, if there was one, came down to the spirit in which the vernacular was appropriated and revived. In its purest forms, vernacular-inspired design was another way of reacting – like punk and deconstruction – against the cloying, impersonal slickness of so much professional design. It was bound to look most suspect when it was recuperated as the latest gimmick by these same commercial forces and to look freshest and most convincing when it was applied in the more open cultural contexts that Kalman cited with approval during his debate with Duffy.

In the work of Art Chantry, based in Seattle from 1978 to 2000, the American vernacular found one of its most enthusiastic and attentive archaeologists – a designer-archivist able to reanimate his sometimes trashy sources without beautifying or sanitizing them to suit a bland, middle-class, supermarket taste. Chantry fashioned hundreds of street posters and album covers infused by the throwaway, unselfconscious visual language of the old newspaper ads, magazines, parts catalogues and clip art that he hoarded in his studio. In one of the most accomplished examples, from 1991, he used spanners, screwdrivers, a toolbox and a drill taken from 1950s tool catalogues and industrial ads to advertise 'The Night Gallery', a performance art series at Seattle's Center on Contemporary Art. Details of the individual performers are scattered across the hardware, like explanatory panels, and a tear-off coupon gives ticket information. In form, the poster mimics a cheap-looking ad, yet its luxurious scale and quality of printing encourage viewers to peer at the details and savour the rhythmic energy and communicative impact of a kind of commercial design that would usually be dismissed by designers

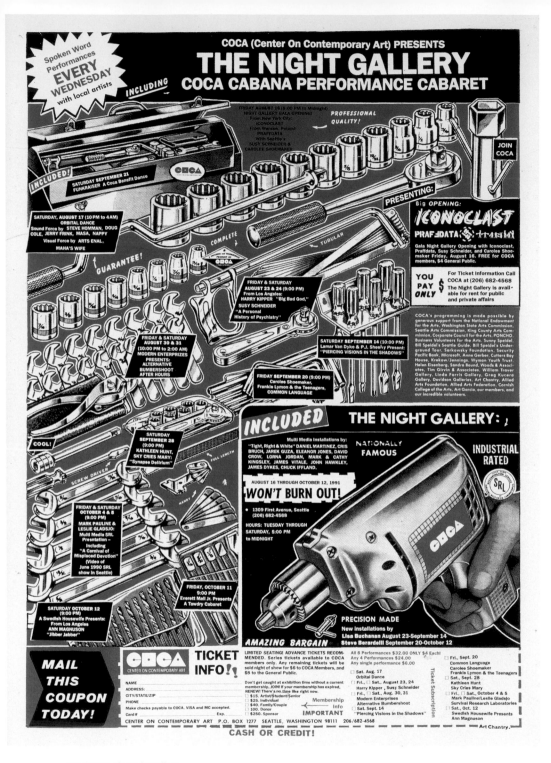

Art Chantry. The Night Gallery,
performance art poster, Center on
Contemporary Art, USA, 1991

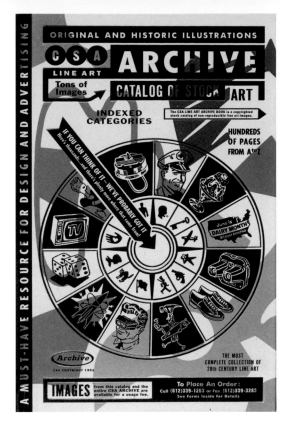

Charles S. Anderson. CSA Line Art Archive Catalog, vol. 1, book cover, USA, 1995

Art Chantry. Logos for Estrus Records, USA, 1990s

as conceptually and æsthetically worthless. Nor is there anything patronizing or cute about Chantry's assimilation of his sources. He used similar material from old advertising for a series of related 'Night Gallery' promotions and, in 1992, designed a CD cover for the band Liquor Giants in the style of a store ad, offering paper towels, baby lotion and grass seeds (marijuana) at bargain prices. His many humorous logos for Estrus Records – a Seattle grunge label that, he notes, 'prides itself on its lack of subtlety' – add up to an alternative history of trademarks.[14]

Equally committed to the evocative power of early Americana is Charles S. Anderson, a designer at Duffy Design Group, before setting up his own Minneapolis studio in 1989. Anderson continued to work for French Paper, producing many promotions in a much-imitated style recalling the commercial art of the 1920s to 1960s that he dubbed 'bonehead'. Anderson's interest in 'un-designed' vernacular imagery began at high school when he met a retired commercial artist, Clyde Lewis, who left him hundreds of hand-drawn cuts, which became the starting point for Anderson's own collection. In 1995, he published *CSA Line Art Archive Catalog* vol. 1, containing 7,777 examples from an archive that now numbered hundreds of thousands of images taken from old books, magazines, catalogues, matchbook designs, cocktail napkins and vintage

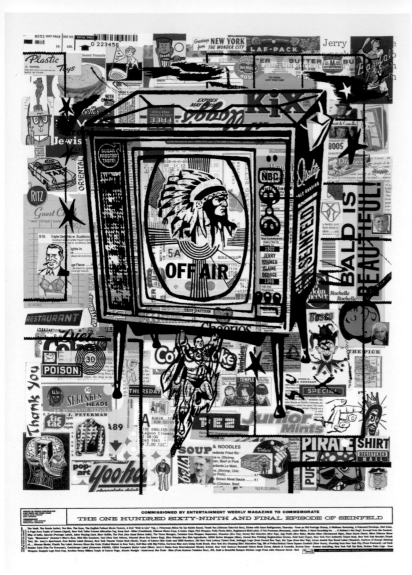

Charles S. Anderson. Seinfeld poster for
Entertainment Weekly, USA, 1998

packaging. Nearly all of these line art images had been cleaned
up and redrawn to simplify them or make them bolder and more
graphic, and to unify the collection. They were organized by
alphabetical category – magic, mail, military, money, monsters –
and, as copyrighted items, could be ordered for a usage fee
from the archive, which functioned much like a library of stock
photography. The archive's clients included Nike, Levi's, *Ray Gun*
magazine, Nissan, Lee Jeans and MTV, and advertising agencies such
as Weiden & Kennedy and Chiat|Day|Mojo, indicating the enduring
popular appeal, however ironic in spirit, of instant, ready-made
signifiers of supposedly simpler, more innocent times. A poster
by Anderson, commissioned by *Entertainment Weekly* to commemorate

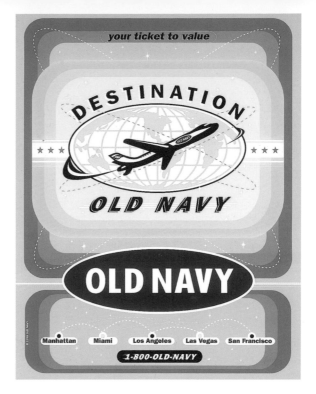

your ticket to value

DESTINATION

OLD NAVY

OLD NAVY

Manhattan   Miami   Los Angeles   Las Vegas   San Francisco

1-800-OLD-NAVY

Alan Disparte. Seasonal advertising campaign for Old Navy, USA, 1998

the 169th and final episode of the situation comedy *Seinfeld*, is an intricate collage of such images, mixed with product logos, packaging and other types of graphic ephemera. This dense textural backdrop flows through the line art image of a television to suggest the way that TV itself contributes to a mental landscape saturated with an easily summoned nostalgia for product experiences we have loved.

In the 1990s, many commercial ventures deployed postmodern nostalgia to trigger reassuring emotions in consumers. In 1994, Gap launched a new division, Old Navy, which would design, manufacture and sell casual clothing and accessories for adults and children. The new stores were committed to a concept of retailing that Old Navy's creative director, Dennis Leggett, labelled as 'shopper-tainment'. To communicate a sense that Old Navy offered fun for all the family, the in-house team devised a graphic identity that was comfortingly old-fashioned, apparently issuing from any point between the 1930s and the 1960s, while simultaneously contriving to look invitingly new – a balancing act characterized by one writer as 'nouveau-retro'.[15] This bright, colourful, vaguely familiar pastiche was splashed across hang-tags, pocket stickers, packaging, advertising and in-store promotions. The personnel who worked on Old Navy's graphics shared a love of popular culture, including music, film and television from the 1950s and 1960s, and senior art director Alan Disparte described how he had 'learned to appreciate the kind of distressed and degenerated

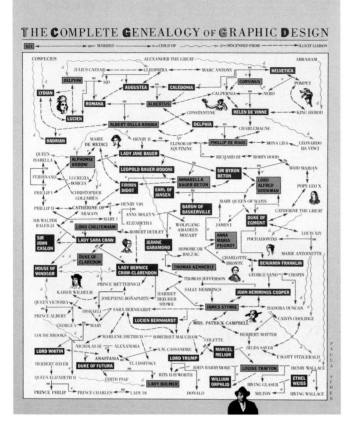

Paula Scher. The Complete Genealogy of
Graphic Design, cover for **Print** magazine,
USA, 1985

beauty of things that are retro. If the packaging worked way back
then, why wouldn't it work now?'[16] Disconnected from any specific
point of origin, a vernacular that was largely commercial in the
first place could be recycled ad infinitum to stimulate further sales.

Yet postmodern forms of reference could also, on occasion,
be put to more pointed, nuanced and even critical uses. Paula Scher's
cover for *Print*'s parody issue, in 1985, inaugurated a trend in which
diagrams, maps, charts and types of information design usually
found in worthy encyclopædias and text books were appropriated
for alternative, often satirical purposes. Scher's 'Complete Genealogy
of Graphic Design' purports to show how an impossibly convoluted
genealogical tree that records every illicit liaison descends from
Confucious, Alexander the Great and Abraham, via the likes of
Caledonia and Helvetica, to arrive eventually, centuries later, at Milton
Glaser. With *Spy* magazine, launched in 1986, the hyperactive info-
graphics look – at once studious and sarcastic – became one of the most
distinctive calling cards of postmodern graphic design. Initially art
directed by Drenttel Doyle Partners, then by Alexander Isley and
B.W. Honeycutt, *Spy* was in all senses a postmodern product, entirely

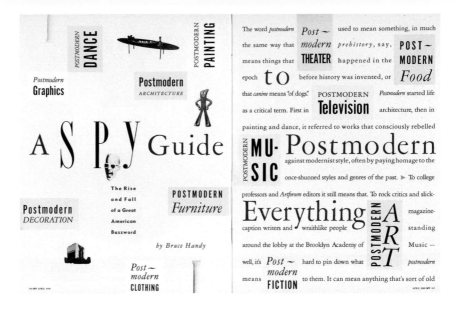

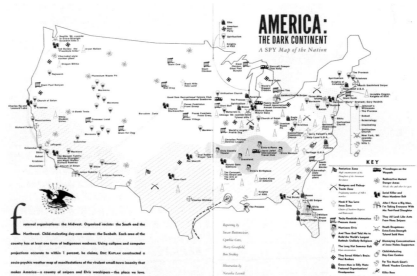

[Top] **Alexander Isley.** Spy, magazine spread, April 1988

[Above] **Alexander Isley.** Spy, magazine spread, June 1988. Illustration by Natasha Lessnik

self-conscious about every detail of its own mechanics. In 1988, it even published 'A Spy Guide to Postmodern Everything', which presented readers baffled by this ubiquitous buzzword with handy hints for recognizing postmodern artefacts in architecture, painting, television, literature, cuisine and graphic design: 'Is it like MTV? Do the layouts look like this one?'[17] The feature's pastel-hued opening spread, art directed by Isley, was a quintessential *Spy* layout: it was fussy, overloaded with words (all of them cutting), an interlocking puzzle that had to be tackled piece by piece. In another issue, *Spy* conducted a graphic analysis of 'America: The Dark Continent', using a stylized map and specially drawn icons explained in a key, to chart the

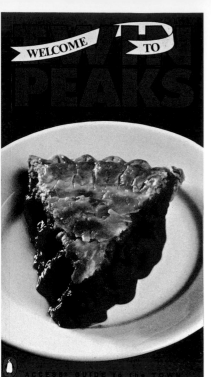
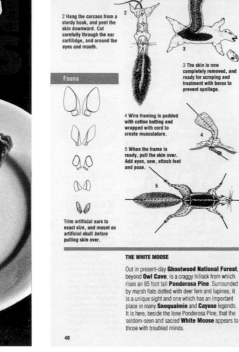
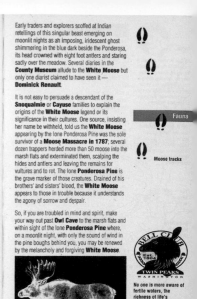

Annie Kook and Stuart L. Silberman.
Welcome to Twin Peaks by Richard Saul
Wurman, David Lynch and Mark Frost, book
cover and spread, Penguin Books, USA, 1991

distribution across the nation of Nazi sympathizers, Ku Klux Klan
members, snipers, serial killers, voodoo conclaves, child-molesting day-
care centres, and 'dismaying concentrations' of supporters of
Republican senator Jesse Helms. A story published after Honeycutt
became art director offered a surefire guide to making Hollywood
hit movies the 'Buddy-o-Matic' way. Readers had to choose between
multiple alternative readings, each one supported by a footnote giving
film references and other information – a mind-bogglingly elaborate
concept for a monthly magazine. Here and elsewhere in *Spy*, writing
and design fused in visual reports that caught the spirit of the
postmodern moment because they were both authoritative and absurd.

A genuine curio, in this regard, was a spin-off from one
of the defining cult television series of the early 1990s, *Twin Peaks*,
created by film-maker David Lynch, a show that came to be seen
as the epitome of postmodern TV. The architect turned publisher
Richard Saul Wurman had become well known in the course of the
1980s for his informative, cleanly designed 'Access' guides to cities
around the world. *Welcome to Twin Peaks* (1991) by Wurman, Lynch and
series producer Mark Frost treats the fictional northwestern town
and its peculiar inhabitants as though they actually exist. TV tie-ins
are commonplace, but the guide's strangeness makes it an intriguing
one-off. Its deadpan layouts and routine illustrative style, detailing
Twin Peaks' flora, fauna, sawmill production and styles of doughnut,
flatten out the fantastical dimension, rendering it almost dull, and

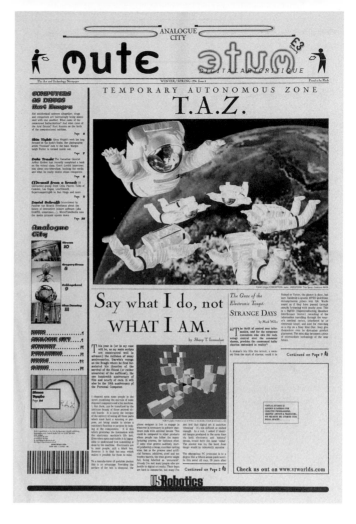

Simon Worthington and Pauline van Mourik Broekman. Mute, no. 4, newspaper front page, UK, 1996

in consequence only serve to heighten its surreality. By pouring fictional content into a format recognized for its authority, the book becomes a parody of the 'Access' series and of the very idea of reliable guides to the world 'out there'.

This strategy of appropriating not merely the graphic form but the entire generic container can prove highly fruitful. It potentially allows a more complex, multifaceted and suggestive interrelationship between the new content and the graphic medium it inhabits. Instead of merely pastiching stylistic fragments, often for no more than superficial æsthetic or nostalgic effect, it opens up the possibility of deeper kinds of parodic resonance. Early issues of the British digital culture publication *Mute*, edited and designed by Simon Worthington and Pauline van Mourik Broekman, were printed on broadsheet-sized newsprint. Features were laid out like news stories and the paper was pale pink, making an instant visual connection with financial publications such as the *Financial Times*. *Mute* was

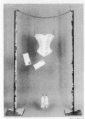
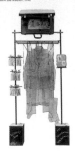
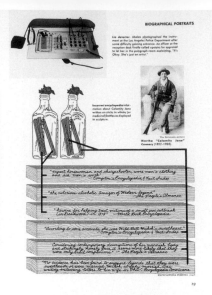

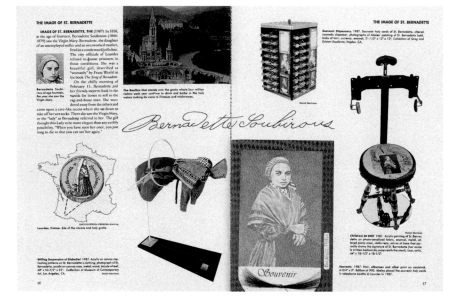

Susan Silton. Encyclopedia Persona by Kim Abeles, catalogue spreads, Santa Monica Museum of Art, USA, 1993

struggling to establish its critical voice and the borrowed format gave it a veneer of seriousness and authority, though one that was playful and ironic for regular readers who were in on the joke. Ironic parody was implemented with even more exacting attention to generic convention and detail in the case of American artist Kim Abeles' 1993 catalogue, *Encyclopedia Persona*, a 15-year survey of her work. Conceived by Abeles, curator Karen Moss and designer Susan Silton, the book mimics the alphabetical structure, matter-of-fact page layout, and typographic and pictorial conventions of an early 1960s encyclopædia; even the textured binding has a hushed, reading-room air about it.

The book's aim is to make a wealth of art and non-art information accessible to the reader and it reflects the artist's research process and methods of presentation. As Moss notes, Abeles 'plays with the pre-conceived idea of an encyclopedia's absolute authority by creating entries that function as meta-histories of her subjects. [She] freely embellishes each entry and compares this process to the art of storytelling. While she sincerely wants people to understand her ideas and her work, parts of the book mimic and mock the didacticism of an encyclopedia.'[18] At the same time, the catalogue's makers readily acknowledge that it is a 'nostalgic tribute' to the simple pleasure – perhaps no longer so popular in a screen-based era – of browsing through reference books in search of knowledge.

Do graphic works such as these represent, in Fredric Jameson's words, 'the failure of the new, the imprisonment in the past'? Certainly, a project such as *Encyclopedia Persona* depends on our familiarity with the conventions being parodied, and this is bound to reaffirm and legitimate them to a degree. Even so, these conventions are interrogated rather than merely parroted and, in the process, they are rendered more problematic than they might otherwise have been. Postmodernist graphic design is often 'about design' just as postmodernist art is often about art, though this is not a wholly new development in applied visual communication: a great deal of graphic design has always worked in this way. Nevertheless, it is significant that design's obsessive preoccupation with the past emerged at a point in the late 1970s when the once fast-flowing waters of innovation had grown stagnant. Designers of all kinds, both the commercially minded and those with the avant-garde aspiration to 'make it new', looked back with a mixture of envy and nostalgia to a time (modernism) when novel inventions seemed to pour from the drawing board. Paradoxically, the arrival of the Apple Macintosh in 1984 only confirmed this strain of retro-futurism among some designers, as the profession struggled to discover whether the computer was simply a handy production tool – as some continued to insist well into the 1990s – or the liberating medium of a new graphic sensibility. It was both of these things, but it was also a boundless, ecstatic, rule-free space, in which cultural tendencies already identified by postmodernist thinkers would find even fuller and more elastic styles of expression.

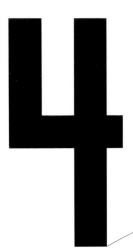

Techno

As some critics were quick to point out, the fragmented and intricately layered designs made possible by the computer often resembled a kind of neo-Futurism or neo-Dada and this was true even when no conscious parody was intended. Yet there were a few attempts, even in the 1980s, when the technology was comparatively new and limited in terms of memory size and processing power, to explore the possibilities for a new æsthetic. American West Coast designers such as April Greiman and the Emigre team, Rudy VanderLans and Zuzana Licko, acquired Apple Macintosh computers as soon as they were introduced in 1984 and set about experimenting enthusiastically with the tools. For Greiman, the computer was 'a new paradigm, a conceptual "magic slate" opening up a new era of opportunity for graphic artists'.[1] Greiman understood immediately that, however much those trained in traditional methods might protest, the computer did change the design process in fundamental ways. In that sense, it was not, as she herself expressed it, 'just another pencil'.[2] A pencil makes physical marks and even if these marks are erased some trace often remains, while other kinds of mark-making – crayon, paint, ink, things cut up and stuck down – leave even more indelible impressions. By contrast, the computer's 'undo' function, as Greiman herself noted, allows something to be removed instantly, without any trace. Ease of deletion gives every aspect of the design a provisional, less certain quality. It no longer exists in such a definite, physical way, so there is much less need to be sure that a particular decision is 'correct', since it can be instantly retracted and changed. This condition of uncertainty and instability extends to the entire design. In digital space, nothing is ever finished; as long as the computer file survives, any element can be rethought – 'The paint never dries in the Mac universe.'[3] Ease of generation allows even more options and variations to be considered.

The fact that accidents need not have lasting or negative consequences means that these chance occurrences and 'mistakes' can potentially be used to provoke unexpected directions in the design process.

To many at the time, low-resolution bitmapped graphics looked like a step backwards, but the earliest exponents of Macintosh design made a virtue of the computer's limitations. In an article titled 'The New Primitives', VanderLans and Licko quoted Piet Zwart with approval – 'We are the primitives of the new technical era' – and argued that coarse bitmaps could be the basis of a new computer æsthetic.[4] Set in bitmapped typefaces designed for use on the Macintosh by Licko and distributed by Emigre, the article showed the æsthetic in action. 'Much of the scepticism and disfavor currently attached to digital images will disappear as a new generation of designers enters the profession,' they prophesy (they were soon proved correct). 'Having grown up with computers at home and school, these designers will assimilate computer technology into the visual communication process as it penetrates everyday practices.'[5] They showed an example by San Francisco illustrator John Hersey, a catalogue cover created in 1987 for 'Pacific Wave', an exhibition of Californian graphic design. Hersey's vibrant image exploits the computer screen's potential as generator of jagged, patterned backgrounds, using its 'primitive' rawness for optical animation. Issues of *Emigre* produced at the time also demonstrated that bitmapped typefaces and images, used sensitively, could convey an unexpected degree of vitality and warmth.

It was Greiman, though, who was responsible for perhaps the most ambitious early attempt to put desktop technology through its paces. Her 2 x 6 foot (0.6 x 1.8 metre), double-sided poster collage, designed for *Design Quarterly* magazine in 1986, is a landmark not only in technical terms, but as a self-authored, cosmological statement that depended on electronic tools for its conception and realization and reflected an exuberant, uncompromised digital sensibility. On the poster itself, Greiman describes her design process: six months spent gathering materials; three months of sketching with MacPaint and digitizing images with MacVision; then three months composing, layering and stretching the image with MacDraw before printing it out on a LaserWriter – a task

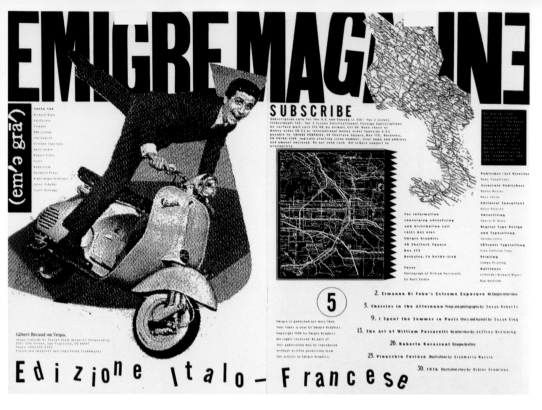

Rudy VanderLans. Emigre, no. 5,
magazine spread, USA, 1986

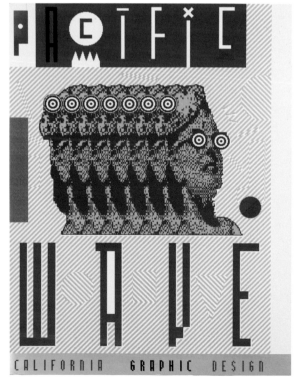

John Hersey. Pacific Wave, catalogue
cover, Magnus Edizione, Italy, 1987

which came close to defeating the technology. The poster shows a life-sized image of Greiman naked and, at her feet, also materializing from a vapour of pixels, her 'spiritual double'. She is surrounded and overlapped by smaller images: a dinosaur, a brain, a spraycan, an astronaut, hands making gestures. A timeline marks various inventions and developments, including her own birth, which culminate in the Mac. It looks a bit like one of those schematic images of humankind despatched across space to extend the hand of friendship to passing extraterrestrials. The cover poses the question 'Does it make sense?' and Greiman answers with a quotation from Wittgenstein: 'If you give it a sense, it makes sense.' On the poster, another Wittgenstein quotation suggests 'the sense lies far in the background'. While some questioned whether the poster made any sense at all, this well-publicized project was significant as a sign of how the designer was becoming increasingly central, as a creative personality, to the presentation, perception and consumption of postmodern graphic design. It was also, as one American critic noted at the time, an important early step in the search to 'determine the computer's unique characteristics and the impact of those characteristics on the future "look" of visual communications'.[6]

The key point about Greiman's poster was that it was *excessive*: in conception, in size, in detail, in the sheer quantity of information with which it deluged the viewer. For many designers, the point of design was still to eliminate extraneous information (noise), to thwart the possibility of ambiguity by reducing a design to its essentials. In the early 1990s, as computer processing power burgeoned, designs created on the screen became increasingly overloaded and complex, overwhelming the viewer with a wild network of pathways to penetrate and decipher, plunging the spectator into the vertiginous reaches and turbulent coordinates of a new kind of digital space. Ten years earlier, thinking about television, advertising and radio rather than the impact of personal computers, Jean Baudrillard described how, in contemporary culture, we inhabit an incessant, instantaneous surfeit of information and solicitation, which invades our private spaces, forcing the 'extroversion of all interiority', obliterating our sense of a separate, inner life. 'We live in the ecstasy of

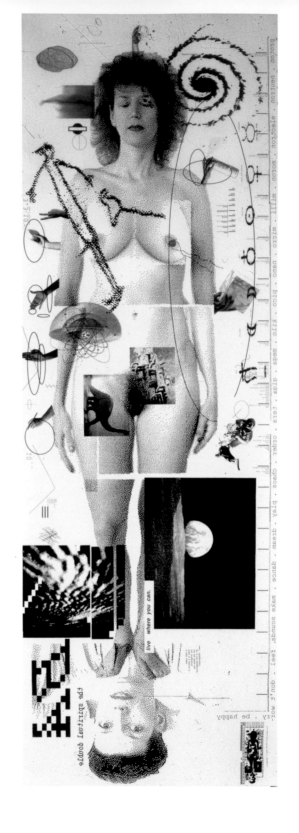

April Greiman. Design Quarterly, no.133,
poster for a magazine, USA, 1986

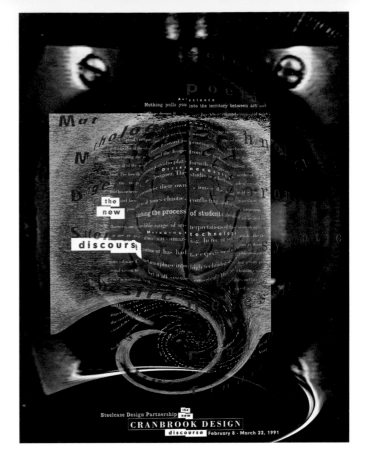

P. Scott Makela. Cranbrook Design:
The New Discourse, exhibition
announcement, USA, 1990

communication,' writes Baudrillard. 'And this ecstasy is obscene.'[7]
This is not, he says, the obscenity of the forbidden or the repressed;
it is 'the obscenity of the visible, of the all-too-visible, of the more-
visible-than-the-visible. It is the obscenity of what no longer
has any secret, of what dissolves completely in information and
communication.'[8] He ends this tirade with a vision of the spectator
as 'a pure screen, a switching center for all the networks of
influence' – an image that possesses even greater resonance in
the era of the Web.[9]

In P. Scott Makela's image of a melting orange brain,
created in 1990 to advertise the 'Cranbrook Design: The New
Discourse' exhibition, the brain itself becomes a 'pure screen'
framed by a pulsing field of video texture, across which lines
of type flow and scroll. At the brain's stem, language dissolves
into a vortex of illegible marks sucked towards a vanishing point
in the darkness, an image both 'ecstatic' and threatening, which
suggests a Baudrillardian surrender to the omnipresent demands
of electronic networks. Inspired by cyberpunk fiction and
'wirehead|hacker technologies', Makela was one of the most
cranked-up, excessive designers of the period; in his own words,

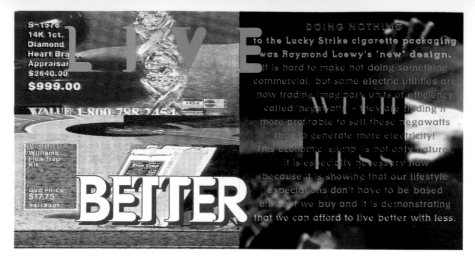

P. Scott Makela. On Doing Nothing
by Tucker Viemeister, spread from
Rethinking Design, Mohawk Paper
Mills, USA, 1992. Digital photography
by P. Scott Makela and Benoit Barbier

Dead History

ABCDEFGHIJK LMNOPQRSTU VWXYZabcdef ghijklmnopqr stuvwxyz012 3456789&@¶

P. Scott Makela.
Typeface for Emigre,
USA, c.1990

'100% digital'.[10] In 'Redefining Display', a project and text published in *Design Quarterly* in 1993, he evokes the unprecedented multitasking possibilities, density of inputs and layering of experience delivered by electronic work environments. 'Awareness of my own working methods has helped me to visualize others' data-processing needs. Every day I make multiple phone calls while my Macintosh runs up to six software programs at once. I send faxes and e-mail, and I am productively addicted to good electronic bulletin boards. I watch obscure TV stations for interesting images or textures, and I enjoy CDs played at high volume.'[11] Makela designed a hybrid font called Dead History and recorded an album of pounding techno music for Emigre with titles like 'Telepresence' and 'Waiting with Baudrillard'. His designs for print, such as a 1992 visual essay for Mohawk Paper's *Rethinking Design* journal, bulge against the edge of the page, straining to burst through its boundaries. Everything communicates at a thunderous volume, as though the controls have been turned up as high as they will go, then jammed on maximum. 'I know all the rules of space and balance and contrast and all the things that make a formal construction work,' he explained, 'but I am after something else. I am after a certain effect. And there might be a hierarchy there, too, but it's very subtle.'[12]

Makela's designs have the hyperreal, super-bright aspect of a dream or hallucination. Like Baudrillard's vision of the individual reduced to a 'switching center', they are a kind of science fiction, but where Baudrillard's cold analysis suggests intellectual disgust, Makela was excited and energized by the prospect of information overload. These were speculations about future technology at a moment in the early 1990s when, despite the media's infatuation with the revolutionary promise of virtual reality, the World Wide Web had yet to arrive, the computer was far from being a household item (especially outside the US) and most people had yet to discover the convenience of e-mail. In his 'Redefining Display' project,

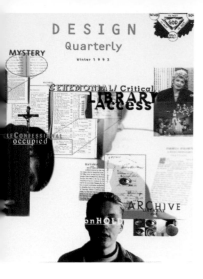

P. Scott Makela with Alex Tylevich.
Design Quarterly, no. 158, magazine
cover, USA, 1993

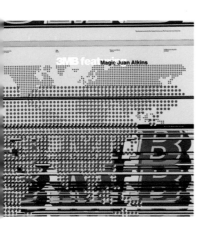

The Designers Republic. 3MB Featuring
Magic Juan Atkins, album cover, Tresor,
Germany, 1993

Makela presented 'subjective forecasts' of how digital 'work walls' might be used by a plumber, a parish priest, a multimedia artist and a motorcycle mechanic. Images flow and collide in temporary formations meant to mirror the concerns, experiences and dramas of the user's everyday life. The priest answers videophone calls, pages through religious texts, keeps an eye on CNN, and hears an on-line confession from behind the red curtain on the left of his screen. Here, as elsewhere, Makela unleashes a torrent of signals in which the separate units of data seem to matter less than the sensation of ecstatic immersion in the information stream.

A similar sense of immersion can be seen in the work of The Designers Republic (DR), founded in Sheffield, England, in 1986 by Ian Anderson. Where Makela favoured photographic or televisual images set in realistic, representational spaces, DR's work is far more graphic, unfolding with kinetic abandon across the two-dimensional flatness of the printed sheet. DR, like Makela, seem fully adapted to postmodern reality, treating it as an invitation to surf opportunistically through the floating world of corporate signs, yet perhaps without Makela's sense of optimism. 'The core of remix culture is the product of sampling both in attitude and experience, and is the inevitable result of the desire for progress in the absence of anywhere to go ... In the context of remixism the original is purely a seed,' writes Anderson.[13] As with postmodern design's use of retro and vernacular imagery, there is a feeling that culture has stalled, that there is nothing left to invent and that 'newness' can only lie in sampling and remixing what already exists into novel constructions with new subjective uses. Nevertheless, in DR's work, a computer-driven æsthetic emerged that would prove highly influential as the 1990s progressed, particularly in Europe. The style's essence is replication. Shapes and symbols – dots, circles, arrows, hearts, parallel lines and graph paper grids – multiply to form sheets of graphic texture that modulate and merge like scientific charts and diagrams in the process of mutation. Embedded in these graphic fields are logos, cartoon characters, fragments of Japanese (DR are obsessed with an imaginary Japan), panels full of fake technical information and cryptic statements from the designers in miniscule type. In a 1993 record sleeve for Magic Juan

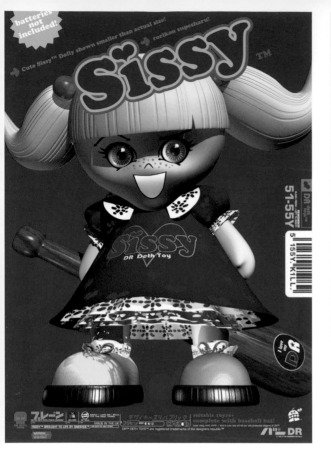

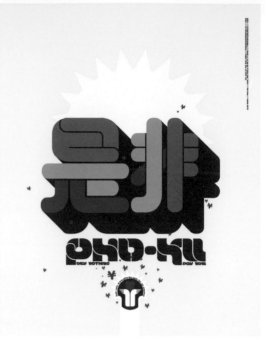

The Designers Republic. Sissy,
poster, UK, 1995

[Right] **The Designers Republic.**
Pho-Ku Corporation, poster,
UK, 2000

Atkins, the banded structure breaks apart as a rogue cloud of dots
swarms down over the titlepiece, which is shattered into horizontal
slices as though it were shooting past in a blur of speed. The design
vibrates with released electric energy.

DR's inspirations were electronic gadgets, 'magic'
technology, UFOs, films such as *Blade Runner* and science fiction
in general, and 'computers as big as planets and as small as
teardrops'.[14] A self-taught designer who originally studied
philosophy, Anderson was an articulate observer who viewed
the postmodern context for design with a mixture of resignation
and subversive wit: 'People may view modern society as being
shallow, riddled with capitalist failure or as being consumed by
senseless consumerism like a dog chasing its own tail – and they
are right. But until I'm in a position to improve its condition, I'm
going to enjoy the game I find intriguing.'[15] DR undertook projects
for Warp Records, Sony, MTV, Warner Brothers and the Ministry
of Sound. While they refrained from overtly critical statements,
a more ambivalent view of the electronic consumer culture they
mostly appear to celebrate surfaced in self-initiated banners
and posters for exhibitions, which featured ad-like incantations

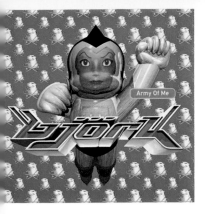

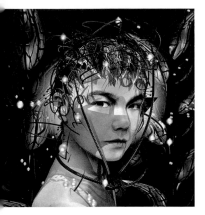

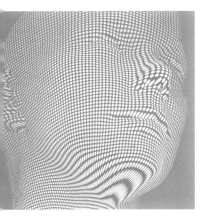

[Top] **Me Company. Army of Me**
by Björk, CD single cover, One Little
Indian, UK, 1995. Astro Boy
modelling by Martin Gardiner

[Middle] **Me Company. Bachelorette**
by Björk, CD single cover, One Little
Indian, UK, 1997. Photography by
Toby McFarlan Pond

[Bottom] **Me Company. Alarm Call**
by Björk, CD single cover. One Little
Indian, UK, 1998

declaring 'Department stores are our new cathedrals', 'Let's hear it
for consumer fascism' and 'Design will eat itself'. To sell their own
products, DR established the Pho-Ku ('fuck you') Corporation, with
the irresistible slogan 'Buy nothing. Pay now'.

The most suggestive expression of this ambivalence is a
fictitious toy called Sissy produced by Dr Deth Toys, a registered
trademark of The Designers Republic. Sissy™ has blue eyes, blond
bunches, a frilly dress and looks about three years old; behind her
back she carries a heavy baseball bat with the slogan 'I love my DR'.
Product advertising informs the viewer that the doll is suitable for
age 16+, that 'she is cute she will kill you' is a protected slogan of
DR (the barcode reads '5 155Y. KILL.' – Sissy kill), and that batteries
are not included. Sissy is sponsored by DR Cola. The figure was
originally rendered in outline, but later versions are three-
dimensionally modelled, giving Sissy the simplified, textureless
look of a character in a computer game or a Japanese anime.
Her face, hair, limbs and clothes have an unreal, plastic sheen.

In the work of Me Company, based in London, three-
dimensional modelling had, by the mid-1990s, become almost a
house style. Science fiction and Japanese popular culture were
once again the inspiration for digital worlds that are entirely
artificial yet obscenely vivid and real, impossible techno-spaces
built up from dazzling reflections and shimmering, glutinous
matter. A recurrent image, in much of this design output, is the
cyborg – an artificial fusion of man and machine. In 'A Cyborg
Manifesto', published in 1991, American theorist of science Donna
Haraway proposes that 'cyborg politics insist on noise and advocate
pollution, rejoicing in the illegitimate fusions of animal and
machine'.[16] Machines, she goes on to suggest, can be 'prosthetic
devices, intimate components, friendly selves'.[17] In a series of
projects for the Icelandic singer Björk, Me Company subjected
the idiosyncratic star to a series of intimate cybernetic couplings
and transformations in which her literal image is sometimes
completely effaced. For the single *Army of Me* (1995), the designers
used a battery of software programs – Elastic Reality, 3D Studio,
Form-Z, Infini-D, Photoshop and Freehand – to gene-splice her with
Astro Boy, the Japanese cartoon character, and so create Astro Björk.

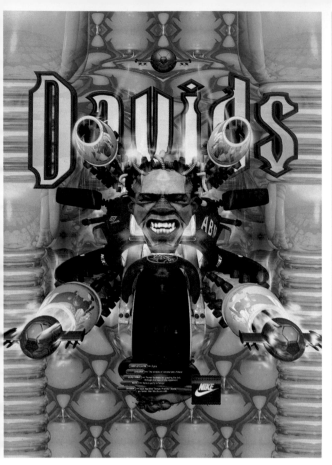

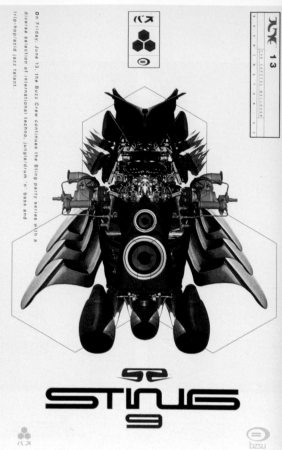

Me Company. Print advertisement for Nike, The Netherlands, 1995

[Right] **Airline Industries. Sting 9,** rave flyer, USA, 1997

On *Bachelorette* (1997), Björk's otherworldly likeness, caught in the reflections and shadows cast by spores of shining pollen, merges with a cyborgian garden in which the 'plants' themselves appear to be organic-robot hybrids. Finally, with *Alarm Call* (1998), her features are reduced to a series of pulsing, cyberscan contours, composed of luminescent dots, as the singer becomes a ghost in the digital machine.

Digital representations of this kind were second nature to a generation that had come to adulthood using computers and spent much of its leisure time in front of the screen, playing *Tomb Raider* and *Myst*. Me Company were soon applying their cyborg style to a series of print ads for Nike, commissioned by Wieden & Kennedy in Amsterdam, in which four Dutch football stars become screaming manga warriors rocketing towards the viewer out of throbbing digital space. Even more than with Makela's work, the viewer is sucked into a maelstrom that borders on delirium. By the mid-1990s, the techno graphic style was recognized everywhere as a lingua franca for techno music events. In the thousands of flyers produced to publicize raves in Britain, the United States, Germany and

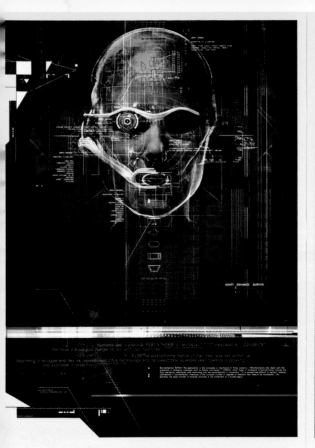

Attik. Noise 3.5: Analytical Experiments
in Graphic Science, book spread, UK, 1998

elsewhere, the preferred graphic mode could involve any or
all of the following: cute little robots, cartoons, insects, UFOs,
spacecraft, futuristic cities, wave forms, scientific diagrams,
neo-psychedelic swirls of colour, Japanese 'transformer' toys,
drifting clouds of plasma, and chunks of three-dimensional
type whizzing through space. Attik was one of the most relentless
exponents and exporters of commercial techno, with offices in
Huddersfield, London, New York, San Francisco and Sydney, and
clients such as Sony, Kodak, Levi's, Coca-Cola and Virgin. In a series
of self-promotional books, Attik's designers presented a mixture
of studio experimentation and client work. *Noise 3.5*: 'Analytical
Experiments in Graphic Science' – includes a spectacularly detailed
computer-generated image of a cyborg's head encrusted with
technological implants and layered with diagrams and information
read-outs. 'Humanic and orgobionic RESYNTHESIS is inevitable
and completely inescapable,' declares a caption, apparently
without irony. 'We have a biological hunger to join with our
machines.' This brings to mind McLuhan's observation: 'We are
all robots when uncritically involved with our technologies.'[18]

Only occasionally did techno's feel-good calls to join the warehouse party and its thrusting commercial offshoots give way to the more detached and ironic style of commentary seen in The Designers Republic's work. Barry Deck's speed-slanted typeface Cyberotica (1994), released by Thirst, captured the genre's rush of libidinal energy with a shrewdly anthropological eye. In Prague, the cultural magazine *Zivel* illustrated a special issue about pornography with a cover showing a computer graphic of a tumescent porno pig – an ambiguous icon for the complexities of 'posthuman' sexuality. In a report published in 1996, J. Abbott Miller of Design|Writing| Research in New York showed examples of 'dimensional typography' in which the normally flat and static realm of the letter was subjected to spatial and temporal extrapolation. In 'Polymorphous', based on Zuzana Licko's Modular Ribbed typeface (1995) – a design seemingly inspired by textured prophylactics – Miller developed the letter 'f' into a rubbery, three-dimensional avatar, bristling with nipple-like protuberances, 'designed for heightened reading pleasure in intimate settings'.[19] Another project, 'Rhizome', takes as its starting point Luc(as) de Groot's typeface Jesus Loves You. In the 1990s, the image of the 'rhizome' – introduced into theoretical discourse by the French philosophers Gilles Deleuze and Félix Guattari – was often invoked in postmodern cyberculture.[20] Where trees have roots, linking them to a single point of origin, plants such as grasses and bamboos have an underground network of stems, a rhizome, which can sprout new plants at any point. As Erik Davies notes in *TechGnosis*, these botanical structures without beginning and potentially without end resemble the myriad networks that make up the Internet, 'that wild digital weed whose very name underscores the interruptions and inbreeding that give postmodernists such interminable delight'.[21] Miller's 'Rhizome', based on the letter 'j', can be seen as a node in this promiscuous network, with dozens of thick and spiky shoots erupting from its tuberous length.

For graphic designers concerned with the relationship between image and text, the computer seemed to promise an end to all the old hierarchies, barriers and restrictions. 'Perhaps the most profound implication for the future is that digital technology

Cyberotica

ABCDEFGHIJKLMNOPQRSTUVWXYZabcdefg
hijklmnopqrstuvwxyz0123456789№°ÆŒ

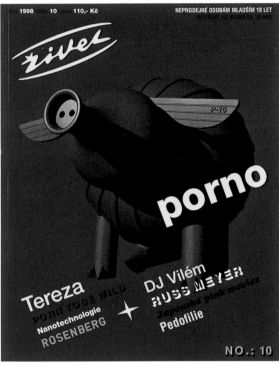

[Top] **Barry Deck.** Typeface
for Thirst, USA, 1994

[Above] **Klára Kvízová and
Petr Krejzek.** Zivel, no. 10,
magazine cover, Czech
Republic, 1998

[Right] **J. Abbott Miller.**
Rhizome typeface, USA, 1996

[Far right] **J. Abbott Miller.**
Polymorphous typeface,
USA, 1996

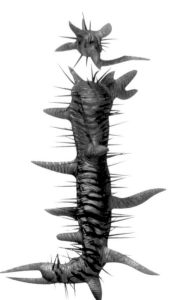

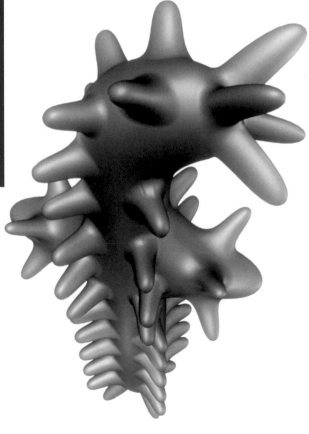

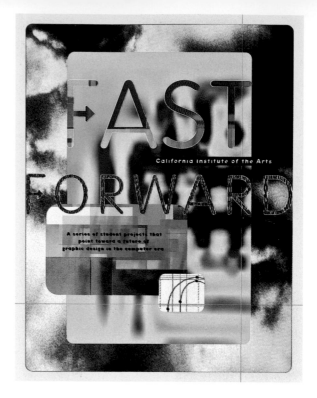

James Stoecker. Fast Forward, book cover,
California Institute of the Arts, USA, 1993

collapses all media into a single desktop tool speaking one digital
language. It is really a *metamedium*,' writes Eric Martin.[22] In *Fast
Forward* (1993), a catalogue for a series of student projects at
California Institute of the Arts, Jeffery Keedy cites science fiction
writer William Gibson's portrayal – in books such as *Neuromancer*
(1984) – of a future in which cybernetics, genetics, neurochemistry,
ecology, designer drugs and technology are on a collision course
with pop culture and there is a 'hallucinogenic melding of mind
and information structures'. 'If this is the construct of our future
world,' notes Keedy, 'then it's the graphic designers that will be
creating our total "human environment".'[23] There is a strain of
wild utopianism in such statements – not to mention an
overestimation of the designer's role – that is typical of a moment
when everything seemed open and it was possible to imagine that
technology itself could be the gateway to a different ordering of
reality. Keedy's text is arranged on the page in a series of floating
blocks that can be read in any order. Lines ripple, cast shadows
and overlap as though they are already part of the 'electronic flow'
into which Keedy expects words, sounds and images to dissolve.
In accordance with deconstructionist theory, the text has been
'decentred'; it no longer feels like the most important thing
happening on the page, but in that case what is? The design itself,
perhaps? Keedy, writing in the least inflected passage on the spread,
explains that the most important aspect of the computer's impact on

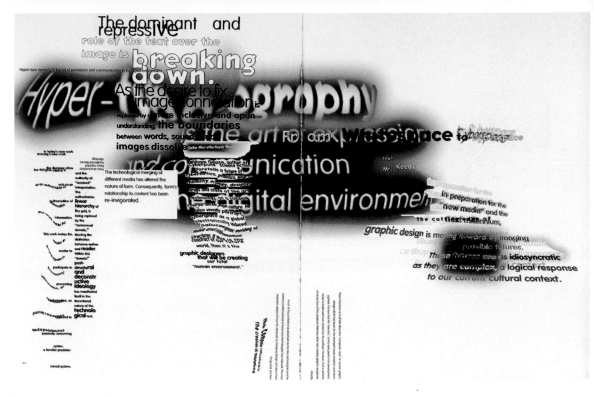

Jeffery Keedy. Fast Forward, book spread,
California Institute of the Arts, USA, 1993

design is not the way that things look, but how 'the computer
influences the creation of meaning'.[24]

The spirit of sweeping digital change was most fully and
persuasively expressed in *Wired* magazine, launched in 1993 by editor
and publisher Louis Rossetto. Under creative director John Plunkett,
Wired's use of design was instantly striking. In the first issue, the
opening words of Marshall McLuhan's *The Medium is the Massage* float
across the surface of three digital collages created by
illustrator|designer Erik Adigard. 'The medium, or process, of our
time – electric technology – is reshaping and restructuring patterns
of social interdependence and every aspect of our personal life. It is
forcing us to reconsider and re-evaluate practically every thought,
every action, and every institution formerly taken for granted.'[25]
Behind McLuhan's words drift melting images of a hand, a keyboard,
a brain and people watching television translated into
hallucinogenic shades of orange, green and pink. This set a pattern
that would be repeated in every issue: *Wired*'s first two or three
editorial spreads were devoted to a visual interpretation of a central
idea extracted from one of the articles (although the second issue
had another McLuhan quote against a background inspired by the
first line of Gibson's *Neuromancer*: 'The sky … was the color of
television, tuned to a dead channel'). While almost every page of
Wired, lavishly printed in pulsating fluorescent inks on a six-colour
press, was a high-impact visual event, it was the magazine's pre-

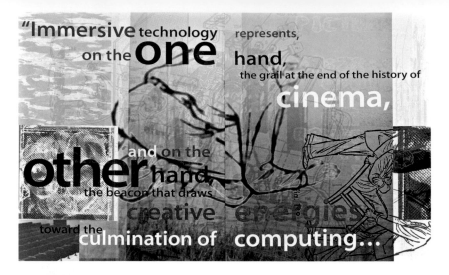

"Immersive technology represents, on the **one** hand, the grail at the end of the history of cinema, and on the other hand, the beacon that draws creative energies toward the culmination of computing...

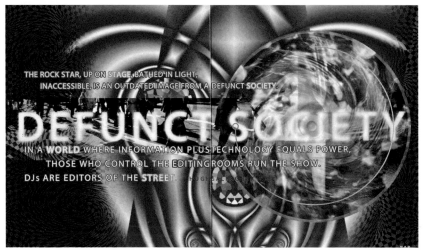

THE ROCK STAR, UP ON STAGE, BATHED IN LIGHT, INACCESSIBLE, IS AN OUTDATED IMAGE FROM A DEFUNCT SOCIETY.

DEFUNCT SOCIETY

IN A **WORLD** WHERE INFORMATION PLUS TECHNOLOGY EQUALS POWER, THOSE WHO CONTROL THE EDITING ROOMS RUN THE SHOW. DJs ARE EDITORS OF THE STREET.

[Top] **Fred Davis. Wired**, no. 1.06, magazine spread, USA, 1993. Creative director: John Plunkett

[Above] **Erik Adigard, M.A.D. Wired**, no. 2.08, magazine spread, USA, 1994. Creative director: John Plunkett

contents page experiments that most vividly transmitted the impression that, as Keedy had claimed, digital design would be central to 'immersive technology'. 'In the world of immersion,' writes Brenda Laurel, a researcher into human-computer interaction, 'authorship is no longer the transmission of experience, but rather the construction of utterly personal experiences.' [26] *Wired*'s pages offered avid readers among the self-styled 'digerati' an intoxicating metaphor for what such immersion in the electronic flow might be like. In 1996, *Wired* published the first three years' worth of spreads as a book, *Mind Grenades: Manifestos from the Future*, a title that suggests – like much of P. Scott Makela's work – a nostalgia for a future that has yet to happen and that seems, on present evidence, unlikely to arrive soon. The Internet, rapidly colonized by commerce, is no longer a wild frontier. The dotcom bubble has burst and virtual reality, once touted as the answer to

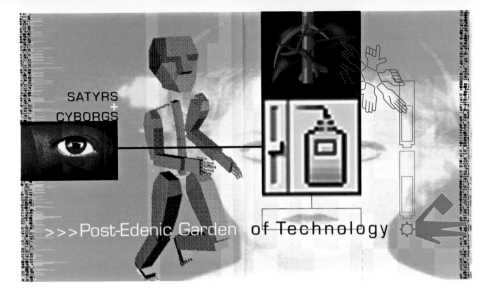

SATYRS
+
CYBORGS

>>>Post-Edenic Garden of Technology

Erik Adigard, M.A.D. Architecture Must Burn by Aaron Betsky and Erik Adigard, visual essay spread, Thames & Hudson, UK, 2000

everything, is the least of our concerns. *Wired* itself, now owned by Condé Nast, has become a business magazine like any other, and people find they are more attached to physical reality (not least paper) than the digital visionaries of the early 1990s liked to think.

The temperature of digital rhetoric may have cooled, but design is still produced, for the most part, on computers and this has irrevocably changed the way that many designers and design theorists think about design. In 2000, Adigard applied his experience with *Wired* to a series of visual essays for the book *Architecture Must Burn* by Aaron Betsky, then curator of architecture, design and digital projects at the San Francisco Museum of Modern Art.[27] Functioning much like *Wired*'s opening pages, Adigard's densely layered compositions are based on key ideas and phrases in the text, and image-led spreads are allowed to alternate on equal terms with text-led spreads. His digital interpretations have a rawness and an awkwardness that often seems deliberate – a textural embodiment of the book's claim that architecture is a form of 'unbuilding, collage and folding' that is ultimately about constructing the self. The text, too, is treated as an image; decentred within the book form's conventional hierarchies – in both the literal and postmodern senses – it flows outwards to the pages' boundaries, changing size and width from column to column and often within the same column. It is an effort to read it in a linear way and there is more text than seems necessary in a book that purports to be a 'manifesto', but ideas still jump out of the page, making their impact sensually as much as sequentially. For Betsky (and, it would seem, for Adigard) the 'electrosphere' composed of advertising, television, film and cyberspace is a postmodern 'floating world' with no material reality, nowhere yet everywhere:

'The floating world is the realm of the graphic designer. Ever more powerful computer technologies have expanded the scope of the floating world, giving them a great deal more freedom. Instead of cutting and pasting, they now assemble; rather than working with images they have prepared for the page, they can scan and manipulate whatever they want.... Information sprawls within the confines of the graphic designer's frame, but it does so in a way that the designer can control with absolute power.... Now that information is free to flow everywhere, graphic designers must invent compositions that no longer depend on physical structure.'[28]

To make sense of the floating world, argues Betsky, 'We must accept that what makes sense is not the law, syntax, rules or structure.'[29] Instead, he finds meaning in the way that information is delivered by the screen, announcing itself, then fading away in a blur, before it disappears behind new layers of information that, in turn, draw us towards other imagery (exactly the quality seen in Adigard's image-fields). In this quintessentially postmodern view, there is no moment of arrival, no meaning to form itself, just a perpetual journey in which signs that no longer refer to a pre- or post-existing reality offer their own mainly sensory forms of satisfaction and solace.

This might sound like an implausibly thin and inward-looking rationale for graphic communication. It takes as its starting point observable facts about the postmodern world, but in the process of formulation and expression it seems to become intoxicated with its own rhetoric and starts to float ecstatically free from the realm of everyday encounters with graphic messages of all kinds. In the enormous and ever-increasing volume of graphic production (which is, in itself, a postmodern phenomenon) most projects do, however, still have to concern themselves with communicating relatively defined and prosaic forms of message, even if the graphic languages they employ no longer conform to out-moded rules, syntax or structure. It may be true, as a generalization, that the viewer, like the designer at his screen, is floating through a boundless media-world with few fixed bearings. Many of the examples shown in this chapter express this sensation. But in a practical sense, people still make continuous choices about what to engage with or ignore and design still tries to seize attention for an instant, sometimes longer, in the hope of conveying an intelligible message. The danger with the simulated world of the screen is that its introverted excitements are so deliriously intense and absorbing that they begin to eclipse all other considerations. From this unreal perspective, scanning, manipulating and assembling at will, everything else also starts to look unreal. The 'process' – a word much used by designers in recent years – becomes an end in itself. [30]

Driven by changes in technology, graphic design is in a process of transition, which, at the time of writing, is still under way. In the last decade, the *look* of graphic design has changed enormously. It is now possible to cram a design with a quantity of imagery and detail that would have been unthinkable in most cases in earlier decades, when mechanical artworks were constructed at the drawing board layer by layer. A glistening perfection of finish that would once have exceeded even the finest draftsman is possible now as a matter of routine. Periodic reassertions of the communicational value of minimalism make no difference; if anything, they simply confirm that easily attainable complexity and spectacular graphic excess have become the new norms.

While the United States was at the forefront of technological design change from the mid-1980s to the mid-1990s, in the late 1990s other graphic cultures, which had been slower to embrace the computer's possibilities, began to pull design in new experimental directions. In Switzerland, birthplace of the International Style, younger designers such as Büro Destruct (founded in Berne in 1994), Martin Woodtli and Norm (both based in Zurich) moved into the professional spotlight. [31] Woodtli combines old and new versions of programs to produce deliberate errors that provoke the unexpected. He invents strange technological icons and pictograms that can be moved around, according to the temporary grammar of a given project, within his autonomous graphic worlds. 'Every work has its own materiality which arises from the tool – the computer.' [32] Norm, too, devise 'laws' for each assignment, discarding them for new rules when the project is completed. Their book, *Introduction*, is a studio manifesto that seeks to return

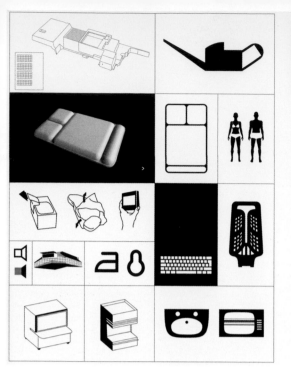

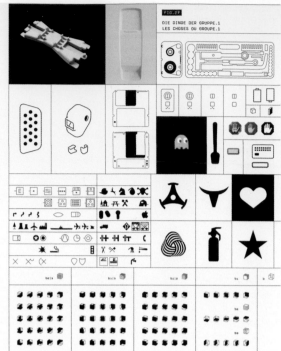

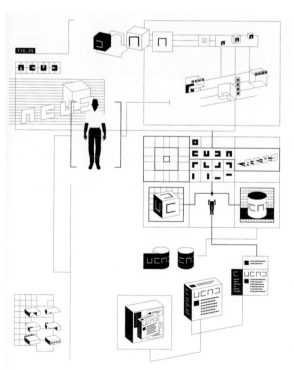

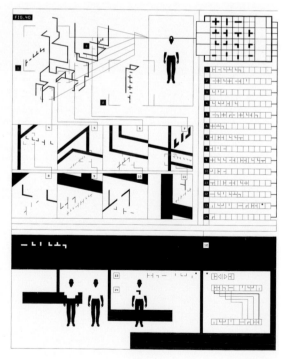

Norm. Introduction, spreads
from a self-published book,
Switzerland, 1999

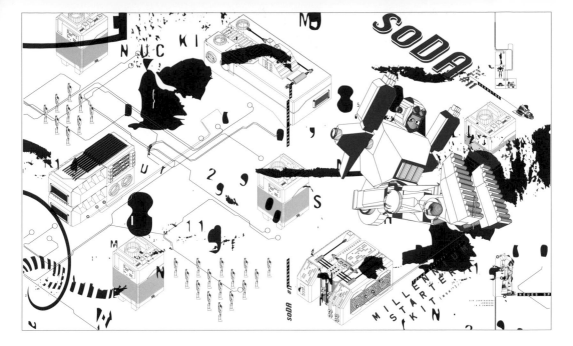

Martin Woodtli. Soda, no. 11,
magazine cover, front and back,
Switzerland, 1999

graphic design to zero. 'We want to talk about graphics via our own
medium – to articulate our reflections graphically. Not as cultural
theoreticians who don't have a clue about fonts,' explains team
member Manuel Krebs.[33] *Introduction* divides graphic representation
into four categories: things that occur in two-dimensional space,
but refer to something that exists in three dimensions; things
with no reference to three-dimensional space; things that refer
to nothing or to themselves; things that are unforeseeable, not
yet known. The diagrams and flow charts that result from this
investigation are fabulously intricate and impenetrable graphic
labyrinths that seem to negate the very clarity they seek. As self-
initiated experiments, they embody the continuing paradox
about contemporary graphic design. On one hand, design is our
omnipresent, everyday reality: 'Everyone lives within it, [yet] no
one discusses it.'[34] On the other, and perhaps for this very reason,
postmodern digital design culture has spawned an inventive and
energetic global subculture that often appears to exist mainly
to talk to itself about itself.

5

AUTHORSHIP

The emergence of the 'designer as author' is one of the key ideas in graphic design of the postmodern period. It is also one of the more problematic ideas, since, as some strands of critical theory would have it, the very notion of an 'author' as a validating source of authority for a cultural work is outdated, backward-looking and reactionary. This idea was most memorably expressed in Roland Barthes' essay 'The Death of the Author', first published in 1968, and the Author's demise has been regularly proclaimed as a desirable goal ever since, even though in every practical sense the author – not least the postmodernist cultural critic – continues to flourish. Barthes makes an argument which is in some ways perfectly logical and reasonable. He notes that, while we continue to search for the explanation of a literary work in the life and experiences of the man or woman who produced it, in reality a piece of writing is a 'tissue of quotations' that owes everything to the mass of writing that preceded it. A text is 'not a line of words releasing a single "theological" meaning (the "message" of the Author-God) but a multidimensional space in which a variety of writings, none of them original, blend and clash'.[1] Take away the author, argues Barthes, and all claims to decipher a text and attribute to it a final, definitive meaning become futile. He proposes instead a process of disentangling the multiplicity of texts: 'the structure can be followed, "run" (like the thread of a stocking) at every point and at every level, but there is nothing beneath: the space of the writing is to be ranged over, not pierced'.[2] With the author pushed into the wings, the reader – usually overlooked by criticism – can take centre stage. It is the reader, not the writer, who decides the meaning of the multiple quotations that compose a text, the reader who gives a text its unity, and it is consequently the reader on whom the future of writing depends. Barthes famously concludes: 'the birth

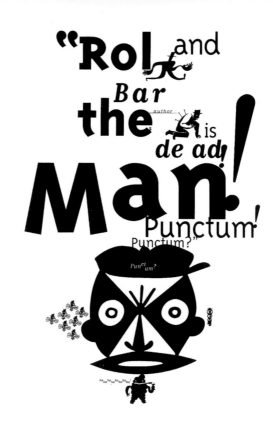

Bob Aufuldish. Selected Notes 2
ZeitGuys by Mark Bartlett, detail from
a feature in **Zed,** no. 2, USA, 1995

of the reader must be at the cost of the death of the Author.'[3]

As we saw in chapter 2, designers attuned to postmodern theory and its popular expressions have often invoked the reader or viewer using similar ideas and terms. Their aim, they said, was not to impose a single closed and restrictive reading, but to provide open structures that encourage the audience's participation and interpretation. Yet there was usually not the smallest hint of self-effacement, let alone a deathwish, in this strategy. Experimental design drew attention to itself and the inevitable result was to throw the spotlight on its makers. Since the earliest days of commercial art, a handful of designers had always become 'stars' of the profession, their work lauded in trade magazines, exhibitions and sometimes in monographs. Nevertheless, professional rhetoric insisted, at least until the 1960s (and sometimes even today), that design was essentially an anonymous activity, and in many ways it was and still is: few members of the public would be able to name even one graphic designer. In the 1980s, as design's sense of its own importance grew, so did its fascination with itself. The number of informal 'show and tell' lectures by designers and well-attended conferences featuring the same travelling band of international design luminaries increased dramatically. The nature of design journalism also changed. Enthusiastic profiles became

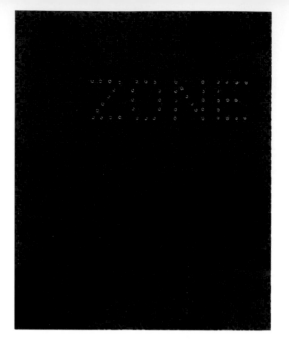

[Right & opposite] **Bruce Mau. Zone,**
no. 1|2, book cover and spread, Zone
Books, USA, 1986

commonplace, paying as much attention to the designers'
personalities as their designs, and many books appeared
celebrating individual bodies of work. A few graphic designers –
Neville Brody, David Carson, Tibor Kalman – even attracted
attention in mainstream media, where they were presented
as significant shapers of contemporary visual culture.

The tendency then, in the last 20 years, has been for
graphic designers of all kinds to assert their presence and
significance. Other people may view them as a group whose job
is to take a client's message and express it as effectively as possible
in a spirit of neutral professionalism, and design rhetoric has often
endorsed this interpretation of design's role. However, the motives
that lead someone to become a designer have always been more
complicated than this suggests. The act of designing can never
be an entirely neutral process, since the designer always brings
something extra to the project.[4] A design cannot fail to be informed,
in some measure, by personal taste, cultural understanding, social
and political beliefs, and deeply held æsthetic preferences.
Moreover, designers have always insisted that, to function
effectively, they need to question and perhaps 'rewrite' the
client's brief. They have argued that the client's understanding
of the communication problem may be imperfect and that this
is why the client needs their help in the first place. At the
same time, designers are motivated by the need for creative
satisfaction and peer approval, significant but sometimes
unacknowledged factors that have a powerful determining
effect on their work.

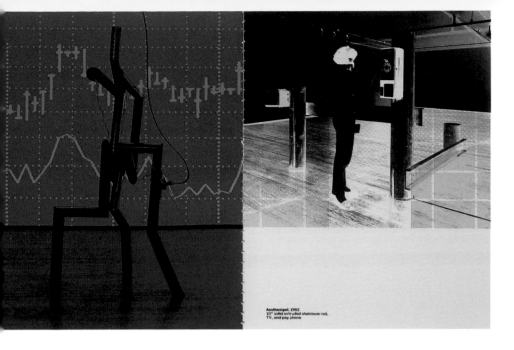

Aesthesigol, 1982
10" solid extruded aluminum rod,
TV, and pay phone

None of this is sufficient, though, to make a designer an
'author' and, before the late 1980s, few designers – not even the
most idiosyncratic – would have described their own design practice
in terms of 'graphic authorship'. The phrase 'designer as author'
did not achieve wider currency until the mid-1990s, although it is
still primarily a North American phenomenon, and remains
controversial and prone to misunderstanding. Canadian designer
Bruce Mau was one of the earliest, most self-aware and deliberate
exponents of the idea. Citing Walter Benjamin's essay 'The Author
as Producer' (1934), and neatly reversing the image, Mau said he
wanted to occupy the role of 'the producer as author'.[5] In the early
1980s, he worked as a designer at Pentagram in London before
returning, disenchanted, to Toronto, where he set up the firm Public
Good, specializing in social, cultural and educational design work.
Bruce Mau Design, his second venture, came to wider attention in
1986, with the publication of *Zone 1|2*, a collection of academic essays
about the contemporary city that was anything but dry or detached.
Mau interspersed the texts, floating elegantly in spacious margins,
with stills from disaster movies, fold-out images by video artists,
city maps on see-through paper, and splashes of colour as vivid as a
Warhol screenprint. *Zone* was a desirable object in which the graphic
designer had clearly played a significant shaping role, and in this
and many subsequent projects for Zone Books, Mau's designs
combined serious intellectual intent with unapologetic sensual
appeal in a way that was soon imitated by other academic
publishers. His aim, he explained in 1994, was to 'roll Bruce Mau
Design on to the field upon which content is developed'.[6] In his

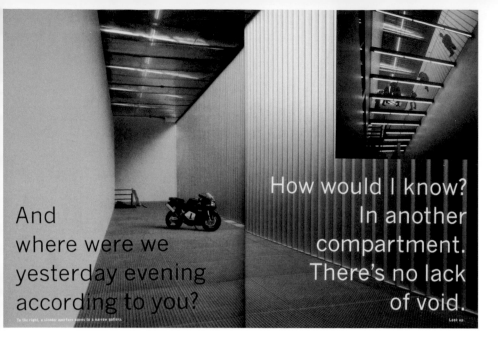

And
where were we
yesterday evening
according to you?

To the right, a slender aperture opens to a narrow gallery.

How would I know?
In another
compartment.
There's no lack
of void.

Look up.

Bruce Mau. S,M,L,XL by O.M.A., Rem Koolhaas and Bruce Mau, book spread, 010/Monacelli Press, The Netherlands|USA, 1995

book *Life Style* (2000), Mau develops this idea by showing two diagrams that represent the typical trajectory of a book project and then the course he would prefer it to take. In the first, the designer arrives on the scene at the end of the research process, after all the key decisions about editorial content have been taken, and is allotted the task of giving form to the content. In Mau's preferred model, the designer undertakes research and the refinement of ideas from the project's inception, sometimes alongside the writer, sometimes exploring other possibilities independently. He writes:

'The new approach replaces division of labor with synthesis, clients and commissions with collaborators and partners, executing tasks with negotiating terrain, maximum output with maximum feedback, and form applied to content with form and content evolving and enriching each other simultaneously.... We are not sure whether this new way of working means the end of design, or whether it means designers become authors, or authors become designers, or all three.'[7]

Mau's collaboration with Dutch architect Rem Koolhaas on the book *S,M,L,XL* (1995) was the most exhaustive and overwhelming example of this approach.[8] The book took five years to complete, expanded from a planned 264 pages to an eventual 1,344 pages, and almost bankrupted Mau's studio in the process. Divided into four main sections corresponding to small, medium, large and extra-large projects, *S,M,L,XL* unfolds with a cinematic momentum and grasp of the relationship between images. Like the film director Chris Marker, whom he admires, Mau is prepared to 'hold a shot too long' to encourage the audience to look more closely.[9] It might be argued that the content is still essentially Koolhaas' – it is his career, his

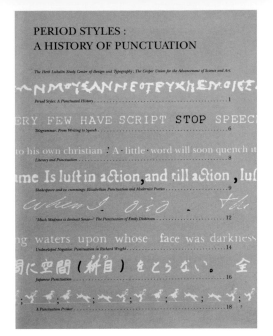

PERIOD STYLES :
A HISTORY OF PUNCTUATION

The Herb Lubalin Study Center of Design and Typography, The Cooper Union for the Advancement of Science and Art.

Period Styles: A Punctuated History 1

Telegrammar: From Writing to Speech 6

Literacy and Punctuation 8

Shakespeare and ee. cummings: Elizabethan Punctuation and Modernist Poetics 9

"Much Madness is divinest Sense–" The Punctuation of Emily Dickinson 12

Underscored Negative Punctuation in Richard Wright 14

Japanese Punctuation 16

A Punctuation Primer 18

Ellen Lupton. Period Styles: A
History of Punctuation, catalogue
cover, The Cooper Union, USA, 1988

body of work, his writing – but Mau's visualization endows this
daunting mass of material with a structural presence that far
exceeds an ordinary monograph's. On the cover, Mau receives equal
billing with Koolhaas as co-author, a degree of recognition achieved
by few other designers.

As Mau argues, a close engagement with content is clearly
essential before anything like authorship can be claimed. Mau's
approach relied on finding clients who would respect and trust
him sufficiently to invite him to become involved in their projects
at an early stage. Other designers initiate their own projects and
are unambiguously responsible for their content, which they generate
entirely or largely themselves. In this respect, Ellen Lupton and
J. Abbott Miller were two of the most significant designer|authors to
emerge in the late 1980s. As with Mau, research was central to their
conception of design practice and they made this commitment explicit
in the three-word manifesto with which, in 1985, they titled their
alliance: Design|Writing|Research. Steeped in the work of theorists
such as Saussure, Derrida and Foucault, they wrote extensively as
critics for design publications such as *Print, Emigre* and *Eye*. As curator
of the Herb Lubalin Study Center at The Cooper Union art school in
New York, from 1986 to 1990, Lupton created many exhibitions about
design in which she combined a number of roles that would usually
be separated: researcher, writer, editor, exhibition designer and
catalogue designer. In an essay about the history of numbers for a
'Writing|Culture' monograph published by The Cooper Union, she
illustrates her text by integrating images into the lines of type,
allowing them to stand as numerical and pictorial representations

of the words they replace. Miller, based at the Design|Writing|Reseach
studio in Manhattan, founded in 1989, undertook editorial design
and exhibition design projects in which he could achieve close
editorial involvement and, from 1997, he was editor and art director
of the visual culture magazine *2wice*. In one of their most ambitious
collaborations as author|curators, *The ABCs of* ▲ ■ ● : *The Bauhaus and
Design Theory* (1991), Lupton and Miller demonstrate how writing and
design might be brought together in a new critical relationship:
'Modern art education often discourages graphic designers from
actively engaging in the writing process … Instead, the graphic
designer could be conceived of as a language-worker equipped to
actively initiate projects – either by literally authoring texts or by
elaborating, directing or disrupting their meaning. The graphic
designer "writes" verbal|visual documents by arranging, sizing,
framing, and editing images and texts.'[10]

Lupton's 'Visual Dictionary' applies this principle to the
exploration of four techniques for organizing textual and pictorial
material: graph, translation, grid and figure. Pages are conceived
graphically, with equal attention to verbal and visual meaning and
a commitment to design possibilities that is highly unusual in
historical and critical documents about visual culture. On a spread
dealing with the grid, Lupton presents a series of observations as
short, separate notes, with their concluding words and phrases
detached from the sentence and shifted by the page grid (here made
visible) into an adjacent column to demonstrate its use for purposes
of discontinuity, cutting and framing. Just as language is a grid which
breaks down experience into repeatable signs – according to Lupton's
reading of Saussure – so the grid itself is a form of language.

Lupton and Miller's positioning of themselves as writers
and their fusion of writing and design gave credibility to any claim
they might make to be 'graphic authors'. In 1996, the publication
of *Design Writing Research*, a compilation of their critical writings on
theory, design and media, confirmed their leading role.[11] With this
book, they joined the ranks of designers who have formulated their
ideas and principles in book form – figures such as Jan Tschichold,
Emil Ruder, Josef Müller-Brockmann and Paul Rand. In the early
1990s, as discussion of authorship became more impassioned, it

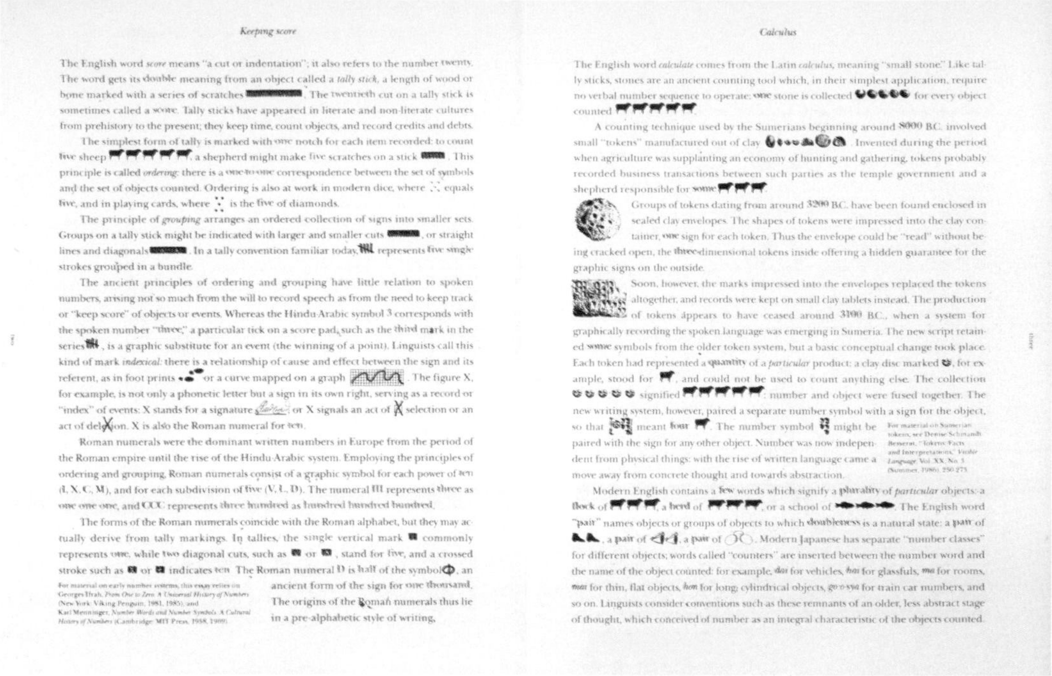

The English word *score* means "a cut or indentation"; it also refers to the number twenty. The word gets its double meaning from an object called a *tally stick*, a length of wood or bone marked with a series of scratches ████. The twentieth cut on a tally stick is sometimes called a *score*. Tally sticks have appeared in literate and non-literate cultures from prehistory to the present; they keep time, count objects, and record credits and debts.

The simplest form of tally is marked with one notch for each item recorded: to count five sheep, a shepherd might make five scratches on a stick. This principle is called *ordering*: there is a one-to-one correspondence between the set of symbols and the set of objects counted. Ordering is also at work in modern dice, where ∴ equals five, and in playing cards, where ♦ is the five of diamonds.

The principle of *grouping* arranges an ordered collection of signs into smaller sets. Groups on a tally stick might be indicated with larger and smaller cuts, or straight lines and diagonals. In a tally convention familiar today, ████ represents five single strokes grouped in a bundle.

The ancient principles of ordering and grouping have little relation to spoken numbers, arising not so much from the will to record speech as from the need to keep track or "keep score" of objects or events. Whereas the Hindu-Arabic symbol 3 corresponds with the spoken number "three," a particular tick on a score pad, such as the third mark in the series, is a graphic equivalent for an event (the winning of a point). Linguists call this kind of mark *indexical*: there is a relationship of cause and effect between the sign and its referent, as in foot prints or a curve mapped on a graph. The figure X, for example, is not only a phonetic letter but a sign in its own right, serving as a record or "index" of events: X stands for a signature or X signals an act of selection or an act of deletion. X is also the Roman numeral for ten.

Roman numerals were the dominant written numbers in Europe from the period of the Roman empire until the rise of the Hindu-Arabic system. Employing the principles of ordering and grouping, Roman numerals consist of a graphic symbol for each power of ten (I, X, C, M), and for each subdivision of five (V, L, D). The numeral III represents three as one one one, and CCC represents three hundred as hundred hundred hundred.

The forms of the Roman numerals coincide with the Roman alphabet, but they may actually derive from tally markings. In tallies, the single vertical mark commonly represents one, while two diagonal cuts, such as V or X, stand for five, and a crossed stroke indicates ten. The Roman numeral D is half of the symbol ⊕, an ancient form of the sign for one thousand. The origins of the Roman numerals thus lie in a pre-alphabetic style of writing.

For material on early number systems, this essay relies on Georges Ifrah, *From One to Zero: A Universal History of Numbers* (New York: Viking Penguin, 1985, 1985); and Karl Menninger, *Number Words and Number Symbols: A Cultural History of Numbers* (Cambridge: MIT Press, 1969, 1969).

The English word *calculate* comes from the Latin *calculus*, meaning "small stone." Like tally sticks, stones are an ancient counting tool which, in their simplest application, require no verbal number sequence to operate: one stone is collected for every object counted.

A counting technique used by the Sumerians beginning around 8000 B.C. involved small "tokens" manufactured out of clay. Invented during the period when agriculture was supplanting an economy of hunting and gathering, tokens probably recorded business transactions between such parties as the temple government and a shepherd responsible for some.

Groups of tokens dating from around 3200 B.C. have been found enclosed in sealed clay envelopes. The shapes of tokens were impressed into the clay container, one sign for each token. Thus the envelope could be "read" without being cracked open, the three-dimensional tokens inside offering a hidden guarantee for the graphic signs on the outside.

Soon, however, the marks impressed into the envelopes replaced the tokens altogether, and records were kept on small clay tablets instead. The production of tokens appears to have ceased around 3200 B.C., when a system for graphically recording the spoken language was emerging in Sumeria. The new script retained some symbols from the older token system, but a basic conceptual change took place. Each token had represented a *quantity* of a *particular* product: a clay disc marked, for example, stood for, and could not be used to count anything else. The collection signified: number and object were fused together. The new writing system, however, paired a separate number symbol with a sign for the object, so that meant *four*. The number symbol might be paired with the sign for any other object. Number was now independent from physical things: with the rise of written language came a move away from concrete thought and towards abstraction.

Modern English contains a *few* words which signify a *plurality* of *particular* objects: a *flock* of, a *herd* of, or a *school* of. The English word "pair" names objects or groups of objects to which *doubleness* is a natural state: a *pair* of, a *pair* of, a *pair* of. Modern Japanese has separate "number classes" for different objects; words called "counters" are inserted between the number word and the name of the object counted: for example, *dai* for vehicles, *ken* for rooms, *mai* for thin, flat objects, *hon* for long, cylindrical objects, *go-sha* for train car numbers, and so on. Linguists consider conventions such as these remnants of an older, less abstract stage of thought, which conceived of number as an integral characteristic of the objects counted.

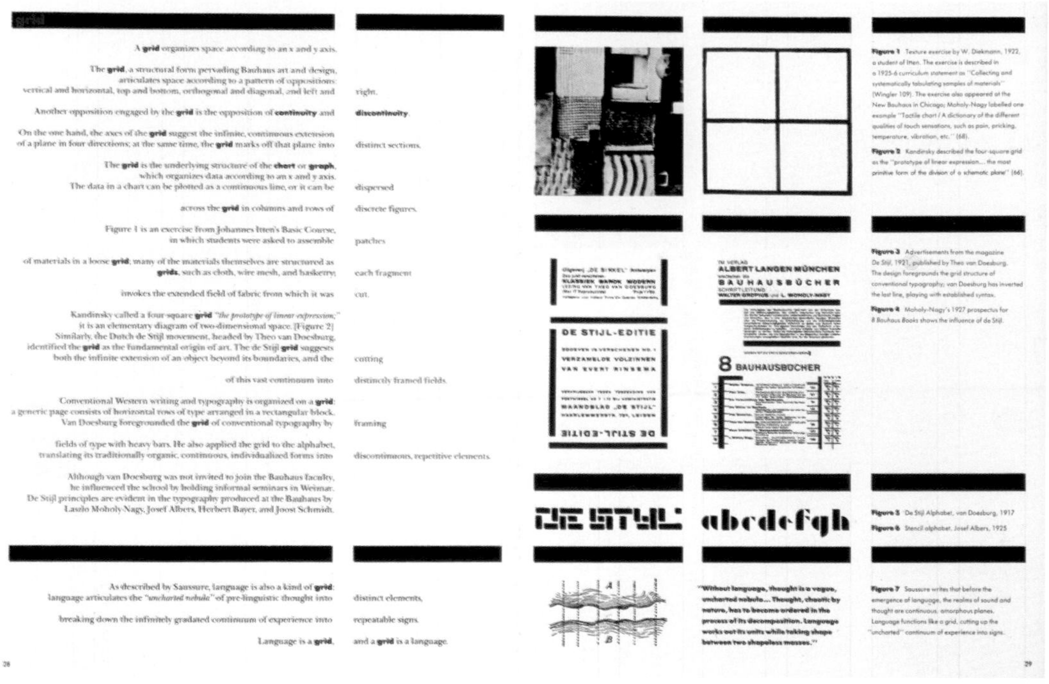

A **grid** organizes space according to an *x* and *y* axis.

The **grid**, a structural form pervading Bauhaus art and design, articulates space according to a pattern of oppositions: vertical and horizontal, top and bottom, orthogonal and diagonal, and left and right.

Another opposition engaged by the **grid** is the opposition of **continuity** and **discontinuity**.

On the one hand, the axes of the **grid** suggest the infinite, continuous extension of a plane in four directions; at the same time, the **grid** marks off that plane into distinct sections.

The **grid** is the underlying structure of the **chart** or **graph**, which organizes data according to an *x* and *y* axis. The data in a chart can be plotted as a continuous line, or it can be dispersed across the **grid** in columns and rows of discrete figures.

Figure 1 is an exercise from Johannes Itten's Basic Course, in which students were asked to assemble patches of materials in a loose **grid**; many of the materials themselves are structured as **grids**, such as cloth, wire mesh, and basketry: each fragment invokes the extended field of fabric from which it was cut.

Kandinsky called a four-square **grid** *"the prototype of linear expression;"* it is an elementary diagram of two-dimensional space [Figure 2]. Similarly, the Dutch de Stijl movement, headed by Theo van Doesburg, identified the **grid** as the fundamental origin of art. The de Stijl **grid** suggests both the infinite extension of an object beyond its boundaries, and the cutting of this vast continuum into distinctly framed fields.

Conventional Western writing and typography is organized on a **grid**: a generic page consists of horizontal rows of type arranged in a rectangular block. Van Doesburg foregrounded the **grid** of conventional typography by framing fields of type with heavy bars. He also applied the grid to the alphabet, translating its traditionally organic, continuous, individualised forms into discontinuous, repetitive elements.

Although van Doesburg was not invited to join the Bauhaus faculty, he influenced the school by holding informal seminars in Weimar. De Stijl principles are evident in the typography produced at the Bauhaus by László Moholy-Nagy, Josef Albers, Herbert Bayer, and Joost Schmidt.

As described by Saussure, language is also a kind of **grid**: language articulates the "uncharted nebula" of pre-linguistic thought into distinct elements, breaking down the infinitely gradated continuum of experience into repeatable signs. Language is a **grid**, and a **grid** is a language.

"Without language, thought is a vague, uncharted nebula... Thought, chaotic by nature, has to become ordered in the process of its decomposition. Language works out its units while taking shape between two shapeless masses."

Figure 1 Texture exercise by W. Diekmann, 1922, a student of Itten. The exercise is described in a 1925–6 curriculum document "Collecting and systematically tabulating samples of materials" (Wingler 109). The exercise also appeared at the New Bauhaus in Chicago; Moholy-Nagy labelled one example "Tactile chart / A dictionary of the different qualities of touch sensations, such as pain, prickling, temperature, vibration, etc." (68).

Figure 2 Kandinsky described the four-square grid as the "prototype of linear expression... the most primitive form of the division of a schematic plane" (64).

Figure 3 Advertisement from the magazine De Stijl, 1921, published by Theo van Doesburg. The design foregrounds the grid structure of conventional typography; van Doesburg has inverted the lost line, playing with established syntax.

Figure 4 Moholy-Nagy's 1927 prospectus for 8 Bauhaus Books shows the influence of de Stijl.

Figure 5 De Stijl Alphabet, von Doesburg, 1917

Figure 6 Stencil alphabet, Josef Albers, 1925

Figure 7 Saussure writes that before the emergence of language, the realms of sound and thought are continuous, amorphous planes. Language functions like a grid, cutting up the "uncharted" continuum of experience into signs.

[Top] **Ellen Lupton. Numbers,** catalogue spread, The Cooper Union, USA, 1989

[Above] **Ellen Lupton, J. Abbott Miller and Mike Mills. The ABCs of ▲■● : The Bauhaus and Design Theory,** catalogue spread, The Cooper Union, USA, 1991

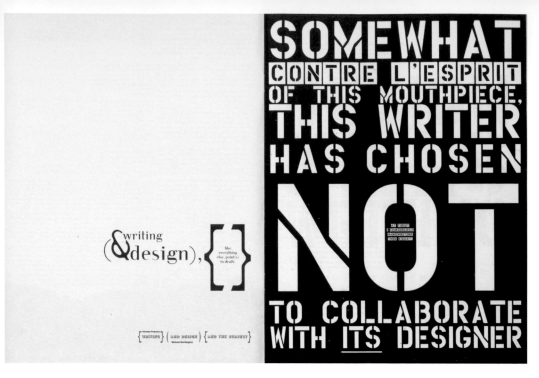

writing
(&design),

{ like
everything
else, point(s)
to death. }

{ Anthony Froshaug
WRITING } (AND DESIGN) { AND THE SUBJECT }
Michael Worthington

SOMEWHAT CONTRE L'ESPRIT OF THIS MOUTHPIECE, THIS WRITER HAS CHOSEN NOT TO COLLABORATE WITH ITS DESIGNER

Michael Worthington. Emigre, no. 35,
'Mouthpiece' issue, magazine spread,
USA, 1995

seemed that writing would need to play a central role and that
only those designers capable of total authorship – undertaking both
writing and design – could hope to become fully fledged graphic
authors. Following Lupton and Miller's example, this period was
marked by an upsurge of interest in theoretical and critical writing
among young designers, particularly in the United States, much
of it published in the pages of Emigre, Eye, Visible Language and Zed.[12]
In 1993, in an essay titled 'What has Writing got to do with Design?',
American designer and design educator Anne Burdick challenged
designers' ingrained reluctance to accept that graphic design is
an inseparable marriage of the verbal and visual, and argued that
design's written content should receive much closer attention.
'Writing can feed the profession in two ways: through the challenge
of critical analysis and through the exploratory freedom of self-
initiated work,' notes Burdick.[13] Her arguments are vigorous and
convincing, yet her concluding words – 'Designers should write not
in order to become better writers, but to become better designers' –
suggest definite though somewhat arbitrary limits to authorial
ambition.[14] In 1995, Burdick guest-edited two issues of Emigre, with
the overall title 'Mouthpiece: Clamor over Writing and Design'.[15]
Some writers undertook the design of their own writing. In other
cases, Burdick brought writers and designers together in more
or less sympathetic pairings intended to 'explore and exploit the
privileged position of authorship'.[16] The essays are hugely disparate
in form, giving rise to the 'clamor' of the title, but considered as

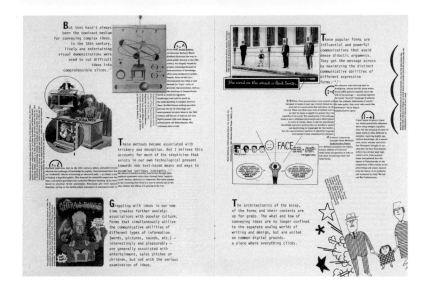

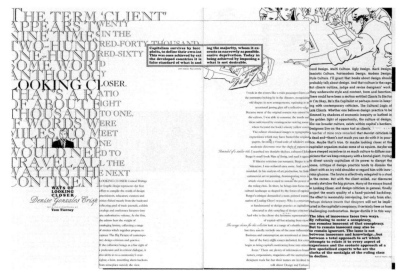

[Top] **Louise Sandhaus. Emigre,** no. 36, 'Mouthpiece' issue, magazine spread, USA, 1995

[Above] **Denise Gonzales Crisp. Emigre,** no. 35, 'Mouthpiece' issue, magazine spread, USA, 1995. Illustrations by Tom Tierney

individual pieces they involve design in a more active process than conventional publishing hierarchies and divisions of labour allow. They are often successful, too, in substantiating Burdick's claim, repeated by many designers at the time, that when words are made material in the form of typography, the meanings of 'writing' and 'design' cannot be separated. The designer, as initiator or working partner, shares responsibility with the writer for the production of meaning, though whether this is an equal responsibility remains a moot point.

Burdick, seemingly aware of the problems of authorship raised by Barthes and others, is careful to avoid suggesting that authorship is an attempt by designers to seize control of areas of the editorial process to which they have traditionally been denied access. Yet the central appeal of authorship for some graphic designers, irrespective of its inherent complexities, is precisely that it recognizes and elevates the position of the designer. The power struggle this is likely to involve was made explicit in the introduction to the exhibition 'Designer as Author: Voices and Visions' in 1996 at Northern Kentucky University. 'Author as authority manifests itself in print and electronic media across most disciplines, from serious scholarship to lowbrow tabloids,' writes co-curator Steven McCarthy. 'Designers as authors realize that despite some influence emanating from the domain of visual image and typographic form, a truly powerful weapon is to control the words themselves, and therefore more of the message.'[17]

In cases where the designer does not have control of the words – that is, in most cases – authorship remains, at best, a questionable concept. Designers have always determined or helped to determine the final form of a text, but this is a relatively minor aspect of its meaning compared to its factual content and the intricacies of argument it might contain. As one of Bruce Mau's former collaborators puts it: 'You can't claim authorship because you made the page pink.'[18] The centrality of form and surface in postmodern culture, often at the expense of content, and a McLuhan-esque belief that it is the overarching medium rather than the specific message that counts, contributes to designers' sense that design deserves greater attention and encourages the view that style itself is a sufficient form of content. Yet, as Burdick recognizes in her criticisms of designers' word-blindness, this argument is often based on a strategy of simply ignoring the communicative potential of words: the designer does not happen to read and concludes that reading must therefore be unimportant to everyone else.

In the most fully realized and persuasive examples of postmodern graphic authorship, the designer has full control over the text, as commissioner, editor or writer. Such work tends to take place in self-determined spaces and venues free from the constraints of client-given design and, for this reason, some see it as peripheral to design's core concerns as a service-providing activity. In the 1980s, some of the most significant and influential designer|authors emerged from the genre of the artist's book. These book artists were

not designers in the professional sense of the term, so they were
not inhibited by the rules and codes of disciplinary practice, even
if they used similar resources and forms. Their primary motivation
was the expression of their own content and they taught themselves
the techniques needed to articulate this effectively. In the United
States, Johanna Drucker combined an academic career as teacher
and author of *The Visible Word* (1994), *The Alphabetic Labyrinth* (1995)
and *The Century of Artists' Books* (1995) with the production, starting
in the early 1970s, of a series of experimental books, which she
wrote, edited, designed and sometimes illustrated and printed by
letterpress. Instead of feeling restricted by the physical limitations
of letterpress, Drucker used its characteristics to structure her
books and extend the investigation of language in printed form.
In *Against Fiction* (1983), her intention was to deconstruct and subvert
the formal conventions of traditional fiction by dismantling the
linear mechanism by which it usually functions. Inspired by Peter
Eisenman's architecture book *House X* (1982), each page is a
transformation of the preceding page, retaining some of its formal
elements and adding or rearranging others. Headlines, subtitles
and short paragraphs help to make Drucker's demanding prose more
accessible. In *The History of the/my Wor(l)d* (1990), an autobiographical
work printed in letterpress in an edition of 70 copies, Drucker
interweaves themes of official history and private memory, using
linguistic play, visual puns and typographic experiment. She divides
the page into a main text in large letters, interrupted by smaller

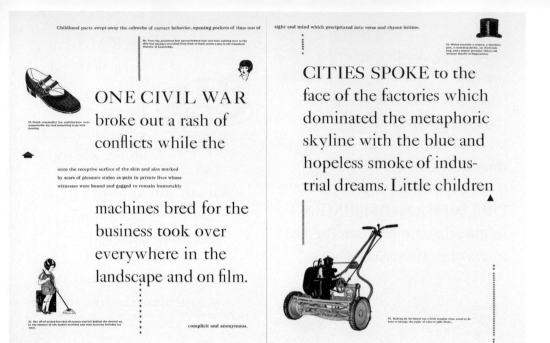

ONE CIVIL WAR broke out a rash of conflicts while the

onto the receptive surface of the skin and also marked
by scars of pleasure stolen as pain in private lives whose
witnesses were bound and gagged to remain immutably

machines bred for the business took over everywhere in the landscape and on film.

complicit and anonymous.

CITIES SPOKE to the face of the factories which dominated the metaphoric skyline with the blue and hopeless smoke of industrial dreams. Little children

Johanna Drucker. The History of the|my
World, spread from an artist's book, USA, 1990

caption-like texts in red and found photo-engravings of glamorous
women, majorettes, tools, machinery and articles of apparel.
Drucker explains the book's theoretical premise:

'The main narrative line offers a feminist critique of history
and memory. The smaller, more intimate red-printed line which
constantly erupts through it is the force of personal memory taking
issue with Lacanian-influenced feminist theory in its assignment
of a masculine and exclusively patriarchal role to language.
The premise of this work was that there was no world, only the
knowing of it in and through language, and that the knowing
of one's self was parallel to this, a construction of and in language
through its acquisition.'[19]

Warren Lehrer, another important American book artist,
studied painting at the City University of New York, where he first
began to combine letterforms and words with hand-drawn marks
and discovered concrete poetry, the collages of Kurt Schwitters
and the books of Diter Rot. Believing that graphic design meant
'avant-garde research into visual literature', Lehrer enrolled at Yale
University to study graphic design, though soon found himself at
odds with the prevailing corporate ethos.[20] His first book, *Versations*
(1980), is a typographically expressive, music score-like transcription
in three languages – English, French and Chinese – of conversations
he had tape-recorded. In *French Fries* (1984), written with Dennis
Bernstein and published in an edition of 1,000 copies, Lehrer
created a fiction of great visual complexity in which dozens of
typefaces, images and shapes, and hundreds of screen tints build up

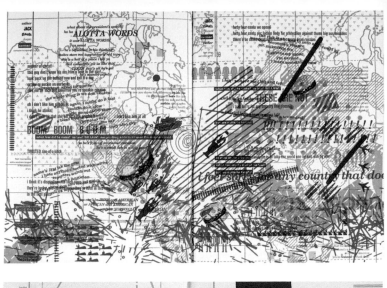

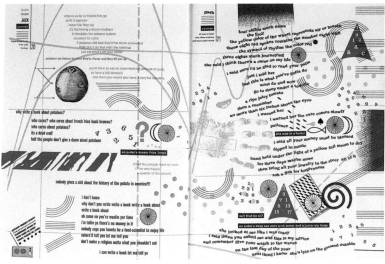

Warren Lehrer. French Fries, spreads from an artist's book, USA, 1984

to form densely layered compositions of immense energy. The story, originally performed as a play, is set in a Dream Queen fast-food restaurant after a murder has taken place and the cast of characters includes a manager, a cashier, four customers and many others, all babbling away in their own voices represented by Univers, Bembo, Helvetica, Kabel, Century Schoolbook, Clarendon, Bodoni, Cooper Black, Futura, and other faces. Other kinds of sound such as a blaring radio, a juke box and people talking on the phone are also expressed graphically.

As one reviewer noted, books such as *French Fries* challenge readers to explore the act of reading: to break with the usual linear pattern, vary the pace, look back at earlier passages, or skip ahead.[21] Lehrer's typographic experiments anticipated new directions in 1990s graphic design by several years. With his 'Portrait Series',

you just lie there on your mat in one position like a statue
with the horrible world buzzing around you
threatening to sting again at any moment

then after an hour or so you have to urinate
only you can't help but remember the times
you've gotten into trouble for having to urinate
asking to urinate or actually urinating in isolation rooms
but you have to do something
so you shove your face back up against
the tiny window in the large door and you look out
but there's no one there
no one to open the door and let you go to the bathroom
like any decent human being would do
for another human being
or even for a quarter of a human being
not to mention an animal

then you get to thinking that if you were a dog
and you had to pee
someone would in all likelihood take you for a walk
and you could breathe the fresh air
and they most likely would pet you and stroke you
and show some affection for you
cause that's a natural tendency
that humans have towards dogs
but nobody comes

you feel like you're gonna pee right then and there
you start knocking against the door
with the palm of your hand
but nobody comes

it gets to the point where
you can hardly hold it in any longer
so you knock some more
you knock and knock and knock
but nobody comes

your bladder feels like it's gonna finally explode
so you just pee right on the floor
the pee spills out beyond the door
the next morning one of the
two-hundred-pound attendants
wakes you up at six o'clock
sticks a broom in your gut and says
now clean it up
asshole!

through a haze of too much weird medication
you feel the broom against your gut

you don't even move
then you hear

either you clean the fuckin floor with this broom right fuckin now or you can use your tongue to do it later

in terms of dignity that's got to be in your top five

you feel proud
fit as a fiddle
and ready to take on a new day

when dennis and connie and warren and biaja come to visit
we all squeeze into the ten-foot-square visiting room
and drum against the plastic lime green chairs
until the inevitable
keep it down in there

one time we were having so much fun
one of the two-hundred-pound attendants opened up
the visiting room door
looked dennis in the eyes
and said
listen
if you don't keep it down
we got straightjackets
for all you people
especially you
mr. bernstein!

unlike my parents and most of my relatives
these friends distrusted the mental health system

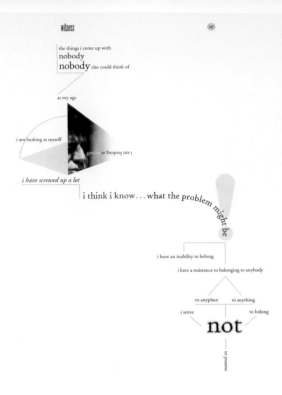

the things i come up with
nobody
nobody else could think of

at my age

i am looking at myself

i am looking at myself

i have screwed up a lot

i think i know… what the problem might be

i have an inability to belong

i have a resistance to belonging to anybody

to anyplace   to anything

i strive   to belong

not

to possess

Warren Lehrer. Charlie, book spread,
Bay Press, USA, 1995

[Right] **Warren Lehrer. Claude,** book
spread, Bay Press, USA, 1995

published in 1995 as a quartet of low-cost trade paperbacks rather than as limited edition artist's books, he showed how 'visual literature' could be used to engage broader audiences. Each of the volumes is a biographical monologue, recounting the life story and experiences of four of Lehrer's male acquaintances: Claude, Brother Blue, Charlie, and Nicky D. The books are unusually tall and narrow, reflecting the human proportions of their subjects, who are shown on their covers. Each character is assigned his own principal typeface, though more than 20 others are used in each book. In *Charlie*, a portrait of Charles Lang, a gifted musician with mental health problems, short lines of lower-case Gill Sans are ranged left like poetry; the text switches fluently into different typefaces and changes in size and layout, depending on the needs of the narrative, which is illustrated by Charlie's sketches. In *Claude*, a portrait of Claude Debs – painter, film-maker, entrepreneur, doctor, fashion photographer and undercover spy – the main type, Garamond, is centred in dense blocks, with individual phrases separated by slashes in an outpouring of reflection and sexual confession. Lehrer's books evoke the subjective experience of their subjects with great particularity and vividness, suggesting the possibility of a new literary genre that makes full use of design's rhetorical dimension. However, experiments of this kind remain a rarity in the bookshops.

In Britain, Jake Tilson's self-published magazines and books share the Pop Art exuberance of Lehrer's *French Fries*. Educated as a

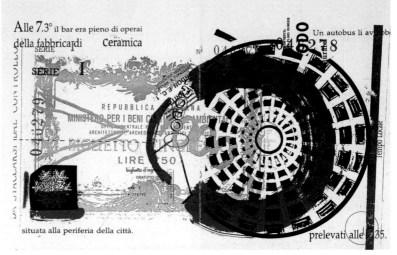

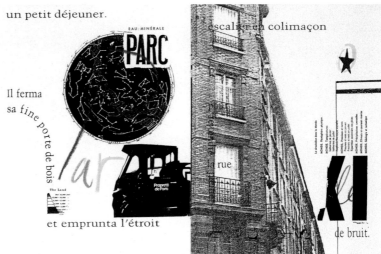

[Top] **Jake Tilson. Breakfast Special No. 1 – El Dottore di Terracotta,** spread from an artist's book, Woolley Dale Press, UK, 1989

[Above] **Jake Tilson. Breakfast Special No. 2 – La Carte Propre,** spread from an artist's book, Woolley Dale Press, UK, 1989

painter, Tilson made the rapid, low-cost, readily available print methods that designers usually shun – photocopying, instantprint, even rubber stamping – central to his work. He did not set out to flout the rules of publishing; he simply did not know what they were. In the late 1970s and 1980s, Tilson made a stream of photocopy editions in which his habitual themes – travel, geography, time – emerge from compressed science fiction narratives inspired by his readings of William Burroughs and J.G. Ballard. *The V Agents* (1981) is a collage tale of global paranoia and possible apocalypse cast in the form of a spiral-bound sketchpad; *The V Agents part 2* (1984) continues the story through a series of alphabetical file cards and interleaved images supplied, like snacks or toys, in a polythene bag. In the five-volume *Breakfast Special* (1989), published in an edition of 100, Tilson presents five alternative views of Mr Emerson, a character who reappears in different guises throughout his *oeuvre*. Mr Emerson leaves an apartment and enters a

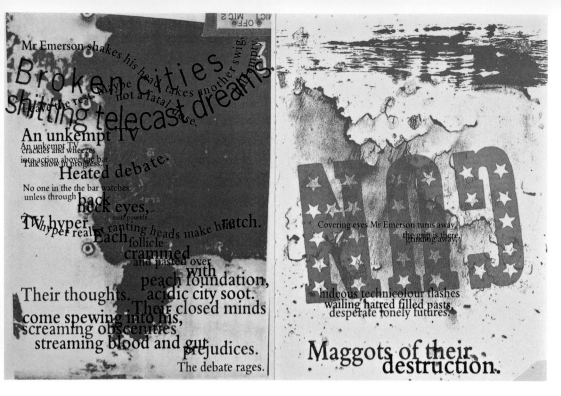

Mr Emerson shakes his head
Broken cities
shitting telecast dreams.
Maybe he takes another swig.
Heave the rest, not a fatal empty.
An unkempt TV
An unkempt TV
crackles and wheezes
into action above the bar.
Talk show in progress.
Heated debate.
No one in the the bar watches
unless through back
neck eyes,
quite possible.
TV hyper
Why hyper real ist ranting heads make him retch.
Each follicle
crammed
and pasted over with
peach foundation,
Their thoughts. acidic city soot.
Their closed minds
come spewing into his,
screaming obscenities
streaming blood and gut
prejudices.
The debate rages.

Covering eyes Mr Emerson turns away
the grin is there,
grinning away.

hideous technicolour flashes
wailing hatred filled pasts,
desperate lonely futures.

Maggots of their
destruction.

Jake Tilson. The Terminator Line,
spread from an artist's book,
Woolley Dale Press, UK, 1991

café for breakfast in Arezzo, Paris, New York, Barcelona and London, and these international scene changes give Tilson the opportunity to mount an exploration of local detail and atmosphere in which typography is as vital to the descriptive effect as the imagery with which it merges. The photocopied pages are sprinkled with tiny hand-glued Xeroxes, individually applied rubber stamp marks and hand-drawn lines, letters and numbers, fusing in informal but delicate compositions. Mr Emerson and the V Agents return in *The Terminator Line* (1991) where Tilson, continuing to avoid the by this time ubiquitous Macintosh computer, weaves lines of free-flowing, hand-positioned type into multilayered photocopy arabesques of considerable complexity.

Few professional designers operate, or seek to operate, at this level of authorship, working with self-initiated content that expresses a strong and consistent individual vision. However, in the course of the 1990s, two British creative teams, Tomato and Fuel, became identified with an authorial approach to design. Tomato, founded in 1991, was unusual in arguing that there was no essential distinction between its projects for clients and self-initiated projects by team members (Steve Baker, Michael Horsham, Karl Hyde, Jason Kedgley, Rick Smith, Simon Taylor, Dirk van Dooren, John Warwicker and Graham Wood). Hyde and Smith also belonged to the techno music group Underworld, and this performance side helped to establish the idea of Tomato as a team able to operate convincingly beyond the borders of professional 'graphic design', a term that they rejected, preferring to describe their creative activities simply as 'work'. Tomato developed an elaborate, passionately held studio philosophy in which 'process' – the act of making their work – was prioritized: 'we are all on a journey; all work is about experience and the mapping of that experience, and for us at tomato [it] is where we go to compare these maps. in effect we bring a map (or maps) from one territory and overlaying [sic] one upon another to see what happens. this is how our individual work evolves, and how we work together.'[22]

In their first book as a collective, *Process; A Tomato Project* (1996), they presented a series of personal projects that flow from one to the next without explanatory labelling in the form of titles or introductory texts, or obvious divisions between each part. There are no individual credits on the different contributions. While they may be the work of particular people – and with inside knowledge of the team, attributions can be made – authorship is effectively shared. As a form of identity-building, this is similar to the approach taken by a more conventionally configured design company such as Pentagram. At Pentagram, projects are led by individual partners, but in the first instance the work is presented to the world as being 'by Pentagram' as a collective entity, rather than by, say, Paula Scher (who became a partner in 1991) or J. Abbott Miller (partner from 1999). However, both of these designers had higher individual profiles before joining Pentagram than most members of Tomato did before joining Tomato. Shared authorship has some obvious advantages in terms of giving Tomato strength through numbers and endowing the collective's public image with a powerful mystique, but it also confers the old-fashioned prestige of authorship on contributions that might not stand up to such consideration if examined in their own right. In Tomato's second book, *Bareback. A Tomato Project* (1999), individual reticence is taken a step further and there is no mention of the members' names anywhere in the book.[23] It could be argued that this frames *Bareback* as an open, Barthesian verbal and visual text, which readers can interpret any way they please, but the effect is distancing. The book is not, in any case, anonymous; it is by one of Britain's best-known experimental design groups and this knowledge

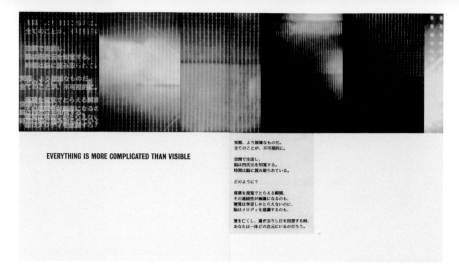

EVERYTHING IS MORE COMPLICATED THAN VISIBLE

実際、より複雑なものだ。
全てのことが、不可視的に。

空間で生活し、
脳は四次元を知覚する。
時間は脳に読み取られている。

どのように？

落屑を視覚でとらえる瞬間も、
その連続性が画像になるのも、
聴覚は単音しかとらえないのに、
脳はメロディを認識するのも、

愛を尽くし、過ぎ去りし日を回想する時、
あなたは一体どの次元にいるのだろう。

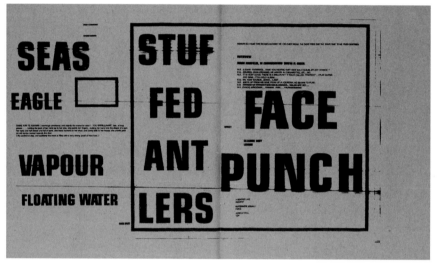

SEAS
EAGLE
VAPOUR
FLOATING WATER
STUF
FED
ANT
LERS
FACE
PUNCH

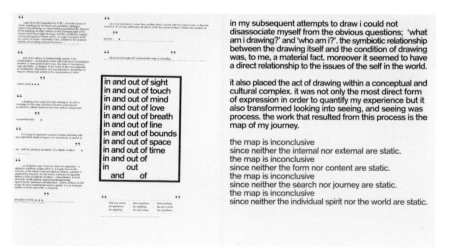

in and out of sight
in and out of touch
in and out of mind
in and out of love
in and out of breath
in and out of line
in and out of bounds
in and out of space
in and out of time
in and out of
in   out
and   of

in my subsequent attempts to draw i could not disassociate myself from the obvious questions; 'what am i drawing?' and 'who am i?'. the symbiotic relationship between the drawing itself and the condition of drawing was, to me, a material fact. moreover it seemed to have a direct relationship to the issues of the self in the world.

it also placed the act of drawing within a conceptual and cultural complex. it was not only the most direct form of expression in order to quantify my experience but it also transformed looking into seeing, and seeing was process. the work that resulted from this process is the map of my journey.

the map is inconclusive
since neither the internal nor external are static.
the map is inconclusive
since neither the form nor content are static.
the map is inconclusive
since neither the search nor journey are static.
the map is inconclusive
since neither the individual spirit nor the world are static.

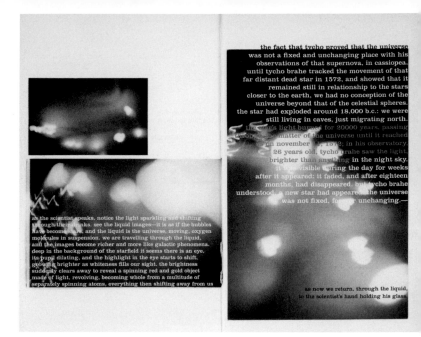

Graham Wood. Tycho's Nova, spread from a self-published book, UK, 2001

[Opposite, top & middle] Tomato. Process; A Tomato Project, two book spreads, Thames & Hudson, UK, 1996

[Opposite, bottom] Tomato. Bareback. A Tomato Project, book spread, Laurence King Publishing, UK, 1999

is bound to shape attempts at interpretation. One of the strongest contributions returns to themes broached in a text in *Process* – mapping, drawing, 'my grandfather' – and shows every sign of an idiosyncratic voice, an author, struggling to articulate the subtleties of private experience and memory. It is hard to see what is gained by withholding the information that the piece is by Warwicker. Subsequently, under his own name, Wood published *Tycho's Nova* (2001), a work of fiction illustrated by his own atmospheric photographs.[24]

Fuel, founded in London in 1991, also pursued the path of collective authorship, but with certain essential differences. First, they were at pains to insist that they regarded themselves as graphic designers rather than as artists or makers of non-specific 'work', and they wanted others to perceive them in this way, too. It is a moot point which is the more challenging position: to reject categorical distinctions, although these distinctions will probably continue to obtain for the most part; or to argue for the tactical expansion of an inherently limited category. Second, Fuel did not suggest that there was an equivalence between client work and personal work. They observed that work for clients usually involved compromises over content that need not be made in self-initiated projects. This may come down to the nature of the content itself. Tomato's imagery was often gestural or abstract, embodying an emotional mood that lent itself readily to inspirational promotional uses. In their self-initiated projects, Fuel tended to work with hard-hitting figurative and textual content that was less amenable to commercial application. Third, in Fuel's case authorship was shared equally. The three designers (Peter Miles, Damon Murray, Stephen

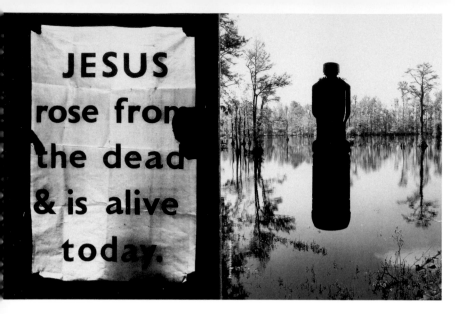

Peter Miles, Damon Murray and
Stephen Sorrell, Fuel. Fuel, spread from
a self-published magazine titled 'Dead',
UK, 1993. Photograph by David Spero

Sorrell) made indivisible contributions to all projects and
consequently 'Fuel' can be regarded as an author of a less ambiguous
kind than 'Tomato', where it was often unclear who had contributed
to a project.

Fuel's authorial method was grounded in the team's
practice as designers. Graphic designers often commission other
creative people – photographers, illustrators and copywriters – to
provide contributions to projects. Fuel applied the same approach
to their self-initiated work. Writing was fundamental to their aims
and they asked regular collaborators to produce copy on specified
subjects, which they then edited and crafted to work in concert
with their visual ideas. They began publishing their own irregular
magazine, *Fuel*, while they were students at the Royal College of Art.
In 1996, they authored their first book, *Pure Fuel*, which is divided
into ten chapters, Function, Leisure, Chaos, Spoilt, Aspire, Product,
Bred, Society, Truth and Space.[25] In both their commercial
commissions for Levi's and MTV and their self-initiated projects,
Fuel employed a graphic style of brutal simplicity and directness,
which, in the early to mid-1990s was completely at odds with the
prevailing taste for layered, expressive typography (exemplified
in Britain by Tomato) and looked more like advertising. In the large
pages of *Pure Fuel*, this is only intermittently effective and, despite
their occasional power, the pared-down, sloganistic spreads do not
cohere into a whole. *Fuel Three Thousand* (2000) is even sparer in its
combinations of type and image – many pages consist of a single
commissioned photograph – but its three sections, Anatomy,
Endings and Translation, unfold with greater fluency, although
the mood, as in their magazine and first book, is ambiguous and
enigmatic.[26] As with *Pure Fuel*, written by journalist Richard Preston,

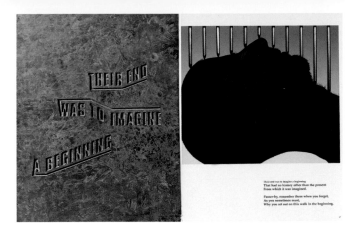

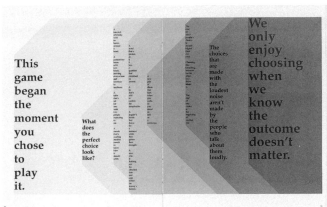

Peter Miles, Damon Murray and Stephen Sorrell, Fuel. Fuel Three Thousand, book spreads, Laurence King Publishing, UK, 2000. Photography by Matthew Donaldson

Fuel Three Thousand has a single writer, Shannan Peckham, an Oxford University academic, who specializes in cultural politics. Like Tomato's books, *Fuel Three Thousand* has an obvious kinship with the artist's book, and the two teams, like many artists, have also initiated their own moving-image projects. However, Fuel's book has a sophistication in its marriage of text and image that gives it a fundamentally different character from artists' often amateurish handling of typography, layout and print. Fuel's presentation of words on the page is highly structured: short passages of text are fashioned to fit boxes and shapes, and words are fitted three-dimensionally into photographic images; carved into surfaces; embroidered on a badge; printed on book covers, Post-it notes and a roll of sticky tape. Some designers professed themselves baffled by the book, but its sense of assurance and control did much to suggest the possibilities of a new graphic genre.

While the concept of 'designer as author' is increasingly familiar, and is also used in other non-graphic areas of design, it is still in some respects quite narrow.[27] Seeing the issue from the point of view of the (graphic) designer, the phrase suggests, as we have seen, that designers might assume a greater degree of influence in the shaping of content and perhaps seek to control it. If the cultural aim is to create new multidimensional forms of communication in which design, writing and content are more closely integrated, one might ask why the graphic designer is necessarily the most suitable person for the task. Why shouldn't content-makers coming from other areas and directions seek greater control of the graphic process? As far back as 1923, El Lissitzky declared that 'The new book demands the new writer.'[28] If the old categorical boundaries are really collapsing as postmodern rhetoric insists, and if the old rules of disciplinary craft no longer apply, then, in theory, the field of graphic authorship is open to anyone able to create 'work' that integrates a verbal and visual dimension. Given the overriding need for a content and for something to say or express in the first place, the specifically 'graphic' component is probably not the most significant part of such a venture. On the other hand, there are many examples of self-initiated design projects that have no discernible content or purpose other than the private satisfaction of making random graphic marks. Their audience, if they have one at all, is limited to other designers.

In the 1990s, intriguing examples of graphic authorship emerged from the fields of illustration, the graphic novel and writing. Where projects by artist|designers such as Drucker, Lehrer and Tilson arose within the genre of the artist's book, were usually produced in limited editions and only sometimes connected with broader audiences, graphic authors coming from outside the art world conceived and presented their work in more populist terms. Their creations could be found in ordinary bookshops, rather than specialist bookshops or galleries. What they shared with the book artists was an ability to take complete control of every aspect of their work, both writing and visual presentation, and a commitment to narrative, though usually of a fictional kind. While the centrality of narrative might seem conventional and even retrograde on one level – avant-garde art sought to banish figuration; avant-garde literature rejected the need for a story – these projects attempted to reach new audiences and to encourage fiction's existing readership to embrace reading experiences with an unfamiliar and sometimes controversial degree of visual content.

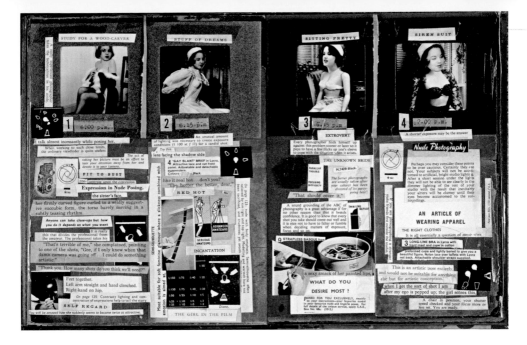

Graham Rawle. Diary of an Amateur
Photographer, book spread, Picador, UK, 1998

Like many postmodern cultural offerings, their creations provided conventional pleasures in unconventional frameworks and forms.

In *Diary of an Amateur Photographer* (1998) by Graham Rawle, the narrator's diary takes the form of a scrapbook.[29] Dated entries, with plentiful crossings out, are typed on a manual typewriter and stuck or stapled into its pages. Photographs, newspaper cuttings, sections of text clipped from books, printed fragments and torn edges give the collage-like pages considerable æsthetic richness. The book's graphic form can be enjoyed in its own right, but Rawle uses these textures to immerse the reader in the mental world of his troubled protagonist, Michael Whittingham, member of a local camera club. When Whittingham finds a strange photograph from 1959 that appears, in his eyes, to show an 'angel' floating against the ceiling, he begins an investigation into the disreputable world of 1950s glamour photography, a seedy milieu that turns out to have unexpected connections with his own disturbed childhood. The *Diary*'s final revelation is concealed in an envelope, stuck in the back of the book, which Whittingham, suspecting the worst, declines to open, though the reader is free to look inside. The book features a cast of models, who pose as the various characters shown in the photographs, and it required the services of make-up artists, hairstylists, and prop and costume suppliers, whose contributions were directed by Rawle.

Rawle's book is not a graphic novel, but there is no doubt that this small but persistent genre has helped to create the conditions in which related forms of experimentation can occur. Ordinary bookshops give shelf-space to graphic novels and in

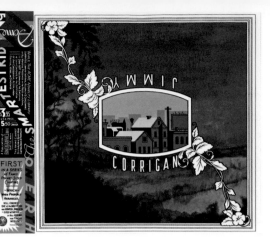

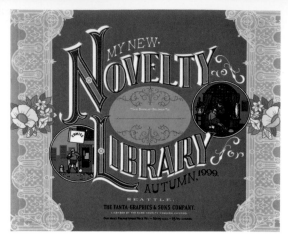

Chris Ware. Acme Novelty Library,
no. 5, comic book cover, Fantagraphics
Books, USA, 1995

[Right] Chris Ware. Acme Novelty
Library, no. 13, comic book cover,
Fantagraphics Books, USA, 1995

exceptional cases the books receive reviews alongside conventional
fiction. In December 2001, Chris Ware's *Jimmy Corrigan: The Smartest Kid
on Earth* (2000) won the Guardian First Book Award, a prize that
usually goes to a conventional piece of writing, though the judges
had trouble deciding whether it was art or literature.[30] Ware's strips
were published over a period of six years in a Chicago newspaper
and periodically gathered together in booklets, which he then
edited into the final form of the novel. The book has a complex
temporal structure, moving between three generations of father-son
relationships, and Ware orchestrates its melancholic mood with
great subtlety. As an artist, he draws with a designer's eye: forms
are simplified and boldly outlined; strong blocks of colour play
against each other graphically; pictorial repetition prolongs time
and creates atmospheres of painful languor and suspenseful ennui.
Much of *Jimmy Corrigan*'s graphic flavour comes from Ware's mastery
of period styles of lettering, a skill used to considerable effect on the
booklets' covers, which parody the look of old publications,
packaging and advertising, while fusing it with Ware's cartoon
imagery. The booklets are supposedly published by The Acme
Novelty Library and Ware fills their inside covers with diagrams of
houses, trees and miniature peep shows to cut out and construct,
surrounded by pedantically elaborate instructions in miniscule type.
The uncategorizable nature of Ware's brand of total authorship can
be seen in the folded poster which covers his graphic novel. This is
clearly 'design' of a complex and accomplished kind, even though
Ware is not a graphic designer. It unites writing, typography, hand-
lettering, information design, cartoon drawing and parodies of
historical graphic styles, and links these elements with
diagrammatic devices – rules, boxes, arrows – to form a
psychological portrait of the hapless Corrigan, placed at its centre.

Another unconventional fiction, Mark Z. Danielewski's
House of Leaves (2000), provides further evidence that new forms
of postmodern graphic authorship are emerging as more than just

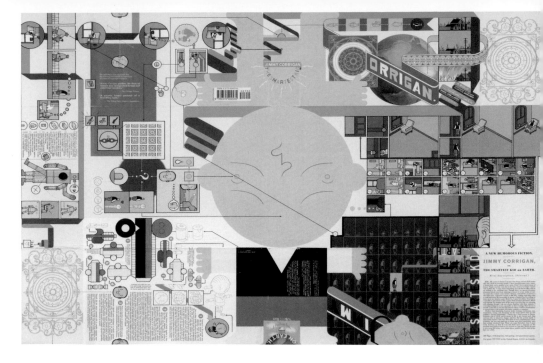

Chris Ware. Jimmy Corrigan: The Smartest Kid on Earth, dust jacket|poster for a graphic novel, Pantheon, USA, 2000

theoretical possibilities.[31] Danielewski, an American first-time author, designed and typeset his entire novel himself in his publisher Random House's New York offices. The positive reaction to *House of Leaves* suggests the degree to which readers' tastes have already been transformed by exposure to the devices, texture and rhetoric of contemporary graphic culture. No one who managed to negotiate *Ray Gun*'s fractured page structures or even the electro-charged layouts of early *Wired* would have any difficulty dealing with *House of Leaves*' teasing pathways and tropes. These include alternating fonts, crazily proliferating footnotes, passages with crossed-out words and missing letters, backwards-reading type, text presented upside down and in strange shapes, and pages consisting of a single sentence. The issue is not so much what Danielewski has done to the text as the way he uses these effects to drive his narrative. For all the book's appearance of wilfulness and mystery, its lack of resolution, there is a carefully stage-managed relationship between typographic form and literary content: one expresses the other. This works especially well during the exploration of photographer Will Navidson's house, subject of the little seen film *The Navidson Record*, analyzed in *House of Leaves* by an army of scholars and critics, imaginary and real. The house is vastly bigger inside than out. A doorway appears where none had been previously, hallways lengthen, a staircase materializes and a deep growl reverberates from the cavernous dark. As a search party navigates these impossible spaces, the men's confusion and mounting panic is reflected in columns of type twisted on the page

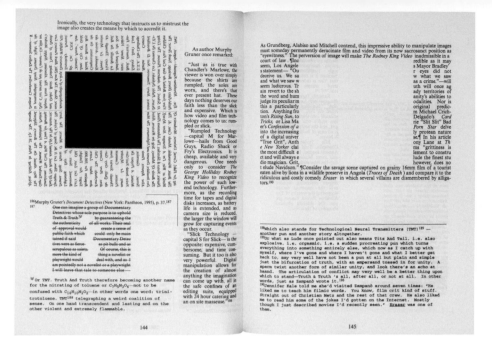

[Above & opposite] **Mark Z. Danielewski.**
House of Leaves, spreads from a novel,
Random House, USA, 2000

to form a maze of interlocking texts that can only be read by
turning the book. In Navidson's final exploration, words shatter
into tiny speech particles, centrally paced within the void of
the page, as he crawls on his belly into the infinite recesses of
a space he has come to think of as God.

In their different ways, Rawle, Ware and Danielewski
answer Lissitzky's call for a new kind of writer able to conceive
and author work both verbally and visually. Indeed, Ware found
it hard to separate the two ways of thinking: 'I tend to think in
all sorts of different ways. I guess more visually. I guess images
flash into my mind [and] they might get transferred into words.'[32]
Ware's work received considerable attention within the design
world and designers often commissioned him for projects of their
own. Danielewski's book, emanating from outside the design scene,
was overlooked by the profession, although it made a considerable
impact among literary reviewers. This oversight suggests the degree
to which graphic authorship is still in the process of emergence.
There is no generally held view of what it is or could be, or where
it might be found, and no clear understanding of the conditions
that would need to be met before work could be regarded as fully
authored, especially in cases where the designer deals with a
content and need supplied by someone else, as in the majority
of commercial commissions. (Outside design, graphic authorship
is not even an issue.) The cover blurb of Bruce Mau's *Life Style* refers
to the designer's 'unique world view' and it seems reasonable to
expect that authored design would aspire to offer a way of looking
at the world that was personal to the designer and different from

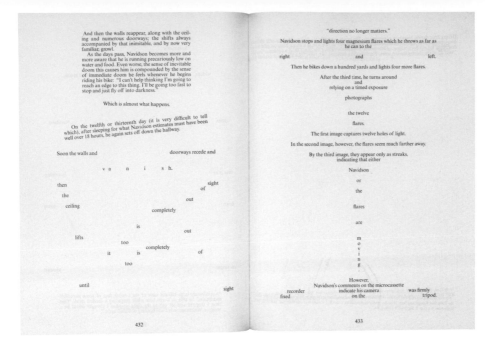

the norm. There is as yet barely any analysis of graphic design in these terms. For the most part, such claims are simply asserted as a way of gaining kudos rather than demonstrated by independent criticism to be a reality in the work itself. [33] Only in cases of total authorship such as Lupton, Lehrer, Tilson or Ware can one confidently address the work as the expression, unique or not, of an individual's 'world view'.

Nevertheless, despite these problems, the cause of authorship advances, particularly in the United States. In 1999, the School of Visual Arts in New York established the first Master of Fine Arts degree in design based on the idea of 'The Designer as Author'. Its founder, art director and design writer Steven Heller, stressed the non-theoretical, practical nature of the course. 'The concept of authorship is, first and foremost, rooted in the independent creation of ideas, which are turned into all manner of product – from books and magazines to toys and television programs, websites to *who knows what*. Our focus is on authorship in the broadest sense.' [34] The course posited the need for designers who wished to become authors to function as entrepreneurs and this made sense, since this is one of the few ways that designers can be sure of proceeding on their own terms. Emigre is an example of an entrepreneurially conceived design project that might be seen as a form of authorship 'in the broadest sense', although it also offered products – publications and typefaces – specifically authored by VanderLans and Licko. But is a designer who sets up a company to manufacture toys designed by other people an author? If so, the word starts to become so diffuse in its meaning that it is no longer

helpful in determining what intrinsic qualities a designer might
bring to a project as an author to make it different in essence from
a non-authored piece of design. Authorship is only useful as a term
to the degree that it opens up a space for thinking about design
that transcends established and possibly limited definitions.

For some critics, though, it is the idea of the designer as
author which imposes restrictions on design. Despite the
persuasive example of her own practice as designer, critic, curator
and author, Ellen Lupton questions the usefulness of authorship
as a model for contemporary design practice, since it hinges 'on a
nostalgic ideal of the writer or artist as a singular point of origin'.[35]
As an alternative, Lupton proposes the idea of the 'designer as
producer', returning to Benjamin's concept of 'The Author as
Producer', which Mau inverted in the 1980s for his own purposes.
In this model, the designer finds opportunities to seize control of
the technological means of production and shares this control
with the reading public, 'empowering them to become producers
as well as consumers of meaning'.[36] It is not necessary for designers
to become writers, notes Lupton, in order for them to take charge
of the content and social function of their work. She compares
the 'designer as producer' role to that of a film producer who
brings together diverse skills in a work whose authorship is shared.
This analogy sidesteps the argument that certain film directors
(and less frequently film producers) can be regarded as the authors
or *auteurs* of their films. According to the 'auteur theory', the
director, through force of artistic personality, imposes a personal
vision on the film, harnessing the talents of others (writer,
cinematographer, costume designer, and so on) to this end.[37]
The 'designer as producer' model could also be charged with its
own form of romanticism. It accepts that there is a struggle for
control of the means of production and trusts in designers' ability
to emerge as victors. Yet it was precisely the realization that
designers have limited power that gave rise to the ambitious claim
that they might become authors. It is far from clear how making
a lesser claim will succeed in challenging the balance of power.

The continuing problem for some critics is that designers'
desire to become authors cannot be reconciled with criticisms of

the author as authority figure by Barthes, Foucault and others.[38] As Michael Rock writes, 'if the proclivity of the contemporary designer is toward open reading and free textual interpretation – as a litany of contemporary theorists have convinced us – that desire is thwarted by oppositional theories of authorship. ... By transferring the authority of the text back to the author, by focusing on voice, presence becomes a limiting factor, containing and categorizing the work. The author as origin, authority, and ultimate owner of the text guards against the free will of the reader.'[39] Rock points out, unarguably, that the few clear examples of design authorship are the exception rather than the rule, and concludes that the authorship model is not adequate as a way of thinking about most design. He proposes three alternatives – designer as translator, designer as performer, designer as director – as better models to describe the processes usually involved in design activity.

Yet the relative smallness at this stage of design authorship as a branch of design does not mean that it lacks potential or that it will not grow. The signs suggest otherwise. Problems of authorship have been exaggerated and it is paradoxical, to say the least, to vest so much authority in speculative critical texts that set out to challenge that authority. It is highly questionable, in any case, whether readers who choose voluntarily to engage with Drucker's *The History of the/my Wor(l)d* or Danielewski's *House of Leaves* are really in nostalgic thrall to oppressive authorities denying them the exercise of their own free will. One could make precisely the opposite argument. We live in a world where authority is increasingly dispersed within vast corporate entities that conceal their inner workings from the public gaze. By committing themselves to complex forms of literary and graphic invention, individual authors (those supposedly problematic 'singular points of origin') encourage readers to explore, experience and question the world in rich, open and ultimately empowering ways.

Opposition

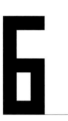

The design approaches discussed so far were always controversial and, during the early to mid-1990s, at the height of these changes, they provoked a number of forceful critiques. In some of these responses, there is a strong sense of an old guard used to working in particular ways refusing to accept that anything about the new work might be valid. It was alarming to see rules of craft that had underpinned whole careers tossed aside so casually. At other times, postmodern design's critics framed arguments which have never received an adequate reply. The answer came, more prosaically, from tidal shifts of emphasis within graphic design practice. In the second half of the 1990s, designers' preoccupations moved on and 'deconstructive' complexity ceased to be a major issue, although visual communication still continued to display symptoms of the postmodern condition of which it was inescapably a part. Print might not have ended, as some had predicted, but there was a deep sense that *something* had changed.

The first critic to let fly, in 1991, was the New York modernist designer Massimo Vignelli. In his view, *Emigre* magazine was a 'national calamity', an 'aberration of culture' and a 'factory of garbage' that could in no way compare with the tradition of quality stretching from Roman times to the Renaissance and on to Malevich in the twentieth century.[1] The following year, Paul Rand, elder statesman of American design, weighed in with an essay titled 'Confusion and Chaos: The Seduction of Contemporary Graphic Design'.[2] For Rand, design's problem was twofold: its lack of humility and originality, and its obsession with matters of superficial style. On the latter point he is exhaustive, detailing a long list of stylistic errors and offences that begins with squiggles, pixels, doodles, dingbats and ziggurats, works its way through

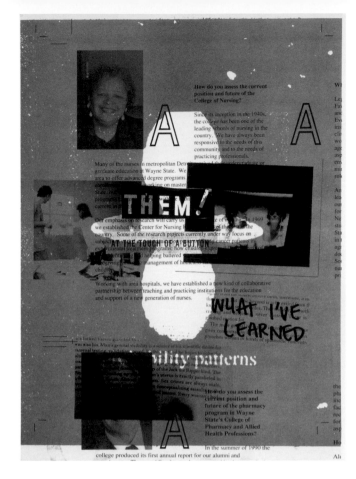

Students of Cranbrook Academy of Art.
Output, loose over-printed sheet, USA, 1992

'indecipherable, zany typography' and concludes with 'whatever "special effects" a computer makes possible'.[3] The most notorious and hotly contested of these attacks was Steven Heller's polemical essay 'Cult of the Ugly', probably because Heller, unlike Rand, singled out individuals for comment and showed examples, including student work from Cranbrook Academy of Art. 'How is ugly to be defined in the current postmodern design climate where existing systems are up for re-evaluation, order is under attack and the forced collision of disparate forms is the rule?' asks Heller. 'For the moment, let us say that ugly design … is the layering of unharmonious graphic forms in a way that results in confusing messages.'[4] Heller's principal concern was that rule-breaking experiments that might have some validity in design schools would be taken up and misapplied by impressionable young designers in the world outside, spreading the confusion and chaos that Rand also deplored. Yet setting out to create 'ugly design' was hardly the purpose of these experiments and their pejorative labelling as 'ugly' was subjective and questionable. In retrospect, it seems that the negative reaction among these designer|critics was largely an initial shock at visual forms that were new, unfamiliar and startling in the context of design. According to Heller, Edward Fella's work could be justified as personal research or art, but 'as a model for commercial practice, this kind of ugliness is a dead end'.[5] Evidently it wasn't, though, because just a few years later, in his capacity as art director of *The New York Times'* Book Review, Heller commissioned Fella to create a series of illustrations in his characteristic style for the paper's summer books review, while Vignelli had modified his views sufficiently to participate with Fella – a key contributor to *Emigre* at the time of his criticisms – in a good-natured public debate.[6]

There were, however, more fundamental criticisms of postmodern typography, which targeted its often repeated claims to be empowering readers by opening up the process of communication and treating them as active participants, rather than as passive receivers. Paul Stiff, a British academic specializing in information design, was one of the most trenchant in his questioning of this 'designer-centred ideology'.[7] Stiff points out that there are many sources of knowledge about reading and communication, including cognitive psychology, ethnology, ergonomics, discourse analysis and feminism, and asks why designers resort instead to sources that neither offer nor require evidence. Reading, he argues, is not the passive, mechanical process that postmodern designers like to imagine. It is an active, complex and purposeful pursuit, requiring strategic choices, inferences and hypotheses about intention, relevance and tone of voice. 'And all this,' he notes, 'is uncontroversially in line with postmodern theories of signifying practices which argue that each reading is a re-writing.'[8] Stiff points to a central omission within the generalizations of postmodern design rhetoric: the mass of communications – educational texts, reports, forms, guide books, reference books, diagrams, dictionaries and manuals – that fall outside the literary and artistic categories of design that it usually prefers to address. This does not, of course, necessarily invalidate its uses in these 'privileged' spheres, though it does set a limit on the application of the 'active participant' approach. However, some critics question the usefulness of deconstructed design in any sphere. 'The idea that design should act out the indeterminacy of reading is a folly ...'

writes Robin Kinross in a self-published polemical pamphlet, *Fellow Readers*. 'Far from giving freedom of interpretation to the reader, deconstructionist design imposes the designer's reading of the text onto the rest of us.'[9] But which texts and which types of reader is Kinross talking about? Nowhere in his discussion does he analyze specific examples and demonstrate the ways in which they fail as communication within their own particular contexts.

What such criticisms also ignore is the degree to which postmodern design might function as a critical practice. In 1983, Hal Foster advanced the idea that there are two kinds of postmodernism, a neo-conservative postmodernism of reaction and a poststructuralist postmodernism of resistance.[10] The postmodernism of reaction repudiates modernism and its radical critique, seeing this as elitist, and in Foster's view, this form is therapeutic and cosmetic. It reduces modernism to a series of styles (which can then be freely plundered), reasserts the verities of tradition and reaffirms the political and economic status quo. Against this, Foster posits the idea of an oppositional postmodernism, which resists both the official culture of modernism and reactionary postmodernism. As always with discussions of postmodernism, there are alternative interpretations. In her book *The Politics of Postmodernism*, Linda Hutcheon modifies Foster's proposal by arguing that separation of the two strands is not possible and that the postmodern enterprise includes both of Foster's types.[11] Postmodernism is engaged in a 'complicitous critique' squarely situated within both economic capitalism and cultural humanism; it is part of the thing it seeks to criticize and, as a result, it cannot be committed to radical change of a utopian modernist kind.

This duality or tension can be seen in the work of a number of designers who, in the 1980s, came to epitomize a postmodern approach to graphic communication. As designer of, first, *The Face* and then of *Arena* magazine, Neville Brody was one of the decade's most visible and influential design figures and his prolific output helped to define the preoccupations of 1980s 'style culture'. Brody intended his stylistic inventions at *The Face* to encourage a closer engagement with the content, which he insisted was the priority,

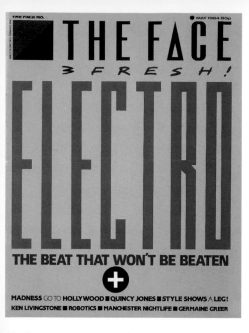

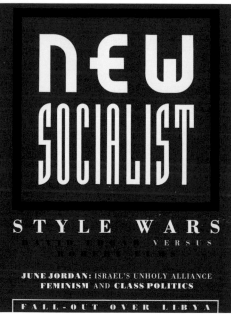

[Top] **Neville Brody.** The Face, no. 49, magazine cover, UK, 1984

[Above] **Neville Brody.** New Socialist, no. 38, magazine cover, UK, 1986

and he rejected the idea that design was about fashion. His public statements at this time were consistently outspoken in their humanism; during a period of Conservative government, he explicitly allied himself with left-wing convictions and causes. A 1986 issue of *New Socialist* magazine, which Brody redesigned at the height of his success, makes this positioning clear. Brody announces the issue's main theme, 'Style Wars', using a graphic language instantly familiar from *The Face*. Inside, Robert Elms, then associate editor of *The Face*, takes the traditional left to task for failing to update its drab, anachronistic image to reflect the new national consciousness of appearances and style. 'Style should be one of our most powerful weapons,' he advises, 'it is one of the mediums that money can never control.'[12] The statement is typical of the confusion that permeated *The Face*, which, in 1985, appeared to proclaim 'The End of Politics'.[13] (Possibly this was meant to be ironic; it can be read either way.) By then it was clear to Brody that money could indeed control style as he watched marketing, advertising and fellow designers assimilate his inventions, stripped of any deeper critical content, as signifiers of fashionable youth culture. At *Arena*, which he art directed from 1986, he responded by switching to simple Helvetica layouts. In 1988, he collaborated with Jon Wozencroft on a front-page feature for *The Guardian*'s review section, which castigated the 'virus' of style and the emptiness of the 'style revolution' and saw design, too, as equally suspect: 'Design is an animal hungry for "fresh" supplies. The process is reductive and the design world faces an abyss of its own making. In the end, design will eat itself. Culture is not a bottomless pit that can be infinitely ransacked – it needs a purposeful present, *lived* experience with which to nourish its context and vocabulary.'[14]

Brody and Wozencroft conclude with a call for *Guardian* readers to 'decode and deconstruct what is presented to you' and for design to encourage a critical perspective.

In the United States, Dan Friedman sought a way of reconciling the positive aspects of modernism and postmodernism. While he was uncomfortable with what he termed the 'darker side' of postmodern philosophy – its cynicism, nihilism and pessimism –

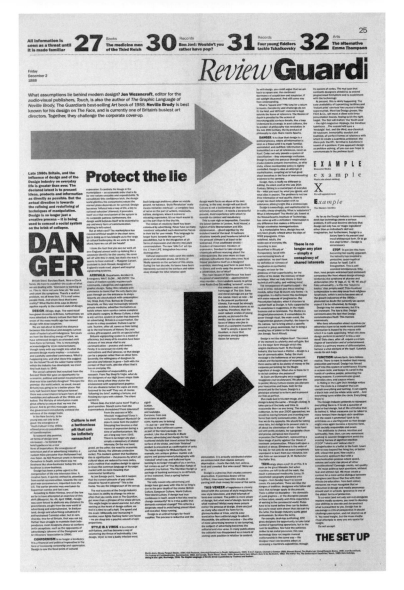

Neville Brody and Jon Wozencroft.
The Guardian, front page of review section, UK, 1988

he embraced the 'radical insights' and 'multiple realities' that it also suggested. For Friedman, it was premature and reactionary to pronounce the end of modernism. In the early 1990s, he termed his own way of thinking and designing 'Radical Modernism', which he defined as 'a reaffirmation of the idealistic roots of our modernity, adjusted to include more of our diverse culture, history, research, and fantasy'.[15] Friedman, like others, questioned whether postmodernism represented a decisive break with modernism, or whether it was a logical continuation, as the word could be taken to imply. He believed it might somehow be possible to embrace modernism's heritage, while also accepting the 'new reality of our cultural pastiche', and yet still hold to a more humanistic purpose.[16]

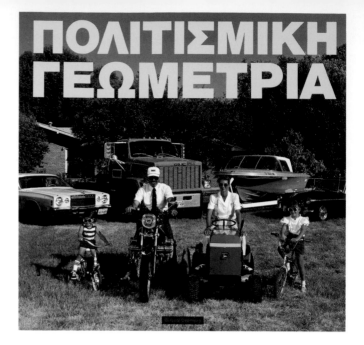

ΠΟΛΙΤΙΣΜΙΚΗ ΓΕΩΜΕΤΡΙΑ

Dan Friedman. Cultural Geometry,
catalogue cover, Deste Foundation for
Contemporary Art Athens, USA, 1988

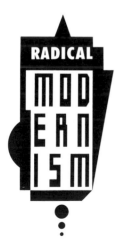

RADICAL MODERNISM

Dan Friedman. 'Radical Modernism'
logo, USA, early 1990s

This attempt to have it both ways inevitably suggests Hutcheon's
notion of postmodernism's complicitous critique. In the 1980s,
Friedman devoted his energies to furniture design and to working
on the ever-evolving interior design of his Manhattan apartment,
which in stylistic terms looked emphatically postmodern. At the
end of the decade, inspired by new developments in graphic design,
he became more involved in it again, designing a series of widely
discussed catalogues for exhibitions curated by the art critic Jeffrey
Deitch: *Cultural Geometry* (1988), *Artificial Nature* (1990) and *Post Human*
(1992). Compared to the hallucinogenic exuberance of his three-
dimensional design projects, these pieces are formally restrained.
Friedman juxtaposes words and phrases selected from Dietch's
essays with well-chosen archival photographs to illuminate
recurrent postmodern themes. *Post Human*, for instance, examines
our attempts to construct new selves by altering our appearance,
behaviour and consciousness. In one spread, Friedman floats
the phrase 'We are already experiencing a new kind of electronic
space' across five images of people using bulky mobile phones.
The unreality of these posed stock shots offers an ironic
commentary on the artificiality and strangeness of a new form
of cyberspace that was universally taken for granted within a
matter of years, as handsets shrunk to a fraction of their
original size. Friedman received criticism for deriving his visual
approach from the artist Barbara Kruger and some apologists
of postmodern complexity expressed dismay at his constrained
typographic palette.[17] Nevertheless, his visual essays communicate
their arguments with precision and wit.

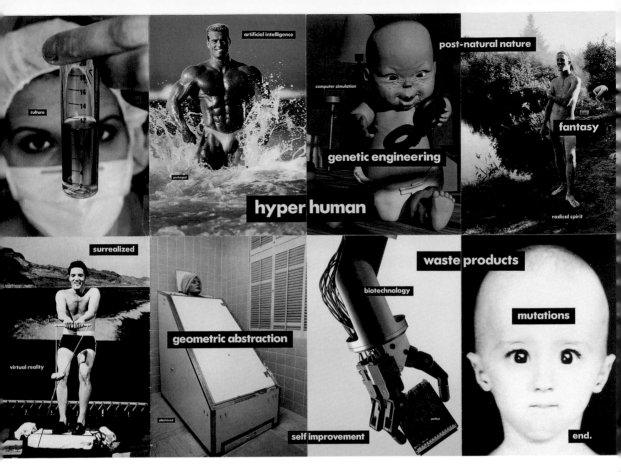

Dan Friedman. Artificial Nature,
exhibition poster (reverse side),
Deste Foundation for Contemporary
Art Athens, USA, 1990

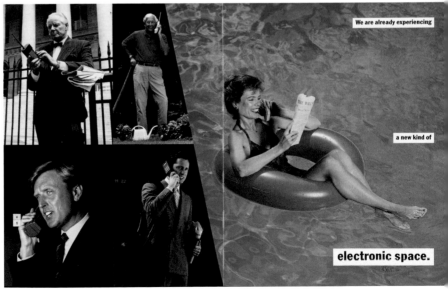

Dan Friedman. Post Human,
catalogue spread, Deste Foundation for
Contemporary Art Athens, USA, 1992

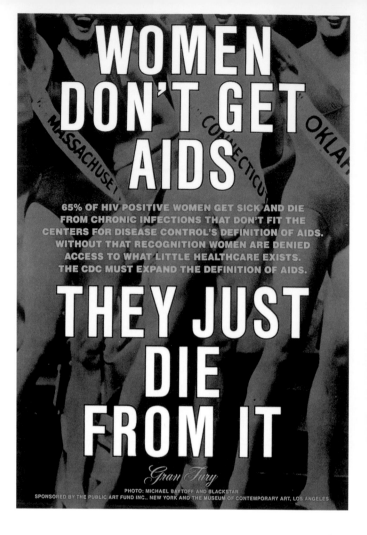

Gran Fury. Women don't get AIDS, poster, USA, 1991

While Friedman's idea of 'Radical Modernism' was perhaps too personal, too much bound up in his own practice as designer and artist, to catch on with other designers, his visual strategies were often seen at this time in the work of those who sought to contest, in Fredric Jameson's phrase, 'the cultural logic of late capitalism'. The most telling appropriation in this kind of message-making was not from art but from advertising. With urgent messages to impart and no room for ambiguity, politically motivated designers opted for straightforward visual formats of a type familiar to all kinds of viewer from a daily diet of posters, billboards and print ads. Gran Fury, a New York collective of artists and designers founded in 1988 to combat the AIDS crisis, favoured forceful statements in combination with a single memorable image.[18] In one illuminated poster used in a bus shelter in 1991, the copyline 'Women don't get AIDS|They just die from it' is illustrated by a beauty pageant photograph, showing three women wearing

THE ADVANTAGES OF BEING A WOMAN ARTIST:

Working without the pressure of success.

Not having to be in shows with men.

Having an escape from the art world in your 4 free-lance jobs.

Knowing your career might pick up after you're eighty.

Being reassured that whatever kind of art you make it will be labeled feminine.

Not being stuck in a tenured teaching position.

Seeing your ideas live on in the work of others.

Having the opportunity to choose between career and motherhood.

Not having to choke on those big cigars or paint in Italian suits.

Having more time to work after your mate dumps you for someone younger.

Being included in revised versions of art history.

Not having to undergo the embarrassment of being called a genius.

Getting your picture in the art magazines wearing a gorilla suit.

Please send $ and comments to: **GUERRILLA GIRLS** CONSCIENCE OF THE ART WORLD
Box 1056 Cooper Sta. NY, NY 10276

Guerrilla Girls. The Advantages of Being a Woman Artist, poster, USA, 1988

sashes representing American states. The message is emphatic in its condemnation of a then inadequate definition of AIDS, but positive in its visual mood. The closely cropped swimsuit line-up, rendered in purple, makes an understated appeal to the contemporary taste for ironic retro imagery. Another highly organized and effective protest group, the anonymous Guerrilla Girls, made equally pointed use of the communicative techniques and codes of advertising design to challenge the American art world's sexist exclusion of women from positions of power.[19] In their many street posters, marked 'Guerrilla Girls Conscience of the art world', they developed a black and white signature style, often without images, based on a headline in heavy sanserif capitals. Trenchant facts, statistics, artists' names and signatures were presented below in a standard body copy typeface. The campaign was arguably postmodern in the way that it disregarded distinctions between high and low culture that would once have confined such a critique to specialized art and cultural magazines and the arts pages of the broadsheets. It used a commercial medium to amplify its arguments to the point where they became highly uncomfortable for its targets and, by occupying public space usually monopolized by advertising, it achieved exceptional public presence and persuasive power. What it

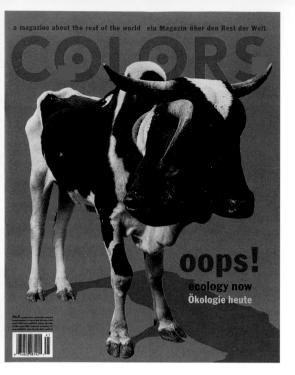

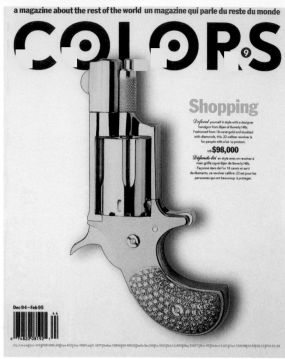

Tibor Kalman and Scott Stowell. Colors, no. 6, magazine cover, Benetton, Italy, 1994

[Right & opposite] **Tibor Kalman and Mark Porter.** Colors, no. 9, magazine cover and spread, Benetton, Italy, 1994

did not do was treat the communication process as an opportunity for any kind of stylistic 'deconstruction'.

In the work of Tibor Kalman, this plain-speaking design approach found one of its most determined, articulate and influential exponents. If M&Co's output in the 1980s had been the epitome of wise-cracking, game-playing, reference-making postmodernism, in 1993 Kalman repudiated this way of working in the most decisive way: he shut down his company. He proposed instead to 'kidnap' advertising's techniques and apply them to 'issues that matter – ecology and racism, for instance – to change people's perception of the world'.[20] Openly didactic, he argued that it should be possible to apply commercial conventions to make ideas interesting and attractive – 'like candy or canapés' – for readers reluctant to spend time working at longer texts. Kalman's most sustained and controversial attempt to explore these possibilities was the 13 issues of Benetton's Colors magazine, which he edited from 1990 to 1996.[21] Like Brody (in his Arena phase), Friedman and the Guerrilla Girls, Kalman and his designers employed a typographic language stripped of complexities and frills. Issues of Colors were picture-led, with the text usually confined to captions and short passages. Pages had a simplicity, clarity and confidence in the communicative power of the relatively unmediated photographic image that was the opposite of the fractured collage-layouts being created in Ray Gun during the same period. Kalman explicitly rejected such mannerisms, regarding

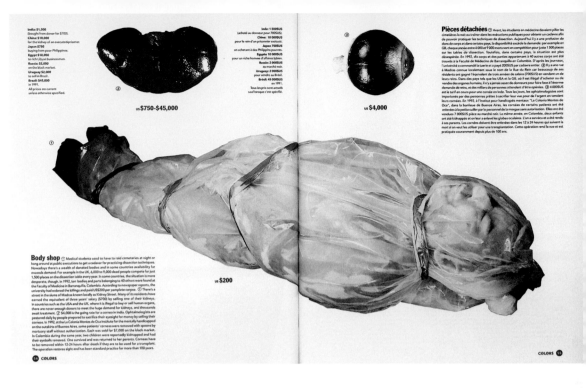

them as masks for a lack of meaningful content. Yet *Colors*, as the creation of a multinational company, was a potent example of complicitous critique – humanistic in intention, but still capitalist in essence. As with Oliviero Toscani's related advertising for Benetton, *Colors* raised awkward questions about the degree to which it was appropriate for a commercial oganization to blur once distinct dividing lines between promotion of its wares (if only by association) and matters of deep social and political concern. For some observers, this was a disturbing instance of the postmodern tendency to collapse established boundaries taken a step too far.

Other designers tried to find ways of reconciling postmodern approaches to graphic communication with the expression of oppositional messages. The British designer David Crow belonged to a generation inspired, in the 1980s, by the example of designers such as Brody, Malcolm Garrett and Peter Saville. An interest in punk music led Crow to Dada and Surrealism, while the punk graphics of Jamie Reid introduced him to Situationist ideas about art, culture and politics. Crow could see a clear link between the Situationist Guy Debord's argument that we live in a 'Society of the Spectacle' and changes designers were making in the high streets of Britain, where design was enjoying a new prominence and glamour.[22] In 1986, while working at Garrett's company, Assorted Images, Crow launched the first issue of his own 'magazine', *Trouble*, which took the form of a poster. He changed themes and formats with each issue, delivering his thoughts on

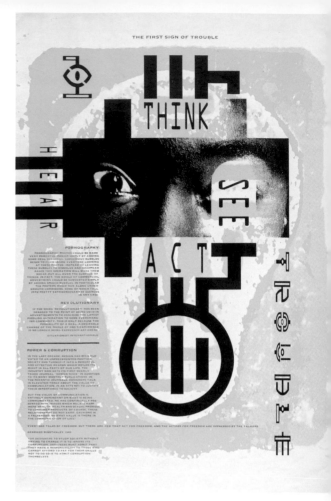

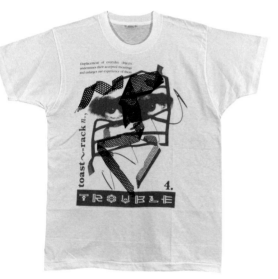

David Crow. Trouble, no. 4,
published as a T-shirt, UK, 1990

[Right] **David Crow. Trouble**, no. 1,
published as a poster, UK, 1986

the 1987 general election as a pack of scratch cards; the meaning of play as a T-shirt; and supermarkets and consumerism as a relatively conventional booklet. All were distinctive for the way in which they applied the Brody-esque graphic style of 1980s consumer culture to political themes that would once have been handled with much less visual sophistication. Their seductive appearance would make them instantly familiar and accessible to a reader of *The Face*, or a buyer of one of Garrett's or Crow's album designs, though small runs meant that *Trouble* had only a limited distribution and audience.

In the early 1990s, Brody and Wozencroft's digital type publication, *Fuse*, launched in 1991, was a significant outlet for designers with experimental inclinations. Its many contributors included Brody himself, Barry Deck, Jeffery Keedy, David Carson, Peter Saville, and Ian Anderson of The Designers Republic. In 1993, Kalman and Crow both devised 'typefaces' for *Fuse* no. 8 on the theme of religion. Kalman's, titled What the Hell, is a series of opposites accessed by typing upper- or lower-case versions of a given

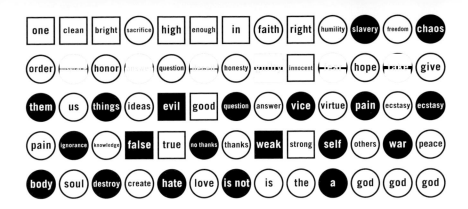

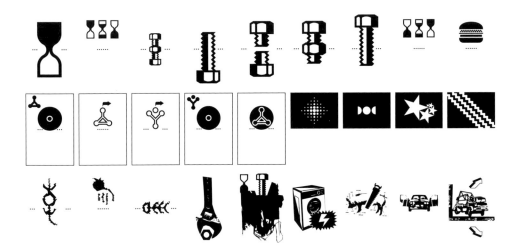

[Top] **Tibor Kalman and Scott Stowell.**
What the Hell, font published in
Fuse, no. 8, UK, 1993

[Above] **David Crow. Creation 6,** font
published in **Fuse,** no. 8, UK, 1993

letter: good|evil, true|false, order|chaos, clean|dirty, right|wrong.
Their proximity within a single key suggests the dependence of
each concept on its binary partner and invites users to decide
which option they prefer. Crow's contribution, Creation 6, is a
series of symbols intended to form the basis of a creation myth.
The area above the baseline represents good, the area below evil.
Different letters stand for such things as boy, girl, god, devil,
conflict, harmony, the great flood, retribution, and death, and
characters can be modified or added in accordance with the user's
beliefs. Creation 6 offers rich possibilities for graphic play, but its
symbols – bolts, a spanner, a washing machine with a lightning
flash – signify little to viewers who do not know the graphic code.

A later *Fuse* project, presented in 1995, challenged the
tendency, often seen in *Fuse* itself, for typographic experiments to
concentrate on communication for a visual elite at the expense of
a broader public discourse. Pussy Galore, created by Teal Triggs,
Liz McQuiston and Siân Cook, members of the Women's Design

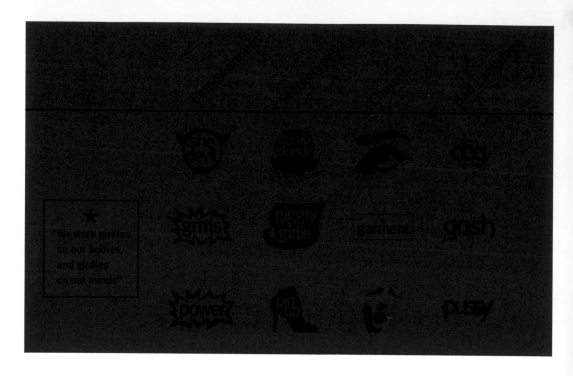

Teal Triggs, Liz McQuiston and Siân Cook, WD+RU. Pussy Galore, font published in **Fuse,** no. 12, UK, 1995

and Research Unit (WD+RU), is a conceptual typeface intended to allow interaction and to encourage users to challenge and reassess how women have been represented by language and to consider the structure of language itself. 'In real life, "women's voices" – their politics, culture, and means of expression – have been constructed and filtered through male visions for too long,' write McQuiston and Triggs. 'The new digital revolution affords opportunities to tear away these and other constraints (both political and creative) and model new structures and languages. We can begin to explore new possibilities, alternative perspectives and ideologies.'[23] In Pussy Galore, four levels can be accessed through the keyboard: normal typing = empowerment of women; shift = ugly stereotypes; option = personal choices; shift + option = vulgar and sexual language. Keyboarding at the first level produces strings of icons containing words such as 'mother', 'home maker', 'career', 'she devil' and 'grrrls', while ugly stereotypes include 'tart', 'dumb blonde', 'lolita' and 'the weaker sex'. Asterisks on selected icons reveal the presence of an additional layer of information, such as quotations and image sequences. Individual characters take on new implications depending on the characters next to them, giving rise to random sequences and pathways charged with adventitious meaning – a further encouragement for the user to engage, explore and respond.

The same desire to interact with and resist public speech can be seen in designers' appropriations of corporate logos. David

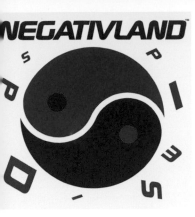

Shawn Wolfe. Dispepsi by Negativland,
CD cover, Seeland Records, USA, 1997

Crow's Creation 6, for instance, features a symbol representing
conflict composed of mangled versions of the Coca-Cola and Pepsi-
Cola logos. Designers Republic have also hijacked and modified the
Pepsi logo for use on a record sleeve by the band Pop Will Eat Itself.
Ian Anderson argued that if a company succeeds in making its logo
ubiquitous in both the environment and viewers' minds, then it
has to accept that people will treat it as part of the scenery and
perhaps answer back.[24] This was certainly the case when the
American experimental musicians and culture jammers Negativland
released a satirical CD titled *Dispepsi* (1997), an audio-collage made
from fragments of cola advertising. The cover by Seattle artist and
designer Shawn Wolfe shows a red and blue yin and yang symbol,
clearly modelled on the Pepsi logo, surrounded by the scrambled
letters of the title.

Designers Republic offered consumers the chance to 'buy
nothing' and other satirically minded designers have taken the
idea of nothingness – the hollow promise at the core of so much
postmodern consumer culture – even further. In 1991, John
Bielenberg, a designer based in San Francisco, invented a fictitious
company, Virtual Telemetrix Inc, to explore the idea of 'design
as means of propagating corporate myth to infiltrate consumer
psychology'. The phantom organization produced an annual
report which declined to give readers any financial information,
a catalogue full of absurd products such as the 'Liver on a Stalk'
('point out the realistic cirrhosis lesions to your dinner guests'),
a web site and a case study for a Las Vegas Casino. The 'dark nature
of consumerism' was also the target of Shawn Wolfe's enigmatic
anti-brand, Beatkit, which began life in 1984 and expired according
to plan in the year 2000.[25] Professional-looking advertisements and
promotional materials proclaimed the virtues of a product line that
had no clear function and did not actually exist. The most enigmatic
of these items, the 'Remover Installer', resembles a machine part
or a sealed electronic component. According to a poster, the device
'Makes any lifestyle choice easy to dispense. Represents every detail
of your life in full dimension, even when you're away.' The ultimate
incomprehensibility of the Remover Installer, even though it
appears in some images to exist in solid form, satirizes the abstract

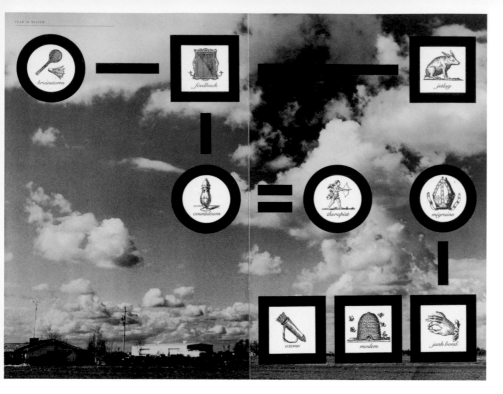

Bielenberg Design. Virtual Telemetrix
1993 Annual Report, spread, USA, 1993

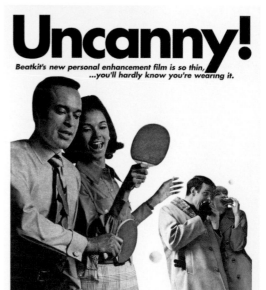

Shawn Wolfe. Uncanny!, poster, USA, 1997

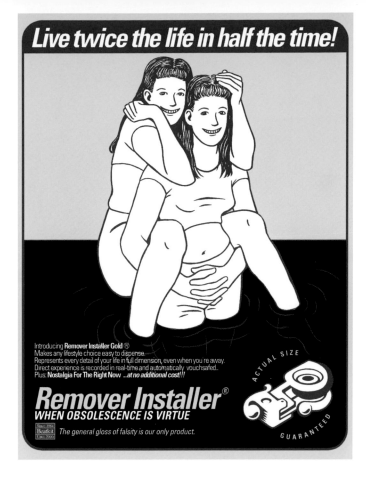

The poster reads:

Live twice the life in half the time!

Introducing **Remover Installer Gold** ®
Makes any lifestyle choice easy to dispense.
Represents every detail of your life in full dimension, even when you're away.
Direct experience is recorded in real-time and automatically vouchsafed..
Plus: **Nostalgia For The Right Now** ...*at no additional cost!!!*

Remover Installer®
WHEN OBSOLESCENCE IS VIRTUE

The general gloss of falsity is our only product.

ACTUAL SIZE
GUARANTEED

Shawn Wolfe. Live Twice the Life
in Half the Time!, poster, USA, 1999

nature of branding's transcendent calls to the consumer. Wolfe was
aiming not at the imperialistic ambitions, omnipresence or failings
of a particular brand, but at an entire system of production and
consumption. As Beatkit freely admits, 'The general gloss of falsity
is our only product.'

The most striking and, in some ways, problematic attempt
to use a postmodern design language to express humanist political
views can be seen in the work of Jonathan Barnbrook. The British
designer's output is so lavish and spectacular in form and, in this
regard, so closely in step with the needs and values of postmodern
commercial culture, that some refuse to accept it can have any
critical content at all. On the other hand, for WD+RU's Teal Triggs,
Barnbrook's 'belief in the socialist construct of Modernism is
housed perfectly in the contemporary language of postmodernist
forms'.[26] Barnbrook, for his part, rejects the idea that his work
belongs in any sense to postmodernism – 'I hate being called a
postmodernist'[27] – precisely because he sees it as signifying the
failure of modernism's idealistic socialist intent. This dichotomy
has been apparent from his earliest commissioned projects.

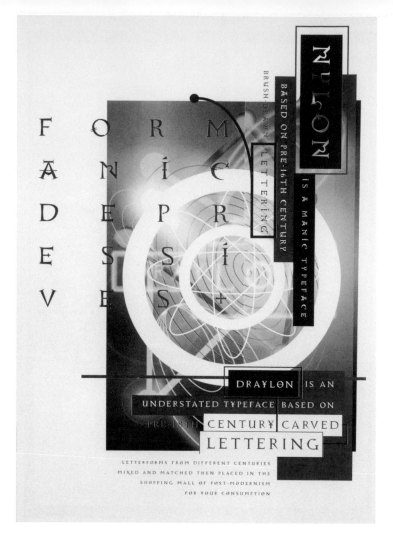

Jonathan Barnbrook. Welcome to the Cult of Virus, brochure page showing Nylon and Draylon typefaces, UK, 1997

Divider pages created in 1993 for the book *Illustration Now* show his preoccupation with consumerism and the military industrial complex. In one page design, a small image of an aeroplane dropping bombs is set into an elaborate graphic frame also containing the words 'we reap as we sow'. Barnbrook gives greater prominence to a second photograph of a hand sowing seeds, but the image's optimism is undercut by the destruction raining down from above, which will obliterate the sower on the ground. He went on to use his carefully titled typeface designs, released by his own Virus Foundry, as vehicles for delivering his acerbic views on commerce (False Idol), advertising and marketing (Prototype), multinational corporations (Bastard), mood-modifying drugs (Prozac), religion (Drone), and postmodernism (Nylon and Draylon). Once purchased, any of these typefaces could, of course, be put to uses at variance with his intentions.

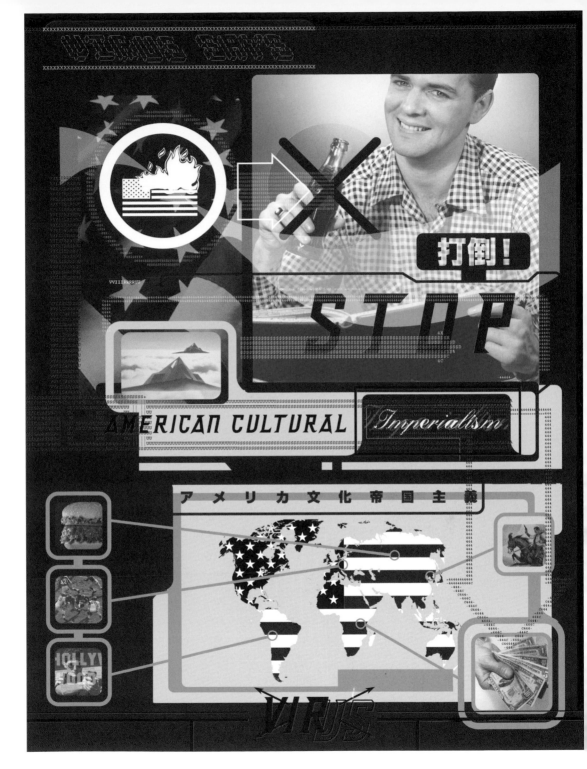

Jonathan Barnbrook. Virus Says Stop
American Cultural Imperialism, poster,
Japan, 1999

While Barnbrook's convictions were evidently sincere, interpretation was complicated by the fact that his work for commercial clients, though devoid of explicit political references, was no different from his personal projects in its formal manipulations. Moreover, he sometimes worked for clients in advertising and the art world who seemed to represent the kind of values he rejected. Does the critical meaning of a Barnbrook design then rest on the presence of artless copylines such as 'Virus says stop American cultural imperialism' – even when the design itself embodies a seductive spectacular excess characteristic of that colonizing process? Any attempt to argue that this poster design enacts its subject matter ironically to strengthen its case is circumvented by the fact that all of Barnbrook's work has this same recognizable look. His complicitous critique would appear to be thoroughly postmodern: he means what he says, but at the same time he cannot escape the prevailing cultural condition.

In 1999, the Canadian anti-corporate magazine *Adbusters* commissioned Barnbrook to create a poster posing the question 'Is economic progress killing the planet?' It was the start of a fruitful collaboration and signalled an increased emphasis on design, as tool and subject matter, in a publication that consistently challenged postmodernism's assumptions and axioms. 'Postmodernism celebrates evanescent flows, a state of no boundaries, the transgressive,' writes John Zerzan, an *Adbusters* contributor. 'If this sounds familiar, it's because these values are shared by the most ardent architects of both consumerism and capitalist globalization.'[28] Postmodernism, Zerzan concludes, 'is the culture of *no resistance*'. In a poster-like spread titled 'Toxic Culture: An Iconography for the Mental Environment', published in an issue devoted to the theme of 'Design Anarchy', *Adbusters* presents a series of icons based on the outline of a human head, graphically depicting noise, erosion of empathy, consumerism, viral marketing, and so on.[29] When it comes to representing postmodernism as an icon, the head contains only an empty space. Elsewhere, a spread written by *Adbusters* and designed by Barnbrook, guest art director of the issue, recycles the received wisdom and clichés of postmodern graphic design rhetoric to scathing effect,

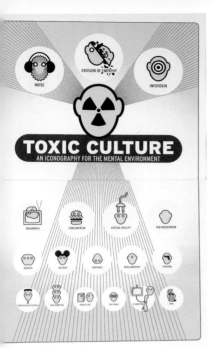

Bill Texas. Adbusters, no.37, 'Design Anarchy'
issue, magazine spread, Canada, 2001

sometimes lifting phrases wholesale from published texts on design:
meaning is arbitrary and without foundation; to impose a unitary
text on readers is authoritarian and oppressive; making texts
visually ambiguous is a way of respecting the reader. 'What if
this subterfuge, irony and disruption is just a postmodern bag
of tricks?' asks *Adbusters*.[30] Here again, though, Barnbrook's design
is ambiguous. It is certainly legible with a little effort for those
familiar with contemporary design's formal repertoire – its 'bag
of tricks' – but the degree of graphic noise might be seen as a
symptom of the very malaise it seeks to condemn, or is that the
point of the design?

In the mid-1990s, *Adbusters'* use of design was comparatively
restrained. Its pages were conventional in editorial structure and
layout and its visual commentary was largely confined to the
creation of parody ads – 'subvertisements' – aimed at global
brands such as Calvin Klein, Marlboro and Camel cigarettes.
In 1998, the magazine published an interview with Tibor Kalman
and the following year, with Kalman's encouragement, it launched
a design manifesto, *First Things First 2000*, attacking consumerist uses
of graphic design.[31] It also introduced a 'Creative Resistance'
competition to encourage young designers to apply their skills to
radical causes. As *Adbusters* became more visual and gave more space
to design issues, it became more appealing to graphic designers.
By the time the 'Design Anarchy' issue appeared, the magazine
had abandoned its earlier editorial structure, familiar from a
thousand news-stand publications, in favour of a loose, open-
ended structure that flowed from one page to the next without
obvious signposting or a clear sense of orientation. These changes
appeared to reflect the view, often expressed by postmodern
designers in the 1990s, that younger readers require a high degree
of visual stimulation to capture their interest and motivate them
to start reading at all. While it was clearly not *Adbusters'* intention
to embrace indeterminacy and jump into the poststructural flow,
'Design Anarchy' showed the difficulty of arriving at a persuasive
contemporary graphic language that is not already tainted
in some way by its association with the forces of capitalist
consumerism and with what Foster calls the postmodernism

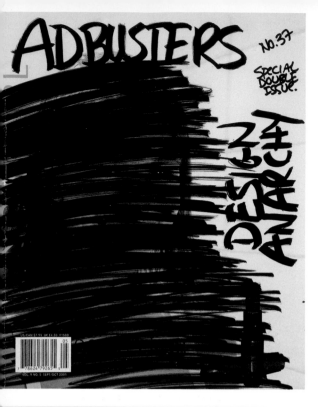

ADBUSTERS No.37 SPECIAL DOUBLE ISSUE. DESIGN ANARCHY

this page is a living surface.

ALL THE WORLD'S A TEXT.　Can you feel it?

Don't be afraid! Jump right into the multicul ural, poststructural, electronic flow.

Meaning Is Ar bitrary And Without Foundation.

to impose a single text on readers is authoritarian and oppressive

Making texts visually ambiguous and difficult to fathom is a way of respecting our readers. Let's lay obstacles, diversions and false trails. Let's halt and disrupt the discourse in devious ways. Use Schmelvetica, Beowolf, Exocet, Pussy Galore...

WE'LL MIX UP HIGH **AND** LOW *Culture* IN THE **BLENDER**

EMBRACE THE VERNACULAR. MAKE MOVIE TRAILERS SO FAST AND FURIOUS THAT THE VIEWER DOESN'T HAVE TIME TO THINK.

sometimes the viewer will feel sick to their stomach,

but that's an appropriate reaction to much of the 20th century.

BUT WHAT IF THIS SUBTERFUGE, IRONY AND DISRUPTION IS JUST A POSTMODERN BAG OF TRICKS?

ARE WE FOLLOWING OUR OWN FOOTPRINTS IN A

HALL OF MIRRORS?

WHY DO WE DISGUISE OUR OPINIONS — WHY DO WE THROW THE RESPONSIBILITY OF UNDERSTANDING BACK ON OUR READERS?

ARE WE JUST CHICKEN — AFRAID TO TAKE A STAND?

how can we hold fast to any vision, any optimism in a world moving towards complacency, cultural conformity and corporate control?

of reaction. Not for the first time it seemed that the only way forward might be to go back, as Rudy VanderLans suggested in 1991 at the height of postmodern experimentation. 'Does all experimentation in graphic design lead to the simplification of graphic design? Are the graphic designers who concern themselves with complex solutions merely slow learners who try out the wildest schemes only to come to one conclusion, that less is more?'[32]

Yet to go back in any stylistic sense, to imitate for instance the typographic language of modernism, also runs the risk of tumbling into the abyss of postmodern pastiche. The problem goes to the heart of the purpose and meaning of graphic design. As it is now understood by most designers, and perhaps especially by those who are not committed to experimental practice, design's purpose is to help business to sell things. This locates even the most unassuming forms of commercial design activity in a complicitous relationship with postmodern consumer culture, which prioritizes the needs of marketing over other kinds of value. It may be possible to resist this to some degree by working on the inside, as Kalman tried to do at Benetton, but any inroads will be provisional until such time as there is a larger political and cultural transformation. After 13 issues of *Colors*, neither Benetton nor the world had changed, though it is certainly the case that individual readers might have done so. If fundamental systemic change feels unlikely, then this tends to suggest that the postmodern condition will be our reality for the foreseeable future, imposing operational constraints or 'rules' of its own, whether we like it or not. Three pressing questions then arise for designers. To what sustained uses, other than its familiar and largely unquestioned commercial uses, might graphic design be applied? How, and even more to the point, where should designers who wish to engage in a rule-breaking postmodernism of resistance position themselves? And finally, given some of the problems of postmodern visual communication discussed in this book, what forms, in terms of style, might an oppositional graphic design assume at this point?

Notes

Introduction

1. See Gerry Beegan, 'An Interview with Judith Williamson', *Dot Dot Dot*, no. 4, winter 2001|2002, p. 32.

2. Richard Kostelanetz, *A Dictionary of the Avant-Gardes*, London and New York: Routledge, 2001 (second edition), p. 488.

3. See, for instance, Angela McRobbie, *Postmodernism and Popular Culture*, London and New York: Routledge, 1994, and Nigel Wheale (ed.), *The Postmodern Arts: An Introductory Reader*, London and New York: Routledge, 1995.

4. David Harvey, *The Condition of Postmodernity: An Enquiry into the Origins of Cultural Change*, Cambridge, MA and Oxford: Blackwell, 1990, p. 27.

5. Jean-François Lyotard, *The Postmodern Condition: A Report on Knowledge*, Manchester: Manchester University Press, 1984 (first published in French 1977).

6. Interviewed in George Plimpton (ed.), *Writers at Work*, second series, 1963.

7. John Lewis, *Typography: Basic Principles: Influences and Trends since the 19th Century*, London: Studio Books, 1963, p. 70.

8. Ibid., p. 70. Fifteen years later, Lewis had revised his earlier, absolutist view. In *Typography: Design and Practice*, London: Barrie & Jenkins, 1978, p. 135, he writes: 'The book page is rarely a medium for self expression' – a significant concession.

9. Bob Gill, *Forget All the Rules about Graphic Design. Including the Ones in this Book.*, New York: Watson-Guptill Publications, 1985 (first published 1981).

10. Peter Hall and Michael Bierut (eds.), *Tibor Kalman: Perverse Optimist*, London: Booth-Clibborn Editions, 1998, p. 14.

11. Quoted in Roger Tredre, 'Typeout!', *Observer Life* magazine, 12 November 1995, p. 46.

12. Kodwo Eshun, 'Universal Magnetic', *i-D*, no. 171, December 1997, p. 52.

13. Fredric Jameson, 'Postmodernism and Consumer Society' in Hal Foster (ed.), *Postmodern Culture*, London and Sydney: Pluto Press, 1985 (published in the US as *The Anti-Æsthetic*, 1983), p. 120.

14. Peter Dormer, *The Art of the Maker: Skill and its Meaning in Art, Craft and Design*, London: Thames & Hudson, 1994. In particular, see chapter 5, 'Do Experts follow Rules?'.

15. David Jury, *About Face: Reviving the Rules of Typography*, Mies, Switzerland: RotoVision, 2002.

16. Ibid., p. 152.

1 Origins

1. Corin Hughes-Stanton, 'What Comes after Carnaby Street?', *Design*, no. 230, February 1968, pp. 42–3.

2. Ibid., p. 43.

3. Charles Jencks, *The Language of Post-Modern Architecture*, London: Academy Editions, 1984 (fourth edition; first published 1977), p. 5.

4. Ibid., p. 7.

5. Wolfgang Weingart, *Typography*, Baden: Lars Müller Publishers, 2000, p. 112.

6. Ibid., p. 112.

7. For the text of Weingart's lecture, see 'How Can One Make Swiss Typography?', *Octavo*, no. 4, 1987. Reprinted in Michael Bierut *et al.* (eds.), *Looking Closer 3: Classic Writings on Graphic Design*, New York: Allworth Press, 1999, pp. 219–37.

8. Dan Friedman, *Dan Friedman: Radical Modernism*,

New Haven and London: Yale University Press, 1994, p. 34.

9. Ibid., p. 35.

10. See J. Abbott Miller, 'The 1980s: Postmodern, Postmerger, PostScript', *Print*, XLIII:VI, November|December 1989, p. 163.

11. Quoted in Valerie Alexander, 'April Greiman', *The Magazine of Kansas City Art Institute*, summer 1982, p. 16.

12. Willi Kunz, *Typography: Macro- and Microæsthetics*, Sulgen: Verlag Niggli, 1998, p. 98.

13. Valerie F. Brooks, 'Triumph of the Corporate Style: Communications Design in the 1970s', *Print*, XXXIV:I, January|February 1980, pp. 30–1.

14. Ivan Chermayeff quoted in 'Play and Dismay in Post-Modern Graphics', *I.D.*, March|April 1980, p. 47.

15. Marc Treib, 'Blips, Slits, Zits and Dots: Some (Sour) Notes on Recent Trends in Graphic Design', *Print*, XXXV:I, January|February 1981, p. 30.

16. Robert Venturi, *Complexity and Contradiction in Architecture*, London: Architectural Press, 1977 (second edition; first published 1966), p. 16.

17. Robert Venturi, Denise Scott Brown and Steven Izenour, *Learning from Las Vegas: The Forgotten Symbolism of Architectural Form*, Cambridge, MA and London: MIT Press, 1977 (revised edition; first published 1972).

18. Barbara Radice, *Memphis: Research, Experiences, Results, Failures and Successes of New Design* (trans. Paul Blanchard), London: Thames & Hudson, 1984, p. 88.

19. Ibid., p. 186.

20. For a mid-1980s use of the term 'new wave' in relation to British graphic design, see Catherine McDermott, *Street Style: British Design in the 80s*, London: Design Council, 1987, pp. 57–88.

21. For a discussion of youth subcultures, see Dick Hebdige, *Subculture: The Meaning of Style*, London: Methuen, 1979.

22. See, for instance, Philip B. Meggs, *A History of Graphic Design*, New York and Chichester: John Wiley, 1998 (third edition; first published 1983); and Steven Heller and Seymour Chwast, *Graphic Style: From Victorian to Post-Modern*, London: Thames & Hudson, 1988 (second edition: *Graphic Style: From Victorian to Digital*, 2000).

23. Quoted in Rick Poynor, 'Peter Saville', *Eye*, vol. 5 no. 17, summer 1995, p. 14. Reprinted in Rick Poynor, *Design Without Boundaries: Visual Communication in Transition*, London: Booth-Clibborn Editions, 1998, pp. 117–23.

2 Deconstruction

1. Paul Feyerabend, *Against Method*, London and New York: Verso, 1993 (third edition; first published 1975), p. 5.

2. Jamie Reid, *Up They Rise: The Incomplete Works of Jamie Reid*, London: Faber and Faber, 1987, p. 105.

3. Art Chantry, *Instant Litter: Concert Posters from Seattle Punk Culture*, Seattle: Real Comet Press, 1985, p. 4.

4. Quoted in Rick Poynor, 'The State of British Graphics', *Blueprint*, no. 46, April 1988, p. 49.

5. Quoted in Kees Broos, 'Hard Werken', *Dutch Art and Architecture Today*, no. 17, May 1985, p. 30.

6. Jacques Derrida, *Of Grammatology*, Baltimore and London: Johns Hopkins University Press, 1997 (corrected edition; first published in English 1976).

7. See Ellen Lupton and J. Abbott Miller, 'Deconstruction and Graphic Design' in *Design Writing Research: Writing on Graphic Design*, New York: Kiosk, 1996, pp. 3–23.

8. Jonathan Culler, *Literary Theory: A Very Short Introduction*, Oxford: Oxford University Press, 1997, p. 126.

9. Christopher Norris, *Deconstruction: Theory and Practice*, London and New York: Routledge, 1991 (revised edition; first published 1982), p. 31.

10. Stuart Sim, *Derrida and the End of History*, London: Icon Books|New York: Totem Books, 1999, p. 31.

11. Philip Johnson and Mark Wigley, *Deconstructivist Architecture*, Boston: Little, Brown, 1988, p. 10.

12. 'Deconstruction at the Tate Gallery', *Architectural Design*, vol. 58 no. 3|4, 1988, p. 7.

13. Philip Meggs, 'De-constructing Typography', *Step-by-Step Graphics*, February 1990. Reprinted in Nancy Aldrich-Ruenzel and John Fennell (eds.), *Designer's Guide to Typography*, Oxford: Phaidon, 1991, p. 135.

14. Chuck Byrne and Martha Witte, 'A Brave New World: Understanding Deconstruction', *Print*, XLIV:VI, November|December 1990, p. 82.

15. Meggs, 'De-constructing Tyography', p. 136.

16. Byrne and Witte, 'A Brave New World', p. 83.

17. Katherine McCoy and Michael McCoy, 'The New Discourse' in Hugh Aldersey-Williams *et al.*, *Cranbrook Design: The New Discourse*, New York: Rizzoli, 1990, p. 16.

18. Quoted in Rudy VanderLans, interview with Jeffery Keedy, *Emigre*, no. 15, 1990, p. 15.

19. Quoted in Jeffery Keedy, 'A Conversation with Edward Fella', *Emigre*, no. 17, 1991, unpaginated.

20. Jeffery Keedy, 'Everything has Changed, Nothing is Different', lecture delivered at 'Fuse 95' conference, Berlin, November 1995.

21. Quoted in Rudy VanderLans, interview with Barry Deck, *Emigre*, no. 15, 1990, p. 21.

22. For a fuller account of these issues, see Rick Poynor, 'Paganini Unplugged' in *Design Without Boundaries: Visual Communication in Transition*, London: Booth-Clibborn Editions, 1998, pp. 219–25.

23. Lewis Blackwell, 'A Hero of Deconstruction', *Independent Saturday Magazine*, 6 December 1997, p. 57.

24. Quoted in Lewis Blackwell, *The End of Print: The Graphic Design of David Carson*, London: Laurence King Publishing, 1995, unpaginated.

25. Ibid., unpaginated.

26. Joshua Berger, 'Regarding the Design, Typography and Legibility of this Publication', *Plazm*, no. 6, 1994, p. 1.

27. Tobias Frere-Jones, 'Towards the Cause of Grunge', *Zed*, no. 1, 1994, p. 32. Reprinted in *Looking Closer 2: Critical Writings on Graphic Design*, pp. 16–8.

28. Jon Wiener, 'Deconstruction goes Pop', *The Nation*, 7 April 1997, pp. 43–4.

29. Quoted in Rick Poynor, 'Katherine McCoy', *Eye*, vol. 4 no. 16, spring 1995, p. 14.

30. Lupton and Miller, 'Deconstruction and Graphic Design', p. 9.

31. Ibid., p. 17.

32. 'A User's Manual' in Avital Ronell, *The Telephone Book: Technology, Schizophrenia, Electric Speech*, Lincoln: University of Nebraska Press, 1989, p. xv.

33. For further discussion, see Gérard Mermoz, 'Deconstruction and the Typography of Books', *Baseline*, no. 25, 1998, pp. 41–4, and Carl Francis DiSalvo, 'Towards an Æsthetics of Intellectual Discourse', *Emigre*, no. 39, summer 1996, pp. 74–8.

3 Appropriation

1. Fredric Jameson, 'Postmodernism and Consumer Society' in Hal Foster (ed.), *Postmodern Culture*, London and Sydney: Pluto Press, 1985 (published in the US as *The Anti-Æsthetic*, 1983), pp. 115–6.

2. Ibid., p. 114.

3. Jessamy Calkin, 'Image Maker', *The Face*, no. 23, March 1982, pp. 44–5.

4. Quoted in Jon Wozencroft, *The Graphic Language of Neville Brody*, London: Thames & Hudson, 1988, p. 8.

5. Malcolm Garrett, 'A Dearth of Typography', *Baseline*, no. 13, 1990, p. 41.

6. Jon Savage, 'The Age of Plunder', *The Face*, no. 33, January 1983, p. 49. Reprinted in Michael Bierut *et al.* (eds.), *Looking Closer 3: Classic Writings on Graphic Design*, New York: Allworth Press, 1999, pp. 267–72.

7. Quoted in Rick Poynor, 'Peter Saville', *Eye*, vol. 5 no. 17, summer 1995, pp. 13–4. Reprinted in Rick Poynor, *Design Without Boundaries: Visual Communication in Transition*, London: Booth-Clibborn Editions, 1998, pp. 117–23.

8. Tibor Kalman, J. Abbott Miller and Karrie Jacobs, 'Good History|Bad History', *Print*, XLV:II, March|April 1991, p. 120. Reprinted in Peter Hall and Michael Bierut (eds.), *Tibor Kalman: Perverse Optimist*, London: Booth-Clibborn Editions, 1998, pp. 76–81.

9. For Scher's reflections on the Swatch poster and surrounding controversy, see Paula Scher, *Make it Bigger*, New York: Princeton Architectural Press, 2002, p. 98.

10. Tibor Kalman, 'Tibor's Typo Tips!', *Baseline*, no. 11, 1989, p. 5. See also Kalman's and Karrie Jacobs' observations on the vernacular in 'We're Here to be Bad', *Print*, XLIV: I, January|February 1990, pp. 122–5. Reprinted in Hall and Bierut, *Tibor Kalman: Perverse Optimist*, pp. 129–31.

11. Paula Scher, 'Lubevitch & Moscowitz: Forgotten Doyens of Deli Design', *Print*, XXXIX: VI, November|December 1985, p. 67.

12. For further discussion, see Ellen Lupton, 'High and Low (A Strange Case of Us and Them?)', *Eye*, vol. 2 no. 7, 1992, pp. 72–7. A revised version, 'Low and High', is reprinted in Ellen Lupton and J. Abbott Miller, *Design Writing Research: Writing on Graphic Design*, New York: Kiosk, 1996, pp. 156–66. See also Jeffery Keedy, 'I Like the Vernacular... Not!' in Barbara Glauber (ed.), *Lift and Separate: Graphic Design and the Quote Vernacular Unquote*, New York: Cooper Union, 1993, pp. 6–11. Reprinted in Michael Bierut et al. (eds.) *Looking Closer: Critical Writings on Graphic Design*, New York: Allworth Press, 1994, pp. 101–3.

13. 'Tibor Kalman vs. Joe Duffy', *Print*, XLIV:II, March|April 1990, pp. 68–75, 158–68. See also responses by Michael Rock and Marc Treib, *Print*, XLV:I, January|February 1991, pp. 123–4, 129–31.

14. Quoted in Julie Lasky, *Some People Can't Surf: The Graphic Design of Art Chantry*, San Francisco: Chronicle Books, 2001, p. 100.

15. Margaret Richardson, 'Buy This', *Print*, LII:VI, November|December 1998, pp. 62–8.

16. Ibid., p. 64.

17. Bruce Handy, 'A Spy Guide to Postmodern Everything', *Spy*, April 1988, p. 104.

18. Karen Moss in Kim Abeles, *Encyclopedia Persona*, Santa Monica: Santa Monica Museum of Art, 1993, p. 10.

4 Techno

1. April Greiman, *Hybrid Imagery: The Fusion of Technology and Graphic Design*, London: Architecture Design and Technology Press, 1990, p. 55.

2. Ibid., p. 55.

3. Eric Martin in Greiman, *Hybrid Imagery*, p. 57.

4. Rudy VanderLans and Zuzana Licko, 'The New Primitives', *I.D.*, vol. 35 no. 2, March|April 1988, pp. 58–61.

5. Ibid., pp. 60–1.

6. Chuck Byrne, 'Miss April', *Print*, XLI:V, September|October 1987, p. 144.

7. Jean Baudrillard, 'The Ecstasy of Communication' (trans. John Johnston) in Hal Foster (ed.), *Postmodern Culture*, London and Sydney: Pluto Press, 1985 (published in the US as *The Anti-Æsthetic*, 1983), p. 130.

8. Ibid., p. 131.

9. Ibid., p. 133.

10. See P. Scott Makela, '100% Digital Design', *I.D.*, vol. 39 no. 3, May|June 1992, pp. 89–90.

11. P. Scott Makela, 'Redefining Display', *Design Quarterly*, no. 58, winter 1993, p. 16–7.

12. Rudy VanderLans, interview with P. Scott Makela, *Emigre*, no. 23, 1992, unpaginated.

13. Ian Anderson, 'Notes on What Button to Push Next' in Martin Pesch and Markus Weisbeck, *Discstyle: The Graphic Arts of Electronic Music and Club Culture*, London: Collins & Brown, 1999, p. 7.

14. Rudy VanderLans, interview with Ian Anderson, *Emigre*, no. 29, winter 1994, p. 19.

15. Ibid., p. 19.

16. Donna J. Haraway, 'A Cyborg Manifesto' in *Simians, Cyborgs, and Women: The Reinvention of Nature*, London: Free Association Books, 1991, p. 176.

17. Ibid., p. 178.

18. Marshall McLuhan and Quentin Fiore, *War and Peace in the Global Village*, Corte Madera, CA: Gingko Press, 2001 (first published 1968), p. 18.

19. J. Abbott Miller, *Dimensional Typography: Case Studies on the Shape of Letters in Virtual Environments*, New York: Princeton Architectural Press, 1996, p. 45.

20. See Gilles Deleuze and Félix Guattari, 'A Rhizome has no Beginning' in *A Thousand Plateaus: Capitalism and Schizophrenia*, London: Athlone, 1988.

21. Erik Davies, *TechGnosis: Myth, Magic and Mysticism in the Age of Information*, London: Serpent's Tail, 1999, p. 329.

22. Eric Martin in Greiman, *Hybrid Imagery*, p. 57.

23. Jeffery Keedy in *Fast Forward*, Valencia, CA: California Institute of the Arts, 1993, p. 62.

24. Ibid., p. 62.

25. Marshall McLuhan and Quentin Fiore, *The Medium is the Massage: An Inventory of Effects*, Corte Madera, CA: Gingko Press, 2001 (first published 1967), unpaginated.

26. Brenda Laurel, 'Immersive Technogy', *Wired*, 1.6, December 1993, p. 107.

27. Aaron Betsky and Erik Adigard, *Architecture Must Burn: A Manifesto for an Architecture beyond Building*, London: Thames & Hudson, 2000.

28. Ibid., unpaginated.

29. Ibid., unpaginated.

30. See, for instance, Tomato, *Process; A Tomato Project*, London: Thames & Hudson, 1996.

31. See *Büro Destruct*, Berlin: Die Gestalten Verlag, 1999, and Robert Klanten, Hendrik Hellige and Mika Mischler (eds.), *Swiss Graphic Design*, Berlin: Die Gestalten Verlag, 2000.

32. Raphael Urweider in Thomas Bruggisser and Michel Fries (eds.), *Benzin: Young Swiss Graphic Design*, Baden: Lars Müller Publishers, 2001, p. 82. See also Martin Woodtli, *Woodtli*, Berlin: Die Gestalten Verlag, 2001.

33. Ruedi Widmer, interview with Manuel Krebs of Norm, *Benzin*, p. 13.

34. Ibid., p. 13.

5 Authorship

1. Roland Barthes, 'The Death of the Author' in *Image-Music-Text* (trans. Stephen Heath), London: Fontana, 1977, p. 146.

2. Ibid., p. 147.

3. Ibid., p. 148.

4. See Robin Kinross, 'The Rhetoric of Neutrality', in Victor Margolin (ed.), *Design Discourse: History, Theory, Criticism*, Chicago and London: University of Chicago Press, 1989, pp. 131–43.

5. See Walter Benjamin, 'The Author as Producer', in *Reflections: Essays, Aphorisms, Autobiographical Writings*, New York: Schocken Books, 1978, pp. 220–38.

6. Quoted in Will Novosedlik, 'The Producer as Author', *Eye*, vol. 4 no. 15, spring 1996, p. 45.

7. Bruce Mau, *Life Style*, London: Phaidon, 2000, p. 327.

8. OMA, Rem Koolhaas and Bruce Mau, *S,M,L,XL*, Rotterdam: 010 | New York: Monacelli Press, 1995.

9. Mau, *Life Style*, p. 322.

10. Ellen Lupton in Ellen Lupton and J. Abbott Miller (eds.), *The ABCs of ▲■● : The Bauhaus and Design Theory*, New York: The Cooper Union, 1991, p. 23.

11. Ellen Lupton and J. Abbott Miller, *Design Writing Research: Writing on Graphic Design*, New York: Kiosk, 1996.

12. For an ambitious American example, see Andrew Blauvelt (ed.), *Visible Language*, 'New Perspectives: Critical Histories of Graphic Design', parts 1–3, vol. 28 no. 3, July 1994; vol. 28 no. 4, October 1994; vol. 29 no. 1, January 1995.

13. Anne Burdick, 'What has Writing got to do with Design?', *Eye*, vol. 3 no. 9, 1993, p. 4.

14. Ibid., p. 5.

15. *Emigre*, no. 35, summer 1995, and *Emigre*, no. 36, fall 1995.

16. Anne Burdick, 'Introduction | Inscription', *Emigre*, no. 36, fall 1995, unpaginated.

17. Steven McCarthy, 'What is "Self-authored Graphic Design" Anyway?', text for 'Designer as Author: Voices and Visions' exhibition leaflet, Northern Kentucky University, 8 February to 8 March, 1996.

18. Nigel Smith quoted in Novosedlik, 'The Producer as Author', p. 53.

19. Johanna Drucker, *Figuring the Word: Essays on Books, Writing and Visual Practice*, New York: Granary Books, 1998, pp. 275–6.

20. Quoted in Philip B. Meggs, 'Performing Art', *Print*, XLVII:III, May | June 1993, p. 82.

21. See Nancy Solomon, 'Bon Appétite', *Afterimage*, February 1986, p. 16.

22. John Warwicker, untitled text in Tomato, *Process; A Tomato*

Project, London: Thames & Hudson, 1996, unpaginated.

23. Tomato, *Bareback. A Tomato Project*, London:
Laurence King Publishing, 1999.

24. Graham Wood, *Tycho's Nova*, London: Tomato, 2001.

25. Peter Miles, Damon Murray and Stephen Sorrell (Fuel),
Pure Fuel, London: Booth-Clibborn Editions, 1996.

26. Peter Miles, Damon Murray and Stephen Sorrell (Fuel),
Fuel Three Thousand, London: Laurence King Publishing, 2000.

27. For discussion in the context of industrial design, see,
for instance, Anthony Dunne, 'Design Noir', *Blueprint*,
no. 155, November 1998, pp. 24–5.

28. El Lissitzky, 'Topography of Typography', 1923.
Reprinted in Michael Bierut et al., *Looking Closer 3: Classic
Writings on Graphic Design*, New York: Allworth Press, 1999, p. 23.

29. Graham Rawle, *Diary of an Amateur Photographer*,
London: Picador, 1998.

30. Chris Ware, *Jimmy Corrigan: The Smartest Kid on Earth*,
New York: Pantheon, 2000.

31. Mark Z. Danielewski, *House of Leaves*, London:
Doubleday, 2000.

32. Quoted in Gary Groth, 'Understanding (Chris Ware's)
Comics', *The Comics Journal*, December 1997, no. 200, p. 143.

33. For an example of the auteur theory applied to the
work of a graphic designer, see Rick Poynor, *Vaughan Oliver:
Visceral Pleasures*, London: Booth-Clibborn Editions, 2000.

34. Steven Heller and Lita Talarico, mission statement
on the School of Visual Arts website, 2002. See also
Steven Heller (ed.), *The Education of a Design Entrepreneur*,
New York: Allworth Press, 2002.

35. Ellen Lupton, 'The Designer as Producer' in Steven
Heller (ed.), *The Education of a Graphic Designer*, New York:
Allworth Press, 1998, p. 159.

36. Ibid., p. 161.

37. On the auteur theory as applied to film, see Andrew
Sarris, 'Notes on the Auteur Theory in 1962' in Gerald Mast
and Marshall Cohen (eds.), *Film Theory and Criticism: Introductory
Readings*, New York: Oxford University Press, 1974, and
Peter Wollen, *Signs and Meaning in the Cinema*, London:
Secker & Warburg, 1972 (revised edition; first published 1969).

38. See Michel Foucault, 'What is an Author?' in Paul
Rabinow (ed.), *Foucault Reader*, New York: Random House, 1984.

39. Michael Rock, 'Graphic Authorship' in Heller, *The Education of
a Graphic Designer*, p. 155. An earlier, illustrated version of Rock's
essay was published as 'The Designer as Author', *Eye*, vol. 5
no. 20, spring 1996, pp. 44–53.

6 Opposition

1. Quoted in 'Massimo Vignelli vs. Ed Benguiat (Sort Of)',
Print, XLV:V, September|October 1991, p. 91.

2. Paul Rand, 'Confusion and Chaos: The Seduction of
Contemporary Graphic Design', *AIGA Journal of Graphic Design*,
vol. 10 no. 1, 1992. Reprinted as 'From Cassandra to Chaos'
in Paul Rand, *Design Form and Chaos*, New Haven and London:
Yale University Press, 1993.

3. Rand, *Design Form and Chaos*, p. 209.

4. Steven Heller, 'Cult of the Ugly', *Eye*, vol. 3 no. 9, 1993,
p. 53. Reprinted in Michael Bierut et al. (eds), *Looking Closer:
Critical Writings on Graphic Design*, New York: Allworth Press,
1994, pp. 155–9.

5. Ibid., p. 59.

6. *New York Times*, 6 June 1999. The Fella and Vignelli event
was organized by the American Institute of Graphic Arts,
New York, 10 March 1999.

7. Paul Stiff, 'Stop Sitting around and Start Reading', *Eye*,
vol. 3 no. 11, 1993, p. 5. Reprinted as 'Look at Me! Look at Me!
What Designers Want' in Michael Bierut et al. (eds), *Looking
Closer 2: Critical Writings on Graphic Design*, New York: Allworth
Press, 1997, pp. 34–7.

8. Ibid., p. 4.

9. Robin Kinross, *Fellow Readers: Notes on Multiplied Language*,
London: Hyphen Press, 1994, p. 11.

10. Hal Foster, 'Postmodernism: A Preface' in Hal Foster (ed.),
Postmodern Culture, London and Sydney: Pluto Press, 1985
(published in the US as *The Anti-Æsthetic*, 1983), pp. ix–xvi.

11. Linda Hutcheon, *The Politics of Postmodernism*, London and New
York: Routledge, 2002 (second edition; first published 1989).

12. Robert Elms, 'Ditching the Drabbies: A Style for Socialism', *New Socialist*, no. 38, May 1986, p. 14.

13. 'Disinfo Special: The End of Politics', *The Face*, no. 61, May 1985, pp. 124–5. For a detailed discussion of *The Face* in relation to postmodernism, see Dick Hebdige, 'The Bottom Line on Planet One: Squaring Up to The Face' in *Hiding in the Light: On Images and Things*, London and New York: Routledge, 1988, pp. 155–76.

14. Jon Wozencroft and Neville Brody, 'Protect the Lie', *The Guardian*, 2 December 1988, p. 25. See also Neville Brody and Stuart Ewen, 'Design Insurgency', *Print*, XLIV:1, January|February 1990, pp. 118–21.

15. Dan Friedman, *Dan Friedman: Radical Modernism*, New Haven and London: Yale University Press, 1994, p. 11.

16. Ibid., p. 115.

17. See Jeffery Keedy, 'Some Kind of Joke?' (letter), *Eye*, vol. 3 no. 10, 1993, p. 4.

18. See Douglas Crimp and Adam Rolston, *AIDS Demo Graphics*, Seattle: Bay Press, 1990.

19. See The Guerrilla Girls, *Confessions of The Guerrilla Girls*, New York and London: HarperCollins, 1995.

20. Quoted in Moira Cullen, 'Tibor Kalman', *Eye*, no. 20 vol. 5, spring 1996, p. 15.

21. See Maira Kalman and Ruth Peltason (eds.), *Colors: Issues 1–13 The Tibor Kalman Years*, London: Thames & Hudson, 2002.

22. Guy Debord, *The Society of the Spectacle*, New York: Zone Books, 1995 (first published 1967).

23. Liz McQuiston and Teal Triggs, 'A Femme Fatale Font with a Mission', *AIGA Journal of Graphic Design*, vol. 14 no. 3, 1996, p. 40. See also Teal Triggs, 'The Making of Pussy Galore', *Baseline*, no. 20, 1995, pp. 25–8.

24. Rudy VanderLans, interview with Ian Anderson, *Emigre*, no. 29, winter 1994.

25. See Shawn Wolfe, 'My Life at the Point of Sale' in *Uncanny: The Art & Design of Shawn Wolfe*, Seattle: Houston, 2000, unpaginated.

26. Teal Triggs and Jonathan Barnbrook, 'The Typo|Language of Jonathan Barnbrook', London College of Printing Design Open Pamphlet Series, no. 1, autumn 1997, p. 1.

27. Ibid., p. 1.

28. John Zerzan, 'Greasing the Rails to a Cyborg Future', *Adbusters*, no. 35, May|June 2001, p. 88.

29. 'Design Anarchy', *Adbusters*, no. 37, September|October 2001, unpaginated.

30. Ibid., unpaginated.

31. Allan Casey, 'Tibor Kalman', *Adbusters*, no. 23, autumn 1998, pp. 24–31. 'First Things First 2000: A Design Manifesto', *Adbusters*, no. 27, autumn 1999, pp. 56–7.

32. Rudy VanderLans, 'Introduction', *Emigre*, no. 19, 1991, unpaginated.

Selected Bibliography

Adair, Gilbert, *The Postmodernist Always Rings Twice: Reflections on Culture in the 90s,* London: Fourth Estate, 1992.

Aldersey-Williams, Hugh, *New American Design: Products and Graphics for a Post-Industrial Age,* New York: Rizzoli, 1988.

——— **et al.,** *Cranbrook Design: The New Discourse,* New York: Rizzoli, 1990.

Aldrich-Ruenzel, Nancy and Fennell, John (eds.), *Designer's Guide to Typography,* Oxford: Phaidon, 1991.

Aynsley, Jeremy. *A Century of Graphic Design: Graphic Design Pioneers of the 20th Century,* London: Mitchell Beazley, 2001.

Barthes, Roland, *Mythologies,* St. Albans, Herts.: Paladin, 1973 (first published 1957).

——— , *Image-Music-Text,* London: Fontana, 1977.

Belsey, Catherine, *Poststructuralism: A Very Short Introduction,* Oxford and New York: Oxford University Press, 2002.

Benjamin, Walter, *Reflections: Essays, Aphorisms, Autobiographical Writings,* New York: Schocken Books, 1978.

Betsky, Aaron and Adigard, Erik, *Architecture Must Burn: A Manifesto for an Architecture Beyond Building,* London: Thames & Hudson, 2000.

Bierut, Michael, Drenttel, William, Heller, Steven and Holland, D.K. (eds.), *Looking Closer: Critical Writings on Graphic Design,* New York: Allworth Press, 1994.

——— **(eds.),** *Looking Closer 2: Critical Writings on Graphic Design,* New York: Allworth Press, 1997.

Bierut, Michael, Helfand, Jessica, Heller, Steven and Poynor, Rick (eds.), *Looking Closer 3: Classic Writings on Graphic Design,* New York: Allworth Press, 1999.

Blackwell, Lewis, *The End of Print: The Graphic Design of David Carson,* London: Laurence King Publishing, 1995.

Bruggisser, Thomas and Fries, Michael (eds.), *Benzin: Young Swiss Graphic Design,* Baden: Lars Müller Publishers, 2001.

Büro Destruct, *Büro Destruct,* Berlin: Die Gestalten Verlag, 1999.

Chantry, Art, *Instant Litter: Concert Posters from Seattle Punk Culture,* Seattle: Real Comet Press, 1985.

Crimp, Douglas and Rolston, Adam, *AIDS Demo Graphics,* Seattle: Bay Press, 1990.

Culler, Jonathan, *Literary Theory: A Very Short Introduction,* Oxford and New York: Oxford University Press, 1997.

Davies, Erik, *TechGnosis: Myth, Magic and Mysticism in the Age of Information,* London: Serpent's Tail, 1999.

Debord, Guy, *The Society of the Spectacle,* New York: Zone Books, 1995 (first published 1967).

Deleuze, Gilles and Guattari, Félix, *A Thousand Plateaus: Capitalism and Schizophrenia,* London: Athlone, 1988.

Derrida, Jacques, *Of Grammatology,* Baltimore and London: John Hopkins University Press, 1997 (corrected edition; first published in English 1976).

Dormer, Peter, *The Art of the Maker: Skill and its Meaning in Art, Craft and Design,* London: Thames & Hudson, 1994.

Drucker, Johanna, *Figuring the Word: Essays on Books, Writing and Visual Practice,* New York: Granary Books, 1998.

Fella, Edward, *Edward Fella: Letters on America,* London: Laurence King Publishing, 2000.

Feyerabend, Paul, *Against Method,* London and New York: Verso, 1993 (third edition; first published 1975).

Foster, Hal (ed.), *Postmodern Culture,* London and Sydney: Pluto Press, 1985 (first published in the US as *The Anti-Æsthetic,* 1983).

Friedman, Dan, *Dan Friedman: Radical Modernism*, New Haven and London: Yale University Press, 1994.

Gill, Bob, *Forget All the Rules about Graphic Design. Including the Ones in this Book.*, New York: Watson-Guptill Publications, 1985 (first published 1981).

Glauber, Barbara (ed.), *Lift and Separate: Graphic Design and the Quote Vernacular Unquote*, New York: Cooper Union, 1993.

Greiman, April, *Hybrid Imagery: The Fusion of Technology and Graphic Design*, London: Architecture Design and Technology Press, 1990.

Guerrilla Girls, The, *Confessions of The Guerrilla Girls*, New York and London: HarperCollins, 1995.

Hall, Peter and Bierut, Michael (eds.), *Tibor Kalman: Perverse Optimist*, London: Booth-Clibborn Editions, 1998.

Haraway, Donna, *Simians, Cyborgs, and Women: The Reinvention of Nature*, London: Free Association Books, 1991.

Harper, Laurel, *Radical Graphics|Graphic Radicals*, San Francisco: Chronicle Books, 1999.

Harvey, David, *The Condition of Postmodernity: An Enquiry into the Origins of Cultural Change*, Cambridge, MA and Oxford: Blackwell, 1990.

Heartney, Eleanor, *Postmodernism*, London: Tate Publishing, 2001.

Hebdige, Dick, *Subculture: The Meaning of Style*, London: Methuen, 1979.

—— , *Hiding in the Light: On Images and Things*, London and New York: Routledge, 1988.

Heller, Steven, *The Education of a Graphic Designer*, New York: Allworth Press, 1998.

—— , *The Education of a Design Entrepreneur*, New York: Allworth Press, 2002.

Heller, Steven and Chwast, Seymour, *Graphic Style: From Victorian to Post-Modern*, London: Thames & Hudson, 1988 (second edition: *Graphic Style: From Victorian to Digital*, 2000).

Heller, Steven and Lasky, Julie, *Borrowed Design: Use and Abuse of Historical Form*, New York: Van Nostrand Reinhold, 1993.

Heller, Steven and Fink, Anne, *Faces on the Edge: Type in the Digital Age*, New York: Van Nostrand Reinhold, 1997.

Hollis, Richard, *Graphic Design: A Concise History*, London: Thames & Hudson, 2001 (second edition; first published 1994).

Hopkins, David, *After Modern Art 1945–2000*, Oxford and New York: Oxford University Press, 2000.

Hutcheon, Linda, *The Politics of Postmodernism*, London and New York: Routledge, 2002 (second edition; first published 1989).

Jameson, Fredric, *Postmodernism, or, The Cultural Logic of Late Capitalism*, London and New York: Verso, 1991.

Jencks, Charles, *The Language of Post-Modern Architecture*, London: Academy Editions, 1984 (fourth edition; first published 1977).

—— , *What is Post-Modernism?*, Academy Editions, 1996 (fourth edition; first published 1986).

Jobling, Paul and Crowley, David, *Graphic Design: Reproduction and Representation since 1800*, Manchester and New York: Manchester University Press, 1996.

Johnson, Philip and Wigley, Mark, *Deconstructivist Architecture*, Boston: Little, Brown, 1988.

Jordan, Joel T. , Hoeckel, Summer Forest and Jordan, Jason A. (eds.), *Searching for the Perfect Beat: Flyer Designs of the American Rave Scene*, New York: Watson-Guptill Publications, 2000.

Jury, David, *About Face: Reviving the Rules of Typography*, Mies, Switzerland: RotoVision, 2002.

Kalman, Maira and Peltason, Ruth (eds.), *Colors: Issues 1–13 The Tibor Kalman Years*, London: Thames & Hudson, 2002.

Kinross, Robin, *Fellow Readers: Notes on Multiplied Language*, London: Hyphen Press, 1994.

Klanten, Robert, Hellige, Hendrik and Mischler, Mika (eds.), *Swiss Graphic Design*, Berlin: Die Gestalten Verlag, 2000.

Kostelanetz, Richard, *A Dictionary of the Avant-Gardes*, London and New York: Routledge, 2001 (second edition; first published 1993).

Kunz, Willi, *Typography: Macro- and Microæsthetics*, Sulgen: Verlag Niggli, 1998.

Labuz, Ronald, *Contemporary Graphic Design*, New York: Van Nostrand Reinhold, 1991.

Lasky, Julie, *Some People Can't Surf: The Graphic Design of Art Chantry*, San Francisco: Chronicle Books, 2001.

Lewis, John, *Typography: Basic Principles: Influences and Trends since* the 19th Century, London: Studio Books, 1963.

Lupton, Ellen, *Mixing Messages: Contemporary Graphic Design in America*, London: Thames & Hudson|New York: Princeton Architectural Press, 1996.

Lupton, Ellen and Miller, J. Abbott, *The ABCs of ▲■●: The Bauhaus and Design Theory*, New York: The Cooper Union, 1991.

—— , *Design Writing Research: Writing on Graphic Design*, New York: Kiosk, 1996.

Lyotard, Jean-François, *The Postmodern Condition: A Report on Knowledge*, Manchester: Manchester University Press, 1998 (first published 1977).

Margolin, Victor (ed.), *Design Discourse: History, Theory, Criticism*, Chicago and London: University of Chicago Press, 1989.

Mast, Gerald and Cohen, Marshall (eds.), *Film Theory and Criticism: Introductory Readings*, New York: Oxford University Press, 1974.

Mau, Bruce, *Life Style*, London: Phaidon, 2000.

McDermott, Catherine, *Street Style: British Design in the 80s*, London: Design Council, 1987.

McLuhan, Marshall and Fiore, Quentin, *The Medium is the Massage: An Inventory of Effects*, Corte Madera, CA: Gingko Press, 2001 (first published 1967).

—— , *War and Peace in the Global Village*, Corte Madera, CA: Gingko Press, 2001 (first published 1968).

McRobbie, Angela, *Postmodernism and Popular Culture*, London and New York: Routledge, 1994.

Meggs, Philip B., *A History of Graphic Design*, New York and Chichester: John Wiley, 1998 (third edition; first published 1983).

Miller, J. Abbott, *Dimensional Typography: Case Studies on the Shape of Letters in Virtual Environments*, New York: Princeton Architectural Press, 1996.

Norris, Christopher, *Deconstruction: Theory and Practice*, London and New York: Routledge, 1991 (revised edition; first published 1982).

Pesch, Martin and Weisbeck, Markus *Discstyle: The Graphic Arts of Electronic Music and Club Culture*, London: Collins & Brown, 1999.

Plunkett, John and Rossetto, Louis, *Mind Grenades: Manifestos from the Future*, San Francisco: Hardwired, 1996.

Poynor, Rick (ed.), *The Graphic Edge*, London: Booth-Clibborn Editions, 1993.

—— **(ed.),** *Typography Now Two: Implosion*, London: Booth-Clibborn Editions, 1996.

—— , *Design Without Boundaries: Visual Communication in Transition*, London: Booth-Clibborn Editions, 1998.

Poynor, Rick and Booth-Clibborn, Edward (eds.), *Typography Now: The Next Wave*, London: Booth-Clibborn Editions, 1991.

Rabinow, Paul (ed.), *Foucault Reader*, New York: Random House, 1984.

Radice, Barbara, *Memphis: Research, Experiences, Results, Failures and Successes of New Design*, London: Thames & Hudson, 1984.

Rand, Paul, *Design Form and Chaos*, New Haven and London: Yale University Press, 1993.

Reid, Jamie, *Up They Rise: The Incomplete Works of Jamie Reid*, London: Faber and Faber, 1987.

Ronell, Avital, *The Telephone Book: Technology, Schizophrenia, Electric Speech*, Lincoln: University of Nebraska Press, 1989.

Scher, Paula, *Make it Bigger*, New York: Princeton Architectural Press, 2002.

Sim, Stuart, *Derrida and the End of History*, London: Icon Books|New York: Totem Books, 1999.

—— , *Irony and Crisis: A Critical History of Postmodern Culture*, London: Icon Books|New York: Totem Books, 2002.

Stone, Allucquère Rosanne, *The War of Desire and Technology at the Close of the Mechanical Age*, Cambridge, MA and London: MIT Press, 1995.

Tomato, *Process; A Tomato Project*, London: Thames & Hudson, 1996.

Turcotte, Bryan Ray and Miller, Christopher T. (eds.), *Fucked Up + Photocopied*, Corte Madera, CA: Gingko Press, 1999.

Venturi, Robert, *Complexity and Contradiction in Architecture*, London: Architectural Press, 1977 (second edition; first published 1966).

Venturi, Robert, Scott Brown, Denise and Izenour, Steven, *Learning from Las Vegas: The Forgotten Symbolism of Architectural Form*, Cambridge MA and London: MIT Press, 1977 (revised edition; first published 1972).

Weingart, Wolfgang, *Typography*, Baden: Lars Müller
Publishers, 2000.

Wheale, Nigel (ed.), *The Postmodern Arts: An Introductory Reader*,
London and New York: Routledge, 1995.

Wolfe, Shawn, *Uncanny: The Art & Design of Shawn Wolfe*,
Seattle: Houston, 2000.

Wollen, Peter, *Signs and Meaning in the Cinema*, London:
Secker & Warburg, 1972 (revised edition; first published 1969).

Woodham, Jonathan M., *Twentieth-Century Design*, Oxford and
New York: Oxford University Press, 1997.

Woods, Tim, *Beginning Postmodernism*, Manchester and New
York: Manchester University Press, 1999.

Woodtli, Martin, *Woodtli*, Berlin: Die Gestalten Verlag, 2001.

Wozencroft, Jon, *The Graphic Language of Neville Brody*,
London: Thames & Hudson, 1988.

Index

Numbers in **bold** refer to illustrations

3D Studio (program) 105

3MB Featuring Magic Juan Atkins, album cover (1993) (The Designers Republic) 103–104, **103**

The ABCs of ▲■● : The Bauhaus and Design Theory, spread (1991) (Lupton|Miller|Mills) 124, **125**

About 2 (1922) (Lissitzky) 70, **71**

About Face: Reviving the Rules of Typography (2002) 16

Abstract Expressionism 73

Acme Novelty Library:
    no.5, comic book cover (1995) (Ware) **142**
    no.13, comic book cover (1995) (Ware) **142**

Adbusters:
    'Design Anarchy' issue 168–169
        cover (Simons) **170**
        spread (Barnbrook) **170**
        spread (Texas) **169**
    First Things First 2000, design manifesto 169
    and Tibor Kalman 169
    'Toxic Culture: An Iconography for the Mental Environment', spread 168

Adigard, Erik 111
    Architecture Must Burn, visual essay (2000) 113, **113**
    (with Plunkett) Wired, no. 2.08, spread (1994) **112**

'The Advantages of Being a Woman Artist', poster (1988) (Guerrilla Girls) **157**

advertising, as social criticism 156–159

Against Fiction, artist's book (1983) (Drucker) 129, **129**

Ahmed, Mimi: The War of Desire and Technology at the Close of the Mechanical Age, book cover (1995) 15, **15**

Airline Industries: Sting 9, rave flyer (1997) **106**

Alarm Call, CD cover (1998) (Me Company) **105**, 106

The Alphabetic Labyrinth, book (1995) (Drucker) 129

alternative reading styles 50–51, 53, 63, 131

Altmann, Andrew 59

amateur designers 38, 40–41

anarchic style 40

Anderson, Charles S. 87–89
    CSA Line Art Archive Catalog, vol.1, cover (1995) 87–88, **87**
    'Seinfeld' poster (1998) 88–89, **88**

Anderson, Ian 103, 104
    and company logos 163
    founder of DR 103
    Fuse contributor 160
    see also The Designers Republic (DR)

The Anti-Æsthetic, book (1983) (Foster) 53

architecture:
    deconstructive 47–48
    modernist 19, 26
    postmodernist 18, 19, 22–23, 36
    Venturi on 26, 27

Architecture Must Burn, visual essay (2000) (Adigard) 113, **113**

Arena magazine 151, 152

Armed Forces, album cover (1979) (Bubbles) 73, **74**

Army of Me, CD cover (1995) (Me Company) 105, **105**

art, design as 26

Art Deco 23, 79, 84

art history, allusions to 72, 73, 84

Art Nouveau 18

'Artificial Nature', poster (1990) (Friedman) 154, **155**

artist's books 128–134, 140

artists as designers 40

Assorted Images 159

Atkins, Martyn: (with Saville) Closer, album cover|sleeve (1980) 36–37, **36**

Attik:
    Noise 3.5: 'Analytical Experiments in Graphic Science', spread (1998) 107, **107**

audience participation 66

Aufuldish, Bob: Selected Notes 2 ZeitGuys, detail (1995) **119**

'The Author as Producer', essay (1934) (Benjamin) 121, 146

authorship:
    Barthes on 118, 146–147
    'designer as author' 17, 118–140, 145–147
    forms of 145–146
    shared 135–137

Bachelorette, CD cover (1997) (Me Company) 105, 106

Baker, Steve 134

Ballard, J.G. 133

Bareback. A Tomato Project (1999) (Tomato) 135, **136**, 137

Barnbrook, Jonathan 165–169
    Adbusters, 'Design Anarchy' issue 168–169
        magazine spread **170**
    Heathen, CD booklet page (2002) **47**
    Illustration Now, divider pages (1993) 166
    'Is economic progress killing the planet?', poster 168
    'Virus Says Stop American Cultural Imperialism', poster (1999) **167**

Welcome to the Cult of Virus, brochure page (1997) **166**

Barthes, Roland 53, 56, 129
    and authorship 118, 146–147
    'The Death of the Author', essay (1968) 118

Basle, Switzerland 19

Baudrillard, Jean 15
    on ecstasy of communication 99, 101, 102

Bauhaus style 79

Bayer, Herbert 75

Beach Culture (magazine) 62

'Beat the Whites with the Red Wedge', poster (1919) (Lissitzky) 75, 76

Beginning Postmodernism, book cover (1999) (River Design Company) **14**, 15

Benjamin, Walter, 'The Author as Producer', essay (1934) 121, 146

Berger, Joshua 63

Bernstein, Dennis 130

Betsky, Aaron:
    Architecture Must Burn (with Adigard) 113
    on 'floating world' 113–114

Bielenberg, John:
    Virtual Telemetrix Inc. (spoof company) 163
    Virtual Telemetrix 1993 Annual Report, spread (1993) **164**

bitmap images 56, 97

Blauvelt, Andrew 54

Bonnell, Wilburn: 'Postmodern Typography: Recent American Developments', exhibition (1977) 22–23

book artists 128–134

Boston 40

Breakfast Special (1989) (Tilson) 133–134
    No.1 - El Dottore di Terrocotta, spread from **133**
    No.2 - La Carte Propre, spread from **133**

Breton, André 35

bricolage 31

Britain:
    early postmodernism 35–37
    and modernism 32–33
    'new wave' 32–37

Brody, Neville 33, 35, 73, 151–152, 159
    engagement with content 151–152
    homage to earlier designers 75–76
    as a media figure 120
    project 61

The Face, no. 23, spread (1982) **75, 76**
The Face, no. 49, cover (1984) **152**
The Face, nos. 50–55, contents page (1984) 49, **49**
(with Jon Wozencroft) *The Guardian*, review page
  (1988) 152, **153**
New Socialist magazine, no.38, cover (1986) 152, **152**
Torchsong, advertisement for (1984) 48–49, **48**
see also Fuse magazine
Broekman, Pauline van Mourik *see* Worthington,
  Simon
Brown, Denise Scott: (with Venturi and Izenour)
  Learning from Las Vegas (1972) 26–27
Bubbles, Barney 33, 34–35, 72–73
  Armed Forces, album cover (1979) 73, **74**
  Do It Yourself, album cover (1979) 73
  The Ian Dury Songbook, spread (1979) 33–34, **34**
  Music for Pleasure, album cover (1977) 72–73, **73**, 76–77
Burdick, Anne:
  'Mouthpiece: Clamor over Writing and Design'
    (editor) (1995) 126
  'What has Writing got to do with Design?', essay 126
  and writing and design 126–128
Büro Destruct 115
Burroughs, William 133
Byrne, Chuck 49–50

CalArts Viewbook, cover (1979) (Greiman) 23, **23**
California Institute of the Arts (CalArts) 41, 56
  poster|brochure for (Greiman|Odgers) 24
  see also Fast Forward
California, 'new wave' 31
Cantor, Fredrich 24
Carlu, Jean: 'US Office of War Information', poster
  (1941) 77
Carson, David:
  and *Beach Culture* magazine 62
  and corporate advertising 61
  designer *Ray Gun* magazine (1992–5) 61, 62–63
  The End of Print, book (1995) 62
  Fuse contributor 160
  'ignorance of rules' argument 13, 16, 62
  as a media figure 120
  repudiation of conventions 61–63
Castle, Phillip: *Mythologies*, book cover (1976) **14**, 15
The Century of Artists' Books (1995) (Drucker) 129
Chantry, Art 85, 87
  Estrus Records, logos (1990s) 87, **87**
  Liquor Giants, CD cover (1992) 87
  'The Night Gallery', poster (1991) 85, **86**, 87
Charlie, visual book (1995) (Lehrer) 132, **132**
Cherry, Jim; *Claro Que Si*, album cover (1981) 30, **30**
Chiat|Day|Mojo 88
Chicago 60
Chirico, Giorgio de 78
City University of New York 130
Claro Que Si, album cover (1981) (Cherry) 30, **30**
Claude, visual book (1995) (Lehrer) 132, **132**

Closer, album cover|sleeve (1980) (Saville|Atkins) 36–37, **36**
Coca-Cola:
  appropriation of logo 163
  and Attik 107
collages 23–24, 111
Colors (Benetton magazine) 158–159, 171
  no.6, cover (1994) (Kalman|Stowell) **158**
  no.9, cover (1994) (Kalman|Porter) **158**, 159
commercial techno 107
communication:
  advertising as 156–159
  postmodern approach 151–152
  potential of words 128
  Radice on 28, 30
  value of minimalism 115
'The Complete Genealogy of Graphic Design', cover
  (1985) (Scher) 90, **90**
Complexity and Contradiction in Architecture (1966)
  (Venturi) 26, 27
computers:
  Apple Macintosh 95, 96–99
  computer generation designers 106
  present reality of 112–113
  utopian forecasts 110–113
  see also digital design
The Condition of Postmodernity (Harvey) 11
'Confusion and Chaos: The Seduction of Contemporary
  Graphic Design', essay (Rand) 148–149
'Connections', poster (1983) (Vanderbyl) 31, **31**
Constructivism 47, 48, 70, 79
consumer culture:
  criticism of 163–165, 169
  effect on design 168, 169
  graphic style of 166
The Cooper Union art school, Herb Lubalin Study
  Center 123
corporate advertising 61
corporate logos 162–163
corporate style 25, 54, 60
The Correct Use of Soap, album cover (1980) (Garrett)
  34–35, **35**
craft, nature of 16
Cranbrook Academy of Art 27, 149
  assault on rules 13
  'Cranbrook Design: The New Discourse',
    exhibition announcement (1990) (Makela) 101, **101**
  Cranbrook Design: The New Discourse (1990)
    (McCoy|Makela|Kroh) 50–51, **51**
  Fella's influence at 56
  'The Graduate Program in Design', poster (1989)
    (McCoy) 50, **50**
  'Output', student work (1992) 149, **149**
  use of theory 51, 53–54
  Visible Language, spreads (1978) (by students) **52**, 53
Creation 6, font (1993) 161, **161**, 162–163
Crisp, Denise Gonzales: *Emigre*, no.35, spread (1995) **127**
critics of postmodernism 148–151

Crosseyed and Painless, record cover (1980) (Kalman)
  81–82, **81**
Crouwel, Wim 43
Crow, David 159–160
  Creation 6, font (1993) 161, **161**, 162–163
  Trouble magazine 159–160
    no. 1 (1986) **160**
    no. 4 (1990) **160**
Croydon Art School, south London 39
CSA Line Art Archive Catalog, vol.1, cover (1995)
  (Anderson) 87–88, **87**
Culler, Jonathan 46
'Cult of the Ugly', essay (Heller) 149–150
Cultural Geometry, cover (1988) (Friedman) 154, **154**
cyberculture 108
'Cyberotica', typeface (1994) (Deck) 108, **109**
cyborg images 105–106, 107
'A Cyborg Manifesto' (1991) (Haraway) 105

Dadaism 60–61, 76, 159
Dance the Night Away, album cover (1980) (Scher) 78, **78**
Danielewski, Mark Z., *House of Leaves* (2000) 142–144,
  144, 145, 147
Davies, Erik, *TechGnosis* 108
Davis, Fred & Plunkett, John: *Wired*, no. 1.06, spread
  (1993) **112**
'Dead History', typeface (1990) (Makela) 102, **102**
De Lucchi, Michele 28
De Stijl 79
'The Death of the Author' (1968) (Barthes) 118
Debord, Guy 159
'decentred' text 110, 113
Deck, Barry:
  'Cyberotica', typeface (1994) 108, **109**
  Fuse contributor 160
  'Template Gothic', typeface (c. 1990) **56**, 57
Decoding Advertisements (Williamson) 8
deconstructed style 60, 61
'De-constructing Typography', article (Meggs) 48
deconstruction:
  and architecture 47–48
  attack on modernism 44
  'decentred' text 110, 113
  and design 44–69
  discussion of 46–47
  and legibility 49
  and meaning 49–50
  and typography 49–51
  as widely-used term 65–66
deconstruction theory 51
'Deconstructivist Architecture', exhibition (1988)
  (MoMA) 47
Deitch, Jeffrey 154
Deleuze, Gilles 108
Depero, Fortunato:
  'Dinamo Futurista' (1933) 78
  Futurist poster (1932) 77

Derrida, Jacques 15, 47, 48, 123
   Glas 67
   On Grammatology (1967) 46, 66
   The Truth in Painting 66
Derridean oppositions 46, 51
design:
   as art 26
   and authorship 17, 118–140, 145–147
   commercial purpose of 171
   as cultural practice 53
   by non-designers 38, 40–41
   'process' as sole end 115, 135
   as subculture 33
   see also digital design; postmodern design
Design magazine 18
Design Quarterly:
   no. 133, collage (1986) (Greiman) 97, 99, **100**
   no. 158, cover (1993) (Makela|Tylevich) **103**
'Design without Designers', invitation (1986)
   (Kalman|Isley) 82, **82**, 84
Design|Writing|Research (Lupton|Miller alliance)
   123, 124
   (with Mills) *The ABCs of* ▲■● *: The Bauhaus and*
     Design Theory, spread (1991) 124, **125**
   critical writings 123
   Design Writing Research (1996) 66–67, 124
   as designer|authors 123–124
'Designer as Author: Voices and Visions', exhibition
   (1996) (McCarthy) 128
designers:
   as authors 118–140, 145–147
   as personalities 119–120
   and writers 126–127
The Designers Republic (DR) 103–105
   3MB Featuring Magic Juan Atkins, album cover
     (1993) 103–104, **103**
   ironic techno style 108
   and Pepsi-Cola logo 163
   Pho-Ku Corporation poster (2000) **104**
   Pop Will Eat Itself (band), record sleeve for 163
   'Sissy', poster (1995) **104**
Detroit Focus Gallery: exhibition posters for (1987|88)
   (Fella) **54**, 55, **55**
Diary of an Amateur Photographer (1998) (Rawle) 141, **141**
A Dictionary of the Avant-Gardes (Kostelanetz) 8
A Different Kind of Tension, album cover (1979) (Garrett)
   75, **75**, **8**
digital design 17, 96–117, 106
   bitmap images 56, 97
   and excess 99–102
   and grunge 65
   image|text relationship 108, 110
   perfection of finish 115
   see also computers
'dimensional typography' 108
Disparte, Alan 89–90
   Gap 'Old Navy', advertising campaign (1998) **89**

Dispepsi, CD cover (1997) (Wolfe) 163, **163**
Do It Yourself, album cover (1979) (Bubbles) 73
Doesburg, Theo van 75
domestic furnishings 28, 36
Dooren, Dirk van 134
Dormer, Peter 16
dotcom bubble 112
double-coded design 35
Doublespace 27
   Fetish, no. 2, cover and spreads (1980) **28**, **29**
Drenttel Doyle Partners 90
Drucker, Johanna 129–130, 140
   Against Fiction (1983) 129, **129**
   The Alphabetic Labyrinth (1995) 129
   The Century of Artists' Books (1995) 129
   The History of the|my Wor(l)d (1990) 129–130, **130**, 147
   The Visible Word (1994) 129
Druckspiegel (trade journal) 20
Duffy, Joe (Duffy Design Group) 84–85, 87
Dumbar, Gert (Studio Dumbar) 58
   and Cranbrook students 58
   performance poster (1987) **59**
   at Royal College of Art 59

Earls, Elliott 63
   'Dysphasia', typeface (1995) 63, **64**
Eckersley, Richard 67
   The Telephone Book, spreads (1989) **68**
eclectic design 18–19, 23, 34, 43, 44
Eco, Umberto 15
Edie, Frank: concert poster (1978) 40–41, **41**
Eisenman, Peter 47, 48
   House X (1982) 129
Elastic Reality (program) 105
Elenga, Henk 43
Eliot, T.S. 12, 13
Ellis, David 59
Emigre magazine (Vanderlans and Licko):
   and computer graphics 96, 97
   criticism of 148
   and entrepreneurship 145
   Keedy and Fella on 'anti-mastery' 55
   Lupton|Miller articles 123
   'Mouthpiece' issues, nos.35|36 (1995)
     (ed.Burdick) 126
     no. 35, spread (1995) (Crisp) **127**
     no. 35, spread (1995) (Worthington) **126**
     no. 36, spread (1995) (Sandhaus) **127**
   'The New Primitives', bitmap article 97
   no. 5, spread (1986) (Vanderlans) **98**
   theoretical writing by designers 126
   typeface for (1990) (Makela) **102**
Emigre Type Specimen Series Booklet No. 4: Keedy Sans (2002)
   (Keedy) **9**
Encyclopedia Persona, spreads (1993) (Silton) 94–95, **94**
The End of Print (1995) (Carson) 62
Enlightenment (18th century) 11

Entertainment Weekly 65, 88–89
entrepreneurship 145
Estrus Records, logos (1990s) (Chantry) 87, **87**
Evans, Walker 78
'excessive' design 60, 99–102, 115
Expressionism 84
Eye magazine 123

The Face 33
   'The Age of Plunder', article (1983) (Savage) 76–77
   Brody and content 151
   Brody and legibility 49
   contents page, nos. 50–55 (1984) (Brody) 49, **49**
   Elms on style as weapon 152
   no. 23, spread (1982) (Brody) **75**, 76
   no. 49, cover (1984) (Brody) **152**
Factory Records 77, 79
Fast Forward (CalArts student catalogue):
   book cover (1993) (Stoecker) **110**
   book spread (1993) (Keedy) **111**
   Keedy on computing future 110–111
Fella, Edward 13, 54
   exhibition poster (1987) 55, **55**
   exhibition posters (1988) **54**, 55, 56
   and Steven Heller 150
   and typography 55–57
feminism 130, 157, 161–162
Fetish magazine 27–28
   'Machine Music', feature 27
   no.2, cover and spreads (1980) **28**, **29**
Feyerabend, Paul 38
Fili, Louise 79
Financial Times 93
'floating world' concept 113–115
Forget All the Rules about Graphic Design. Including the Ones
   in this Book. (Gill) 12–13
Form-Z (program) 105
Foster, Hal 169, 171
   The Anti-Æsthetic (1983) 53
   on types of postmodernism 151
Foucault, Michel 15, 123
   and authorship 146–147
Freehand (program) 105
Frej, David 54, 58
French Fries, artist's book (1984) (Lehrer|Bernstein)
   130–131, **131**
Frere-Jones, Tobias 65
Friedman, Dan 20, 21, 23, 152–156
   'Artificial Nature', poster (1990) 154, **155**
   Cultural Geometry, cover (1988) 154, **154**
   Post Human, spread (1992) 154, **155**
   poster based on letter 'N' (1968) 21
   and 'Radical Modernism' 152–153, 156
   'Radical Modernism' logo (early 1990s) **154**
   'Space', poster (1976) 21, **21**
   and 'Swiss Punk' 34
   Typografische Monatsblätter, no. 1, cover (1971) 21, **21**

Fuel (Miles, Murray & Sorrell) 137–139
   Fuel, self-published magazine 138, **138**
   Fuel Three Thousand (2000) 138–139, **139**
   Pure Fuel (1996) 138
functionalist tradition 43
Fuse magazine (Brody & Wozencroft) 160–162
   font (1995) (WD+RU) 161–162, **162**
   'What the Hell', font (1993) (Kalman|Stowell)
    160–161, **161**
Futurism 76, 77–78, 80–81

Gap 'Old Navy' 89–90
   advertising campaign (1998) (Disparte) **89**
Garrett, Malcolm 33, 35, 73, 159
   The Correct Use of Soap, album cover (1980) 34–35, **35**
   A Different Kind of Tension, album cover (1979) 75, **75**, 76
   homage to earlier designers 76, 81
   and 'Retrievalism' 76
   Someone Somewhere (In Summertime), record cover
    (1982) 35, **35**
Gehry, Frank 47
Geissbuhler, Steff 23
'Generation X' youth culture 61
Gibson, William, *Neuromancer* (1984) 110, 111
Gill, Bob, *Forget All the Rules about Graphic Design.*
   Including the Ones in this Book. 12–13
Glas (Derrida) 67
God Save the Queen, record cover (1977) (Reid) **39**, 40
Goldberg, Carin 79
   'The Graduate Program in Design', poster (1989)
    (McCoy) **50**, 51
   'Graduate Studies in Fiber', poster (1984) (Keedy)
    53–54, **53**
Gran Fury: 'Women don't get AIDS', poster (1991)
   156–157, **156**
graphic authorship 140–145
graphic design *see* design
graphic designers *see* designers
The Graphic Language of Neville Brody (Wozencroft) 33
graphic novels 140–145
Graves, Michael 31
   Portland Building, Portland, Oregon (1982) 19
Great Beginnings, spread (1984) (Koppel & Scher) 79, **79**
The Great Rock 'n' Roll Swindle, promotional materials
   (Reid) 40
Grego, Valentina: Memphis logo (1983) **28**
Greiman, April 21, 23, 24, 34, 35
   CalArts Viewbook, cover (1979) 23, **23**
   and computer graphics 96, 97, 99
   Design Quarterly, no. 133, collage (1986) 97, 99, **100**
   (and Odgers) poster|brochure 24
   (and Odgers) *Wet*, cover (1979) 23–24, **23**
grid systems 13, 24, 31, 62, 124
Groot, Luc(as) de 63
   'Jesus Loves You', typeface 108
   'Jesus Loves Your Sister', typeface **65**
grunge 63, 65–66

Guardian First Book Award 142
The Guardian, review page (1988) (Brody|Wozencroft)
   152, **153**
Guattari Félix 108
Guerrilla Girls 157–158
   'The Advantages of Being a Woman Artist',
    poster (1988) **157**
   'Guerrilla Girls Conscience of the art world',
    street posters 157

Hadders, Gerard 43
Hadid, Zaha 47
hand graphics 56
Haraway, Donna, 'A Cyborg Manifesto' (1991) 105
Hard Werken Association 42–44
   Hard Werken, no. 1, cover (1979) **42**
   Hard Werken, no. 3, spread (1979) **43**
   'The Year of Japanese Film', poster (1981)
    (Haspel) 44, **45**
Hard Werken magazine 42, 43
Harvey, David, *The Condition of Postmodernity* 11
Haspel, Tom van den 43
   'The Year of Japanese Film', poster (1981) 44, **45**
Hawkwind (group) 72
Heathen, CD booklet page (2002) (Barnbrook) **47**
Heller, Steven 145, 149–150
   'Cult of the Ugly', essay 149–150
   and Edward Fella 150
Hersey, John: 'Pacific Wave', cover (1987) 97, **98**
Hiding (1997) (Taylor) 67
'high' vs. 'low' culture 11, 38, 84, 157
Himmelblau, Coop 47
historical references 70, 72, 73, 75, 76–81, 84
historicism 34, 37
The History of the|my Wor(l)d (1990) (Drucker) 129–130,
   130, 147
homage 34
Honeycutt, B.W. 90, 92
Hori, Allen 54, 58
   'Typography as Discourse', poster (1989) **58**, 59
Horsham, Michael 134
House Industries 63
   'Bad Neighborhood' series, typeface (1995) **65**
House of Leaves (2000) (Danielewski) 142–144, **144, 145**, 147
House X (1982) (Eisenman) 129
Hughes-Stanton, Corin 18, 19
Hutcheon, Linda, *The Politics of Postmodernism* 151, 154
hybrid design 11, 19, 26, 35, 36–37
Hyde, Karl 134

i-D magazine:
   i-D, no. 20, cover (1985) (Jones) **42**
   launch of 41–42
The Ian Dury Songbook, cover and spread (1979)
   (Bubbles) 33–34, **34**
identity-building 135
images:

as text 123–124
and words 128
Infini-D (program) 105
info-graphics 90
innovation, impossibility of 76
Innovation, promotional mailer (1985) (Vanderbyl)
   31–32, **32**
'instant design' 42
International Style 115
International Symposium on Deconstruction, Tate
   Gallery 48
Internet 108, 112
Introduction, self-published book (1999) (Norm) 115, **116**, 117
irony 12, 15
Isley, Alexander 90
   (and Kalman) promotional postcard (1986) 82, **83**
   Spy magazine spreads (April|June 1988) **91**
   see also Kalman, Tibor
Izenour, Steven: (with Brown & Venturi) *Learning*
   from Las Vegas (1972) 26

Jacobs, Karrie 79–80
Jameson, Fredric 14, 156
   impossibility of innovation 76, 95
   on pastiche vs. parody 71–72
Jancourt, Jan 58
Jencks, Charles:
   Jencksian postmodernism 35
   The Language of Post-Modern Architecture (1977) 19
'Jesus Loves You', typeface (Groot) 108
'Jesus Loves Your Sister', typeface (Groot) **65**
Jimmy Corrigan: The Smartest Kid on Earth (2000) (Ware)
   142, **143**
'jive modernism' 80
Johnson, Betsey 27, **28**
Johnson, Philip 48
   'Deconstructivist Architecture', exhibition
    (with Wigley) 47
   proposals for AT&T building, New York 36
Jones, Terry:
   i-D, no. 28, magazine cover (1985) **42**
   launches *i-D* 41–42
   Not Another Punk Book, book design (1977) 41
Joy Division:
   Closer, album cover|sleeve (1980) (Saville|Atkins)
    36–37, **36**

Kalman, Tibor (M&Co) 158–159, 171
   and *Adbusters* magazine 169
   and design rules 13
   design as social comment 158–159
   history debate with Joe Duffy 84–85
   as a media figure 120
   use of vernacular sources 81–85
   projects:
    (and Stowell) *Colors*, no.6, cover (1994) **158**
    (and Porter) *Colors*, no.9, cover (1994) **158, 159**

Crosseyed and Painless, record cover (1980) 81–82, **81**
  (with Isley) 'Design without Designers',
    invitation (1986) 82, **82**, 84
'Modernism and Eclecticism', lecture 79–80
Restaurant Florent:
  print advertisement (1987) 82, **83**
  promotional literature (1985–93) 82
  (Isley and) promotional postcard (1986) 82, **83**
(and Stowell) *What the Hell*, font (1993)
  160–161, **161**
Kars, Willem 43
Kedgley, Jason 134
Keedy, Jeffery:
  on computers and meaning 110–111
  on digital design 112
  Fuse contributor 160
  rejection of modernism 54–55
  projects:
    Emigre Type Specimen Series Booklet No.4: Keedy Sans
     (2002) **9**
    event programme (1988) **57**
    Fast Forward, text and spread (1993) 110–111, **111**
    'Graduate Studies in Fiber', poster (1984) 53–54, **53**
    Keedy Sans, typeface (1990) 57
Kinross, Robin, *Fellow Readers*, pamphlet 150–151
Klefisch, Karl: *Die Mensch-Maschine*, album cover (1978)
  70–71
Kook, Annie & Silberman, Stuart L.: *Welcome to Twin
  Peaks*, cover and spread (1991) 92–93, **92**
Koolhaas, Rem 47, 122–123
Koppel & Scher (Terry Koppel & Paula Scher):
  Great Beginnings, spread (1984) 79, **79**
Kosstrin, Jane 27
Kostelanetz, Richard:
  A Dictionary of the Avant-Gardes 8
  on postmodernism 8
Kraftwerk 70, 75
Krebs, Manuel 117
Kroh, Mary Lou 50
Kruger, Barbara 154
Kunstgewerbeschule, Basle 19–20, 21, 24
'Kunstkredit 1976|77', poster (Weingart) (1977) 22, **22**
'Kunstkredit 1978|79', poster (Weingart) (1979) 22, **22**
Kunz, Willi 23
  'Strange Vicissitudes', poster (1978) 24, **25**
Kvízová, Klára & Krejzek, Petr: *Zivel*, no.10, cover
  (1998) 108, **109**

Lacan, Jacques 130
'The Language of Michael Graves', poster (1983)
  (Longhauser) 32, **32**
The Language of Post-Modern Architecture (1977) (Jencks) 19
LaserWriter 97, 99
Laurel, Brenda 112
lead type 20
Learning from Las Vegas (1972) (Venturi|Brown|Izenour)
  26–27

Leggett, Dennis 89
legibility 20, 27, 43, 49, 63
Lehrer, Warren 130–132, 140, 145
  Charlie, visual book (1995) 132, **132**
  Claude, visual book (1995) 132, **132**
  (with Bernstein) *French Fries* (1984) 130–131, **131**
  Versations (1980) 130
letterpress 20, 129
letterspacing 24, 27, 31–32, 55–56
Levine, Sherrie 78
Levi's 88, 107, 138
Lewis, Clyde 87
Lewis, John, *Typography: Basic Principles* (1963) 12
Libeskind, Daniel 47, 53
Licko, Zuzana 96
  'Modular Ribbed' typeface (1995) 108
  see also Emigre magazine
Life Style (2000) (Mau) 121–123, 144
linearity 24
Liquor Giants, CD cover (1992) (Chantry) 87
Lissitzky, El 70, 75, 76, 140
  About 2 (1922) 70, **71**
  'Beat the Whites with the Red Wedge', poster
   (1919) 75, 76
  verbal|visual writing 144
literary criticism 56
'Live Twice the Life in Half the Time!', poster (1999)
  (Wolfe) 163, 165, **165**
Longhauser, William: 'The Language of Michael
  Graves', poster (1983) 32, **32**
Los Angeles Contemporary Exhibitions (LACE),
  programme (1988) (Keedy) **57**
'low' vs. 'high' culture 11, 38, 84, 157
Lupton, Ellen 123–124, 145
  on 'designer as producer' 146
  Numbers, catalogue spread (1989) **125**
  Period Styles: A History of Punctuation, cover (1988) **123**
  'Visual Dictionary' 124
  'Writing|Culture' monograph, essay in 123
  see also Design|Writing|Research
Lynch, David 92
Lyotard, Jean-François, *The Postmodern Condition: A
  Report on Knowledge* 11

McCarthy, Steven: 'Designer as Author: Voices and
  Visions', exhibition (1996) 128
McCoy, Katherine 53, 54
  Cranbrook Design: The New Discourse (1990) (with
   Makela & Kroh) 50–51, **51**
  on deconstruction 65–66
  'The Graduate Program in Design', poster (1989)
   50, 51
McCoy, Michael 50
McCracken, Pete: Plazm typeface (1993) **65**
McDonald, Edward 58
MacDraw (program) 97
McLaren, Malcolm 39–40

McLuhan, Marshall 107
  The Medium is the Massage 111
MacPaint (program) 97
MacVision (program) 97
Magic Mountain (Mann) 79
Makela, P. Scott 50
  'Cranbrook Design: The New Discourse',
   announcement (1990) 101, **101**
  'Dead History', typeface (1990) 102, **102**
  (with Tylevich) *Design Quarterly*, no.158, cover
   (1993) **103**
  digital forecasts 102–103
  Emigre, techno music recording for 102
  and information overload 101–103
  'On Doing Nothing', spread (1992) 102, **102**
  'Redefining Display', project and text (1993)
   102–103
Malevich, Kasimir 148
Marker, Chris 122
Martin, Eric 108–109
Mastroianni, Marcello 24–25, **25**
Matter, Herbert: travel poster (1934) 80–81, **80**
Mau, Bruce (Bruce Mau Design) 121–123
  and designers as authors 121–123, 146
  Life Style (2000) 121–123, 144
  S,M,L,XL (1995), spread (1995) 122–123, **122**
  Zone, no. 1|2, cover and spread (1986) **120**, 121, **121**
Me Company 105–107
  Alarm Call, CD cover (1998) **105**, 106
  Army of Me, CD cover (1995) 105, **105**
  Bachelorette, CD cover (1997) **105**, 106
  Nike, advertisement for (1995) 106, **106**
meaning:
  and deconstruction 49–50, 66–67
  visual meaning 51
Mechanix, record cover (1982) 77
The Medium is the Massage (McLuhan) 111
Meggs, Philip, 'De-constructing Typography', article 48
Memphis: The New International Style, book cover (1981) 30, **30**
Memphis design group 28–30, 31
  logos, 1982 and 1983 (Radl) **28**
  logos, 1983 (Grego) **28**
Die Mensch-Maschine, album cover (Klefisch) 70–71
Metamorphosis (Kafka) 79
Michael Peters Group 84
Microsoft 61
Miles, Peter 137
Miller, J. Abbott 79, 123–124, 135
  and 'dimensional typography' 108
  'Polymorphous', typeface (1996) 108, **109**
  (with Jacobs) *Print* article 79–80
  'Rhizome', typeface (1996) 108, **109**
  and *2wice* magazine 124
  see also Design|Writing|Research
Mills, Mike 124
Mind Grenades: Manifestos from the Future, Wired
  magazine 112

minimalism 115
Ministry of Sound 104
mistakes 42, 97, 115
Miyake, Issey 31
modern architecture 19, 26
moderne style (1920s) 18
modernism:
    and postmodernism 11, 153
    progressive ideals of 11, 165
    'Radical Modernism' 152–153, 156
'Modernism and Eclecticism', lecture (Kalman) 79–80
modernist design:
    and corporate style 25, 54
    deconstructionist attack on 44, 54–55
    and montage 15
    typography of 20, 25, 27
'Modular Ribbed' typeface (1995) (Licko) 108
Moholy-Nagy, Laszlo 75
Mondrian, Piet 73
montage 15, 42
Moss, Karen 94, 95
Movement, album cover (1981) (Saville) 77, **77**
MTV 88, 104, 138
Müller-Brockmann, Josef 124
Murray, Damon 137
Museum of Modern Art (MoMA), New York
    'Deconstructivist Architecture' exhibition (1988) 47
music:
    new wave 33–34
    punk rock 33, 38–41, 159
    techno 102, 106–107
Music for Pleasure, album cover (1977) (Bubbles) 72–73, **73**, 76–77
Mute, no. 4, newspaper page (1996)
    (Worthington|Broekman) 93–94, **93**
Myst (computer game) 106
Mythologies, book cover (1976) (Castle) **14**, 15

Nabokov, Vladimir 56
Nakata, Robert 58
Nelson, Ricky **23**, 24
neo-classicism 36, 37
neo-Dada 96
neo-Futurism 96
Neuromancer (1984) (Gibson) 110, 111
Never Mind the Bollocks Here's the Sex Pistols, album cover (1977) (Reid) 40, **40**
New Socialist magazine, no. 38, cover (1986) (Brody) 152, **152**
new wave music 33–34
The New York Times 65
    Book Review 150
Newman, Robert 40
New Order:
    Movement, album cover (1981) (Saville) 77, **77**
    Procession, album cover (1981) (Saville) 77–78, 80
    Thieves Like Us, record cover (1984) (Saville) 78, **78**

newspaper clippings 41
Next Directory, cover (1991), (Why Not Associates) 59–60, **59**
'The Night Gallery', poster (1991) (Chantry) 85, **86**, 87
Nike 61, 88
    advertisement for (1995) (Me Company) 106, **106**
Nissan 88
'noise' 26, 27, 99, 169
Noise 3.5: 'Analytical Experiments in Graphic Science', book spread (1998) (Attik) 107, **107**
non-designers, designs by 38
Norm 115
    Introduction, self-published book 115, **116**, 117
Norris, Christopher 46–47, 48
nostalgia 84–85, 89, 95
Not Another Punk Book, book design (1977) (Jones) 41
Numbers, spread (1989) (Lupton) **125**

Odgers, Jayme:
    (with Greiman) poster|brochure 24
    (with Greiman) *Wet*, cover (1979) 23–24, **23**
'On Doing Nothing', spread (1992) 102, **102**
Of Grammatology (1967) (Derrida) 46, 66
Op Art 73

'Pacific Wave', cover (1987) (Hersey) 97, **98**
Pappas, Michael: (with Valicenti), spread (1990) 60, **60**
parody 12, 80, 90, 142, 169
    ironic parody 93–95
    vs. pastiche 71–72
participation, audience 66
pastiche 12, 80, 89, 171
    vs. parody 71–72
pattern-making, ornamental 23
Peckham, Shannan 139
Pentagram 121, 135
Pepsi-Cola 61, 163
Period Styles: A History of Punctuation, cover (1988) (Lupton) **123**
Pevsner, Nikolaus 18
Pho-Ku Corporation poster (2000) (The Designers Republic) **104**
Photoshop (program) 105
phototypesetting 20
Pictorial Modernism 79, 84
'Play and Dismay in Post-Modern Graphics', article 26
Playboy 65
Plazm Fonts 63
    typeface for (1993) (McCracken) **65**
Plazm (magazine) 63
Plunkett, John 111
pluralistic style 34
poetics 56
The Politics of Postmodernism (Hutcheon) 151, 154
'Polymorphous', typeface (1996) (Miller) 108, **109**
'Pop' design 18
Portland Building, Portland, Oregon (1982) (Graves) 19
Post Human, spread (1992) (Friedman) 154, **155**

The Postmodern Condition: A Report on Knowledge (Lyotard) 11
postmodern design:
    and advertising 156–159
    commercial pillaging of 152
    and complexity 17
    as a critical practice 151–152
    influence of theory 13
    and social criticism 156–169
'postmodern graphic design' 18
postmodern typography *see* typography, postmodern
'Postmodern Typography: Recent American Developments', exhibition (1977) (Bonnell) 22–23
postmodernism:
    critics of 148–151
    as a description 8, 10, 18–19, 22–23
    types of 151
Preston, Richard 138
Print magazine:
    article on uses of history (Miller|Jacobs) 79–80
    Kalman|Duffy on historical sources 84–85
    Lupton|Miller articles 123
    Scher on delicatessen design (1985) 82
    'The Triumph of the Corporate Style', article 25
print methods:
    letterpress 20, 129
    low-cost 39, 40, 42, 133, 134
'process' 115, 135
Process; A Tomato Project (1996) (Tomato) 135, **136**, 137
Procession, album cover (1981) (Saville) 77–78, 80
Pruitt-Igoe housing scheme, St Louis, Missouri 19
Public Good (design firm) 121
punk design 39–45, 63, 65, 159
punk rock 33, 38–41, 159
Pure Fuel (1996) (Fuel) 138
Pussy Galore, font in *Fuse* (1995) (WD+RU) 161–162, **162**

'Radical Modernism' 152–153, 156
Radice, Barbara 28
Radl, Christoph: Memphis logos (1982 and 1983) **28**
Rand, Paul 124
    'Confusion and Chaos: The Seduction of Contemporary Graphic Design', essay 148–149
rave flyers 106–107
Rawle, Graham, *Diary of an Amateur Photographer*, graphic book (1998) 141, **141**
Rawlings, Steve: *Umberto Eco and Football*, cover (2001) **15**
Ray Gun (magazine) 61–63, 88, 143
    feature on Deconstruction (band) (1994) 62
    irregular typography 62–63
readers vs. authors 118–119
reading:
    active participation 118–119, 147, 150–151
    and illegible text 63
    and non-linear texts 50–51, 53, 113, 131
    and visual stimulation 169
'Redefining Display', project and text (1993) (Makela) 102–103

Reid, Jamie 38–40, 159
  détourne campaign 39
  God Save the Queen, record cover (1977) **39**, 40
  The Great Rock 'n' Roll Swindle, promotional
    materials 40
  Never Mind the Bollocks Here's the Sex Pistols, album
    cover (1977) 40, **40**
  Suburban Press, graphics for 39
Renner, Paul 79
Restaurant Florent:
  print advertisement (1987) (Kalman) 82, **83**
  promotional literature (1985–93) (Kalman) 82
  promotional postcard (1986) (Isley|Kalman)
    82, **83**
Retrievalism 76
retro style 30, 79, 103
  decorative retro 84–85
  ironic retro 157
  'nouveau-retro' 89–90
revivalist typography 37
rhizome image 108
'Rhizome', typeface (1996) (Miller) 108, **109**
River Design Company: *Beginning Postmodernism*, book
  cover (1999) **14**, 15
Riviera, Jake 72
Rock, Michael 147
Rodchenko, Alexander 47, 75
Roman, Cliff: 'The Weirdos are Loose', poster (1977) 41, **41**
Ronell, Avital, *The Telephone Book* (1989) 67, 69
Rossetto, Louis 111
Rot, Diter 130
Rotterdam 42–44
Royal College of Art 59, 138
Ruder, Emil 124
rules:
  'ignorance of' argument 13, 16, 38, 62
  and typography 12–13, 16
Russian Constructivism *see* Constructivism

S,M,L,XL (1995), book spread (1995) (Mau) 122–123, **122**
St Louis, Missouri: Pruitt-Igoe housing scheme 19
San Francisco Museum of Modern Art 113
Sandhaus, Louise: *Emigre*, no. 36, spread (1995) **127**
Saussure, Ferdinand de 123, 124
Savage, Jon, 'The Age of Plunder', article (1983) 76–77
Saville, Peter 33, 35–36, 73, 159
  (and Atkins) *Closer*, album cover|sleeve (1980)
    36–37, **36**
  Fuse contributor 160
  Movement, album cover (1981) 77, **77**
  Procession, album cover (1981) 77–78, 80
  Thieves Like Us, record cover (1984) 78, **78**
Scher, Paula 60, 135
  'The Complete Genealogy of Graphic Design',
    cover (1985) 90, **90**
  Dance the Night Away, album cover (1980) 78, **78**
  Print design article (1985) 82

Swatch watches, poster (1986) 80–81, **80**
  see also Koppel & Scher
School of Visual Arts, New York 145
Schuitema, Paul 75
Schwitters, Kurt 75, 130
Seattle 40
'Seinfeld' poster (1998) (Anderson) 88–89, **88**
Selected Notes 2 ZeitGuys, detail (1995) (Aufuldish) **119**
self-initiated projects 128–139, 140–145
self-taught designers 38
semiotics 51, 56
Sex Pistols 39–40
  The Great Rock 'n' Roll Swindle (film) 40
Silberman, Stuart L. *see* Kook, Annie
Silton, Susan: *Encyclopedia Persona*, spreads (1993)
  94–95, **94**
Simons, Mike: *Adbusters*, no.37, cover **170**
'Sissy', poster (1995) (The Designers Republic) **104**
Situationists 39, 159
Smith, Rick 134
social criticism 156–169
Soda, no. 11, cover (1999) (Woodtli) **117**
software programs 105
Someone Somewhere (In Summertime), record cover (1982)
  (Garrett) 35, **35**
Sony 104, 107
Sorrell, Stephen 137–138
Sottsass, Ettore 28
sounds as graphics 131
sous rature ('under erasure') 47, 69
'Space', poster (1976) (Friedman) 21, **21**
spacing, of letters 24, 27, 31–32, 55–56
Spencer, Herbert, *Pioneers of Modern Typography* (1969)
  73–74
Sports Illustrated 65
Spy magazine 90–92
  'America: The Dark Continent' 91–92
  spread (April 1988) (Isley) **91**
  spread (June 1988) (Isley) **91**
  'A Spy Guide to Postmodern Everything'
    (1988) 91
Steelcase Design Partnership, New York 50
'Stereotypes', magazine insert (1990) (Valicenti|Thirst) **61**
Sterling, David 27
Stiff, Paul 150
Stiff Records 72
Sting 9, rave flyer (1997) (Airline Industries) **106**
Stoecker, James: *Fast Forward*, book cover (1993) **110**
'Strange Vicissitudes', poster (1978) (Kunz) 24, **25**
street posters 40–41
structuralism 56
'style culture' 151–152
Suburban Press 39
Surrealism 23, 159
Swatch watches, poster (1986) (Scher) 80–81, **80**
'Swiss Punk' 34
Switzerland 115–117

and International Style 115
modernist design 20, 24

Tatlin, Vladimir 47
Taylor, Mark C., *Hiding* (1997) 67
Taylor, Simon 134
TechGnosis (Davies) 108
techno graphic style 106–107, 108
techno music 102, 106–107
The Telephone Book (Ronell) 67, 69
  spreads (1989) (Eckersley) **68**
television 89, 92–93
'Template Gothic', typeface (c. 1990) (Deck) **56**, 57
The Terminator Line (1991) (Tilson) 134, **134**
Texas, Bill: *Adbusters*, no.37, spread (2001) **169**
text:
  'decentred' 110, 113
  destabilization of 25, 69
  free interpretation of 147
  integrated images 123–124
  legibility 20, 27, 43, 49, 63
  and visual stimulation 169
theory:
  and authorship 123, 124
  deconstructive 51, 53–54, 67
  designers' aversion to 10
  influence on designers 13, 126
Thieves Like Us, record cover (1984) (Saville) 78, **78**
Thirst:
  (Valicenti & Pappas) spread (1990) 60, **60**
  (Valicenti) 'Stereotypes', magazine insert (1990)
    60–61, **61**
three-dimensional design 28, 105–106, 108
Tilson, Jake 132–134, 140, 145
  Breakfast Special (1989) 133–134
    No.1 – El Dottore di Terrocotta, spread (1989) **133**
    No.2 – La Carte Propre, spread **133**
  The Terminator Line (1991) 134, **134**
  The V Agents (1981) 133
  The V Agents, part 2, (1984) 133
Times Square, Manhattan 21
Tomato (creative team) 134–135, 137
  Bareback. A Tomato Project (1999) 135, **136**, 137
  Process; A Tomato Project (1996) 135, **136**, 137
Tomb Raider (computer game) 106
Toscani, Oliviero 159
Total Design 43
tradition 35
Treib, Marc 26
Triggs, Teal, McQuiston, Liz & Cook, Siân (WD+RU),
  Pussy Galore, font (1995) 161–162, **162**
'The Triumph of the Corporate Style', magazine article 25
Trouble magazine 159–160
  no.1, published as a poster (1986) (Crow) **160**
  no.4, published as a T-shirt (1990) (Crow) **160**
The Truth in Painting (Derrida) 66
Tschichold, Jan 75, 76, 124

Tschumi, Bernard 47, 48
2wice magazine 124
Twin Peaks (television series) 92–93
Tycho's Nova, book spread (2001) (Wood) 137, **137**
Tylevich, Alex: (with P. Scott Makela) *Design Quarterly*,
    no. 158, cover (1993) **103**
Typografische Monatsblätter (magazine) 20
    no. 1, cover (1971) (Friedman) 21, **21**
    no. 12, cover (1972) (Weingart) **20**
Typography: Basic Principles (1963), John Lewis 12
'Typography as Discourse', poster (1989) (Hori) **58**, 59
typography, postmodern:
    criticisms of 150
    and deconstruction 48–51
    destabilization of text 25, 69
    intentional imperfection 57
    legibility 27, 43, 49, 63
    letterspacing 24, 27, 31–32, 55–56
    mixed type weights 27, 31–32

Umberto Eco and Football, book cover (2001) (Rawlings) **15**
'Uncanny!', poster (1997) (Wolfe) **164**
Underworld (techno group) 134
United States:
    and design change 115
    designers as authors 145
    new wave and design 25–32
    punk scene 40–41
    theoretical writing 126
'US Office of War Information', poster (1941) (Carlu) 77

The V Agents (1981) (Tilson) 133
    part 2, (1984) 133
Valicenti, Rick 60–61
Vanderbyl, Michael:
    American Institute of Architects, poster (1983) 31
    'Connections', poster (1983) 31, **31**
    Innovation, mailer (1985) 31–32, **32**
VanderLans, Rudy 96, 171
    Emigre, no.5, spread (1986) **98**
    see also *Emigre* magazine
Venezky, Martin 58
Venturi, Robert:
    Complexity and Contradiction in Architecture (1966) 26, 27
    (with Brown & Izenour), *Learning from Las Vegas*
    (1972) 26–27
Vermeulen, Rick 43
vernacular 17, 103
    and modernism 27
    as source material 81–89
Versations (1989) (Lehrer) 130
Vienna Secession 79
Vignelli, Massimo 148, 150
Virgin 107
virtual reality 112–113
Virtual Telemetrix 1993 Annual Report, spread (1993)
    (Bielenberg Design) **164**

'Virus Says Stop American Cultural Imperialism',
    poster (1999) (Barnbrook) **167**
Visible Language:
    critical writing by designers 126
    spreads from (1978) (Cranbrook students) **52**, 53
The Visible Word (1994) (Drucker) 129
'Visual Dictionary' (Lupton) 124
'visual literature' 131–132, 140–141
visual meaning 51
visual stimulation, and reading 169
Vogue magazine 41

Wall Street Journal 84
The War of Desire and Technology at the Close of the
    Mechanical Age, book cover (1995) (Ahmed) 15, **15**
Ware, Chris 144, 145
    Acme Novelty Library, no. 5, cover (1995) **142**
    Acme Novelty Library, no. 13, cover (1995) **142**
    Jimmy Corrigan: The Smartest Kid on Earth (2000) 142, **143**
Warp Records 104
Warwicker, John 134
Weiden & Kennedy 88, 106
Weingart, Wolfgang 19–20, 25, 35
    design as art 26
    'Kunstkredit 1976/77', poster (1977) 22, **22**
    'Kunstkredit 1978/79', poster (1979) 22, **22**
    poster commissions 22
    and 'Swiss Punk' 34
    Typografische Monatsblätter, no. 12, cover (1972) **20**
    and typography 20, 27
'The Weirdos are Loose', poster (1977) (Roman) 41, **41**
Welcome to the Cult of Virus, brochure page (1997)
    (Barnbrook) **166**
Welcome to Twin Peaks, cover and spread (1991)
    (Kook|Silberman) 92–93, **92**
Werkman, H.N. 75
Weston, Edward 78
Wet, cover (1979) (Greiman|Odgers) 23–24, **23**
'What has Writing got to do with Design?', essay
    (Burdick) 126
What the Hell, font (1993) (Kalman|Stowell) 160–161, **161**
Why Not Associates 59
    Next Directory, cover (1991) 59–60, **59**
Wiener, Jon 65
Wigley, Mark 47, 48
Williamson, Judith:
    Decoding Advertisements 8
    on postmodernism 8
Wired magazine 111–113, 143
    bought by Condé Nast 113
    Mind Grenades: Manifestos from the Future, spreads
    (1996) 112
    no. 1.06, spread (1993) (Davis|Plunkett) **112**
    no. 2.08, spread (1994) (Adigard|Plunkett) **112**
Witte, Martha 49–50
Wittgenstein, Ludwig 99
Wolfe, Shawn:

Beatkit (anti-brand) 163, 165
Dispepsi by Negativland, CD cover (1997) 163, **163**
'Live Twice the Life in Half the Time!', poster
    (1999) 163, 165, **165**
'Uncanny!', poster (1997) **164**
Wolff, Bernard Pierre 36
'Women don't get AIDS' poster (1991) (Gran Fury)
    156–157, **156**
Women's Design and Research Unit (WD+RU) (Teal
    Triggs, Liz McQuiston & Siân Cook):
    'Pussy Galore', font in *Fuse* (1995) 161–162, **162**
Wood, Graham 134
    Tycho's Nova, book spread (2001) 137, **137**
Woodtli, Martin 115
    Soda, no. 11, cover (1999) **117**
word pictures 62
word presentation 50–51, 53
Worthington, Michael: *Emigre*, no. 35, spread (1995) **126**
Worthington, Simon & Broekman, Pauline van
    Mourik: *Mute*, no. 4, (1996) 93–94, **93**
Wozencroft, Jon 152
    The Graphic Language of Neville Brody 33
    see also *Fuse* magazine
writing:
    and design 126–127
    theoretical 123, 126
Wurman, Richard Saul:
    Access city guides 92–93
    (with Lynch & Frost) *Welcome to Twin Peaks* (1991)
    92–93, **92**

Yale University 130
'The Year of Japanese Film', poster (1981) (Haspel) 44, **45**
youth culture 33
    'Generation X' 61

Zed magazine 126
Zerzan, John 168
Ziggy Stardust, by Bauhaus, record cover (1982) 77
Zivel magazine, no. 10, cover (1998) (Kvízová|Krejzek)
    108, **109**
Zone, no. 1|2, cover and spread (1986) (Mau) **120**,
    121, **121**
Zwart, Piet 75, 97

Picture Credits

Laurence King Publishing Ltd and the author wish to thank the individuals and institutions who have kindly allowed their works to be reproduced in this book. Every effort has been made to contact copyright holders, but should there be any errors or omissions we would be pleased to insert the appropriate acknowledgment in the subsequent edition of this publication. Designers are credited in the captions alongside the illustrations. Additional information is given below. Numbers refer to page numbers (T = top; B = bottom; R = right; L = left).

22L and R Museum für Gestaltung, Zurich
30L photograph courtesy of Studio Michele de Lucchi; **30**R © YELLO; courtesy of Mercury Records, a division of Universal Music Germany
34 reproduced by permission of Andrew King, Temple Mill Music, London
42L Lizzy Tear (cover star); William Faulkner (hair & make-up)
47 Jonathan Barnbrook (design); Indrani (post-production); © 2002 ISO Records|Sony Music Entertainment Inc.
71 reproduced by permission of the British Library Board, London
73 © Sanctuary Records Group, London
74 © Elvis Costello
80L Museum für Gestaltung, Zurich
81 reproduced by permission of Maira Kalman|M&Co
82 reproduced by permission of Maira Kalman|M&Co|Alexander Isley
83T reproduced by permission of Maira Kalman|M&Co; **83**B reproduced by permission of Maira Kalman|M&Co|Alexander Isley
89 Alan Disparte (senior art director); Roger Groth (designer illustrator); Anne Buhl (senior editorial director); Helee Hatlestad (senior copywriter)
91T and B © 1988 Spy Publishing Partners, LLP
94 reproduced by permission of the Fellows of Contemporary Art, Los Angeles
101, 102T, **103**T reproduced by permission of Laurie Haycock Makela
106R Airline Industries|Todd Baldwin (illustration); Paul Miller (typography)
119 Bob Aufuldish (design); Mark Bartlett (text); Eric Donelan and Bob Aufuldish (ZeitGuys dingbats)
158L reproduced by permission of Maira Kalman|M&Co|Scott Stowell
158R and **159** reproduced by permission of Maira Kalman|Mark Porter
161T reproduced by permission of Maira Kalman|M&Co|Scott Stowell
169 Kalle Lasn (concept); Bill Texas (illustration); courtesy www.adbusters.org
170T Mike Simons; courtesy www.adbusters.org